Elvis Presley:

"I'm not putting down the people who've written so much junk about me, because I realize that they have to fill their columns and pages with something. But right now I'm setting the record straight."

Las Vegas showgirl Kitty Dolan:

"I remember the fresh, clean smell of him. He didn't use colognes or even a hair tonic, because Elvis is just himself. And that's pretty wonderful. . . . When Elvis takes you into his arms, he's not a boy, he's a full-grown man."

The Memphis Mafia:

"He works ten times harder than any one of us. Yet we live like kings with the King."

Elvis' ex-wife, Priscilla:

"I saw the demands on Elvis and I wouldn't ever want to live my life like he does. I want to do what I want to do, to have freedom—and that's not possible for Elvis. . . . We respect and care for each other and we always will."

The psychic George Dareos:

"Elvis will be an idol till the day he dies."

Books by May Mann

Jayne Mansfield
The Private Elvis (Original title: Elvis and the Colonel)

Published by POCKET BOOKS

The
PRIVATE
ELVIS

(Original title: ELVIS AND THE COLONEL)

by

MAY MANN

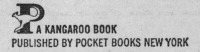

A KANGAROO BOOK
PUBLISHED BY POCKET BOOKS NEW YORK

THE PRIVATE ELVIS

Drake edition published 1975

Second POCKET BOOK edition published August, 1977

This POCKET BOOK edition includes every word contained in
the original, higher-priced edition. It is printed from brand-
new plates made from completely reset, clear, easy-to-read type.
POCKET BOOK editions are published by
POCKET BOOKS,
a Simon & Schuster Division of
GULF & WESTERN CORPORATION
1230 Avenue of the Americas,
New York, N.Y. 10020.
Trademarks registered in the United States
and other countries.

ACKNOWLEDGMENT

The obituary which appears on pp. v-ix is copyright, ©, 1977,
by The New York Times Company. Reprinted by permission.

The following is a page one article, reprinted by permission from *The New York Times*, Wednesday, August 17, 1977:

ELVIS PRESLEY DIES; ROCK SINGER WAS 42

Heart Failure is Cited by Coroner— Acclaim Followed Early Scorn

---

By MOLLY IVINS

Elvis Presley, the first and greatest American rock-and-roll star, died yesterday at the age of 42. Mr. Presley, whose throaty baritone and blatant sexuality redefined popular music, was found unconscious in the bedroom of his home, called Graceland, in Memphis yesterday at 2:30 P.M.

He was pronounced dead an hour later at Baptist Memorial Hospital, after doctors failed to revive him.

Dr. Jerry Francisco, the Shelby County coroner, who conducted a two-hour examination of the body, said "preliminary autopsy findings" indicated that the cause of death was "cardiac arrhythmia," which a hospital spokesman defined as "an irregular and ineffective heart beat." The coroner was not immediately able to determine the cause of the "cardiac arrhythmia."

Mr. Presley was once the object of such adulation that teen-age girls screamed and fainted at the sight of him. He was also denounced for what was considered sexually suggestive conduct on stage. Preachers inveighed against him in sermons and parents forbade their children to watch him on television. In his first television appearance on the Ed Sullivan show, his act, which might be thought of as tame by today's standards, was considered by the broadcasters to be so scandalous that the cameras showed him only from the waist up, lest his wiggling hips show.

Mr. Presley's early hit songs are an indelible part of the memories of anyone who grew up in the 50's. "Hound Dog," "Heartbreak Hotel" and "Blue Suede Shoes" were teen-age anthems. Like Frank Sinatra in the decade before and the Beatles a decade later, Mr. Presley was more than a singer—he was a phenomenon, with 45 gold records that sold more than one million copies each.

Mr. Presley was a show-business legend before he was 25 years old. At the age of 30 he was the highest-paid performer in the history of the business. He made 28 films, virtually every one of them frivolous personality vehicles and nearly all of them second-rate at best, but they grossed millions.

In recent years, Mr. Presley, who used to carry about 175 pounds on a 6-foot frame, had been plagued with overweight.

A recently published book called *Elvis, What Happened?* by three of his former bodyguards alleged that the singer was given to using amphetamines.

History of Mild Hypertension

Dr. Francisco said yesterday that Mr. Presley had a history of mild hypertension and that he had found evidence of coronary artery disease. Both of these, the coroner said, could have been "contributing causes" in Mr. Presley's death.

"But the specific cause may not be known for a week or two pending lab studies," he said, adding, "It is possible in cases like this that the specific cause will never be known."

A hospital spokesman said that the coroner is required by law to conduct an examination if the cause of death is not immediately apparent.

Responding to repeated questions about whether the autopsy had revealed any signs of drug abuse, the coroner said the only drugs he had detected were those that had been prescribed by Mr. Presley's personal physician for hypertension and a blockage of the colon, for which he had been hospitalized twice in 1975.

Dr. George Nichopoulos, Mr. Presley's personal physician, told the Associated Press that Mr. Presley was last seen alive shortly after 9 A.M. Dr. Nichopoulos said that Mr. Presley had been taking a number of appetite depressants, but the physician said they had not contributed to his death.

Elvis Aron Presley was born in a two-room house in Tupelo, Miss., on Jan. 8, 1935. During his childhood, he appeared with his parents, Gladys and Vernon Presley, as a popular singing trio at camp meetings, revivals and church conventions.

The family moved to Memphis when Mr. Presley was 13. He attended L. O. Humes High School and worked as an usher in a movie theater. After graduation, he got a job driving a truck for $35 a week. In 1953, Mr. Presley recorded his first song and paid $4 for the privilege; he took the one copy home and played it over and over.

A shrewd song promoter called "Colonel" Thomas A. Parker was impressed by the early records and took over the management of Mr. Presley's career. Mr. Presley toured in rural areas under the sobriquet "The Hill Billy Cat." Colonel Parker, a character of P. T. Barnum proportions, followed the credo, "Don't explain it, just sell it." He once observed, "I consider it my patriotic duty to keep Elvis up in the 90 percent tax bracket."

When Colonel Parker went to negotiate with 20th Century-Fox on a film deal that would be Mr. Presley's screen debut, the studio executives dwelled on the singer's youth and inexperience. "Would $25,000 be all right?" one executive finally asked. Colonel Parker replied: "That's fine for me. Now, how about the boy?"

"Heartbreak Hotel," Mr. Presley's first song hit, was released by RCA in January 1956. A blood-stirring dirge about love and loneliness, it burned up the jukeboxes and eventually sold two million copies.

A phenomenal string of hit songs followed, and Elvis Presley fan clubs sprouted all over the world; membership at one time numbered 400,000.

In 1957, he went to Hollywood to make his first film, *Love Me Tender*. It opened to unanimous jeers from the critics and grossed between five and six times what it cost to make.

His later films were considered equally obnoxious by cinéastes. One critic remarked of *Jailhouse Rock* that Mr. Presley had been "sensitively cast as a slob." Mr. Presley responded, "That's the way the mop flops."

Drafted Into the Army

In the spring of 1958, Mr. Presley was drafted into the Army as a private, an event that caused as much stir as an average Super Bowl. "The Pelvis," as he was known, was stationed in West Germany for two years and was given an ecstatic welcome home by his fans.

In 1967, Mr. Presley married Priscilla Beaulieu, the daughter of an Air Force colonel. They met during his military service, and had a daughter named Lisa Marie, born on Feb. 1, 1968. Although concrete details of their private life remained sketchy through his deliberate design, the fan magazines were full of reports of marital difficulties, and the couple separated in February 1972. They were divorced in Santa Monica, Calif., in 1973.

Mr. Presley was said to have been a shy person, and rarely granted interviews. He seems to have been scarred by some of the early heavy publicity, and returned from his stint in the Army more withdrawn than he had been.

In the early 60's, he made no personal or even television appearances, but earned $5 million a year simply by cutting a few records and making three movies a year. He made a picture called *Harem Holiday* in 18 days and was paid $1 million.

In the 70's Mr. Presley appeared with some frequency in Las Vegas, Nev., nightclubs. Although he sometimes appeared bloated, he was still an excellent showman and audiences always loved him.

In his nightclub act, he would occasionally parody himself. "This lip used to curl easier," he joked, referring to his one-time trademark of singing with a sneer.

It was believed that Mr. Presley neither smoked nor drank, but according to the book by his former aides, he depended heavily on stimulant and depressant drugs. He is also said to have been depressed by the book's "iconoclastic" treatment of him.

He was a generous and often sentimental man. He deeply mourned the death of his mother, and kept a suite for his grandmother, Minnie Presley, at his home in Memphis.

The house, Graceland, was an 18-room $1 million mansion with a jukebox at the poolside. Mr. Presley surrounded himself with a retinue of young men called the Memphis Mafia, who served as bodyguards, valets and travel agents. He had a passion for cars, especially Cadillacs, which he tended to acquire in multiples.

Mr. Presley also gave Cadillacs away with startling frequency. He would from time to time see some stranger, nose pressed against a car-showroom window, and invite the person to go inside and pick out the color he or she liked best. Mr. Presley would then pay the entire cost of purchase on the spot.

Mr. Presley was a nocturnal person who thrived when most others were asleep.

Maurice Elliott, a vice president and spokesman for Baptist Hospital, said Mr. Presley had gone to sleep yesterday morning at 6 A.M. Some time during the evening or early morning hours, Mr. Elliott said, Mr. Presley visited a dentist. Then, between 4 A.M. and 5:30 A.M. he played racket ball on the court of his mansion, the hospital official reported.

When Mr. Presley was a patient in the hospital, Mr. Elliott recalled, "he would put tin foil over the windows. He would normally not get up until noon or thereafter, and not go to bed until 2, 3, 4 A.M."

Mr. Presley's movie career ended in 1970, and in that year he made a successful television special. Critics remarked on how little he had aged. He kept in shape for years with karate, in which he had a black belt. But his penchant for peanut butter and banana sandwiches washed down with soda finally caught up. In one of his last appearances, his trademark skintight pants split open.

After his death became known yesterday, radio stations around the country began playing nothing but old Presley records. Mr. Presley recorded about 40 albums, many of them soundtracks of his films. They include "Loving You," "King Creole," "Frankie and Johnny," "Paradise, Hawaiian Style," "Clambake" and "Speedway."

At his death, Mr. Presley had been an indelible part of the nation's musical consciousness for 20 years.

The funeral is being handled by the Memphis Funeral Home. A spokesman said late yesterday that arrangements had not been completed.

Mr. Presley is survived by his 9-year-old daughter, father and grandmother. His father and his daughter were reportedly at Graceland at the time of his death.

PREFACE

IN 1975, THE world of "rock 'n' roll" celebrated the 21-year mark in Elvis Presley's phenomenal career, and along with it, his fortieth birthday. His record as an entertainer (including his combined gross income in the multi-millions) stands him resolutely as "The King"— head and shoulders over his nearest contenders. Offers for Elvis Presley concerts come from all parts of the world with the highest fees ever to be paid; these have yet to be tapped. Now into his third decade, the King of Rock 'n' Roll will without a doubt continue for as many more years—until he himself chooses to abdicate.

This is to acknowledge a debt to Elvis Presley, who through the years, has spent considerable time with me, to help me record who he is, what he is, how he thinks and reacts. And to discuss with me, with no questions barred, the highly dramatic and unknown side of "the public image" and "the legend," going behind the scenes of the widely speculated, yet unknown Elvis Presley—both heartaches and triumphs.

A very private person who always considered his personal life "nobody's business," he has had the confidence and respect to permit me to bring Elvis Presley into focus as a reality. It has taken us from 1956 to the present to compile the many interviews and facts herein.

I also want to thank the eminent producer, Hal B. Wallis, Colonel Parker, and all of those kind people who have known Elvis along with those from the South, often so close-mouthed, and the legions of Elvis fans who have been so cooperative. They reveal Elvis Presley as a genius as well as a very human being instead of a mysterious legend. And behind Elvis has been The Colonel.

CHAPTER ONE

Our First Kiss

THE PROS AND cons had weighed in the balance, with Mr. Hal Wallis for, and Colonel Parker against, our meeting. But obviously, it had all been settled by some mutual agreement—for there I was, and there was Elvis Presley glancing in my direction with a courteous yet quizzical smile. During the next four hours, Elvis Presley would have kissed me three times with approval and sincere affection.

That first meeting took place in 1957 at the behest of the powers that contractually master-minded the Presley career. Behind the throne were Hal B. Wallis, the widely heralded award-winning producer who exclusively discovered and signed Elvis for motion pictures, and "Colonel" Tom Parker, who originally discovered Elvis in Tennessee and started him on his most amazing and enduring career.

At the time of our meeting, Elvis was already long accustomed to commanding instant attention and breathless admiration. Before the cameras in a nightclub scene for a picture entitled, *King Creole,* playing the scene over and over, he was bored—and it showed—while the director went on asking, "Just one more, Elvis. You need to put more sparkle into it!" The extras who formed the nightclub group were middle-aged, and the electricity that makes sparks between performer and audience was lacking. But "rock 'n roll"—or any kind of music with a beat—turns me on. I was fascinated with Elvis singing "Anyway You Want Me." It was as though he were singing it just to me where I was seated in a box just outside camera range. I was his enthusiastic audience-of-one, completely captivated, and his response was immediate. The music seemed to ripple

1

from his body in the sheath of shimmering sex that no one has ever been able to emulate.

It was then that I fell helplessly in love, on the spot, with Elvis and with his talent—though I'd no intention at all of even liking this so-called "vulgar hip swinger sex symbol." But he was so alive, so with it, that the turn-on was instantaneous.

The director hollered out, "That's it! Wow, Elvis! You come to life! That's the take we've waited for all day!!!!!" To me—"We should have paid you long ago to be here. You set Elvis off!"

Then Elvis himself was standing before me saying, "I'm Elvis and you're—Miss Mann." He took my arm and was helping me up and out of the box; then we were walking to his portable dressing room nearby.

So this is Elvis! I gasped literally, admiring his tall boyish handsomeness, his hazel eyes (which are sometimes brown and sometimes blue). What a complete surprise he is! Wow! He'd sung with rhythm—crazy, mad, wild, urgent, and demanding! And now in a happy mood, he was humming "Love Me Tender," caressing each syllable. The words came softly with a quality of magnetism inherent and effortless—plainly hypnotic. I became momentarily like all of the millions of kids who idolize him—kids who love the escape, the happy, carefree, spontaneous laughter, who love gaiety and not to feel so alone or lost.

Now I was beginning to understand the charisma of Elvis Presley, and why the kids dig him! These are kids trying to assess their values and goals in the various processes of growing into life, of their hopes and their dreams for direction for happiness. In the fifties, kids were evidencing the fact that already they felt bewildered, that they were not sure of what was important and necessary for emotional security. Their wonder, their hesitation at approaching responsible future commitments, swept the headlines and the pulpits. What were their goals? What was their ambition? Fathers worried about supporting their families; too many mothers were away from home to earn money for that second car to fill the two-car garage. Left on their own, this generation of nice confused children was growing up without direction of what for, what to do or to be.

Then like a burst of warm sunshine, there was Elvis Presley! They joyfully wrapped him and his new music, to which they could relate as their very own, close to their hearts; absorbing the understanding of love and belonging. His songs were extensions of their emotions at loving and being loved. True, they giggled, screamed, and laughed, because they were self-conscious or stimulated into an adult elation not heretofore experienced. They let off steam with various squeals. But to them Elvis was love.

"Elvis," I said, wondering if he would permit the abruptness and direct honesty of my prodding, "Why do you think your Christmas Album was banned by some radio stations, even after your million record sellers like 'Heartbreak Hotel' and 'All Shook Up' which were sung in 'rockabilly' time?" Despite the adverse publicity, the Christmas Album was a complete sell-out.

"I don't know why those two stations banned it," he replied frankly. "It was perhaps because I sang 'White Christmas' with a beat. 'Silent Night' and 'I'll Be Home for Christmas' were straight. Oh well," he sighed, "Sometimes every knock can be a boost." Then he smiled, "When everybody agrees on something and everyone says 'I like it,' they start talking about something else. When there's no controversy, there's no news. When they quit talking," he concluded, "you're dead!"

Elvis could well have turned my next remark aside, but he didn't even try to sidestep it. "People and your critics," I mused, "say your gyrations on stage are vulgar! And they call you 'Elvis the Pelvis'."

"No, I don't think they are vulgar! I know that I get carried away with the music and the beat sometimes," he acknowledged. "And I don't know quite what I'm doing. But it is all rhythm and the beat—it's full of life. I enjoy it. The kids understand. It's the newness. I think older people will grow to understand it. It's the way I feel when I play, and I respond to the music accordingly. It's today, as it is. It's being young—you know—being this generation!"

Elvis' directness surprised me. Our introduction had been based completely on the honor system. No press agent was present to protect him. Would there be hell to pay later on when it was discovered I had been questioning Elvis on matters that weren't asked at all! And for all his good humor and evident faith and trust in me—was I overstepping the bounds of good taste?

We sat there side-by-side on a little settee, touching ever so slightly. In this warmth of camaraderie without warning to myself, let alone Elvis, I was again wondering out loud. How in heaven's name could he account for all of that hullabaloo—flagrant headlines, editorials—that his act was a disgrace at Los Angeles Pacific Auditorium? Why the police had sent for an entire squadron on Elvis' second night there, threatening arrest! The Elvis I was spending the afternoon with was refined and gentlemanly. Any crude behavior on his part just didn't seem possible.

Ministers and churches and the P.T.A. denounced Elvis as going straight to the devil! And all of the young people viewing his actions were being contaminated!

"In general, everyone liked the show," Elvis replied with a smile. "A few came with the object in mind of finding it wrong. 'How do you get away with it?' some asked. But you can't stop with the rock 'n roll beat! The music, it goes right through me. You can't stop. Every generation goes through an era of music. What about cheek-to-cheek moonlight dancing—and tight body-holds with the last one! This, today is young and alive and fun. I never plan my reactions, and I can never do anything twice. It is the mood and the music." Five years later, Elvis was to exclaim, "If I had done what today's rock 'n' rollers (his imitators by the hundreds) are doing on stage, I'd have been put in jail!"

Elvis was relaxed and quite at ease, and at times when he thought I was becoming somewhat abashed at my own daring questions, he reached over and kissed me lightly on the forehead or reassuringly on

4

the cheek. It was hard to believe he was Elvis Presley, the fabulous King of Rock 'n' Roll, so completely different from his public image.

Elvis was then twenty-two, six-feet tall, with 175 pounds distributed over a virile lithe body. And he radiated charm and magnetic masculinity plus—which was at the same time surprisingly almost naive—and even wholesome. More, he was completely unspoiled and unaffected. With such fame and success, how could he be all of this and remain all of that?

The most eligible young movie queens in town—stars such as Natalie Wood, daughters of studio executives, and society debutantes like Judy Spreckles (heiress to the sugar millions) were completely and openly enamored with him. And what about all those girls, hundreds of them, standing outside the Paramount Studio gates, rain or shine, from dawn-till-dusk, lunchless and dinnerless, waiting endless hours in the hope of glimpsing Elvis Presley driving in or out in his limousine. Had he fallen in love with one of them or one of the glamor movie stars who clearly pursued him?

"I've been in love yes, very much so," he sighed. "To be truthful, exactly twice. It was when I was going to Humes High School in Memphis, and that was being in love for almost two years. I thought it was real, but it turned out that I just thought it was. There was this girl who lived next to us and I was really in love. But when I began working trucks and then into music, I was gone a lot; another fellow moved in and beat my time. It sure hurt. My little old heart has had a lot of aches. That was the only time I went steady. Today she's married and has a kid. I was seventeen then, a little young maybe, but my love was sincere and very real. I wanted to marry her someday, and all of my love was meant to be forever, too." The other love?

"It has happened in the last two years. I can't say, it wouldn't be the right thing for me to say who, but I thought she was my girl, that maybe this time the real love. But again she wasn't. I am sincere about anything that I can feel from the heart, so a few have given me a bad time. A real bad time. I've learned the hard way

5

that a girl doesn't want a man who is too anxious and one she can lead by his ears. It is best, I've finally concluded, to have an understanding at the start. I now at last know that is insurance against getting hurt. I will, if love ever comes to me again, say quite clearly, 'I'm in love with you but respect my affection, for I am not allowing myself to be so in love that I'll be unhappy without you.' "

"A girl always takes advantage of the situation and makes it rough for me, once she knows I care. I know all too well—but I don't like to play games. I like honesty. I like to know I am honest."

There was a silence between us. Elvis called out the door for a couple of cokes. While we sipped our ice-cold drinks, Elvis lost in his thoughts and perhaps vivid recall, without my asking, returned to the subject. "Love is something you can't explain to a sixteen- or seventeen-year-old kid. It's like life. You listen to your mother and your daddy tell you these things. You listen, but you don't understand until you experience it. Then you say, 'That's what they were talking about. That's what they meant.' "

So this is Elvis Presley with millions of girls idolizing him—rushing after him—and the two girls he had offered his love chose to ignore it and hurt him deeply. Those two love affairs had apparently wrapped his emotions in caution and hesitancy, for it was years before Elvis was to acknowledge love again. While Elvis played the field, he became known as a loner.

"Once you're hurt, you tend to be more careful, more watchful. You can't let go. It's like you burn your hand on a hot stove. You don't put your hand down on it a second time. Not knowingly, you don't. At the same time I'm not cynical. I know someday I'll risk it and fall in love again."

"I'm very sensitive. I can get hurt way-down deep inside and it leaves a lasting mark. Now I find I'm afraid to trust my heart because maybe the girl might think she loves me because I'm Elvis Presley the record star—and not just for me. If the other two girls couldn't love me for me when I was nobody, how will I ever know now if it is real love or just a passing fancy or whim of a girl who likes my records?"

It was growing twilight when Elvis walked me to the door. On the way, a cameraman offered, "Would you two like your picture?" "Oh, yes," I exclaimed. Elvis agreed. In one, he was kissing my cheek. And oh, what trouble that picture was to cause—but that was in the future, one we happily did not anticipate.

CHAPTER TWO

Elvis Tells Me of Childhood, Poverty and Riches

THEN IT WAS Elvis' last day as a civilian in Hollywood. He was heading back to Memphis that night to become Private Presley in Uncle Sam's Army. There are a lot of things to do on your last day in town—not just the wind-up scene of *King Creole* for Hal Wallis. Yet Elvis was entirely agreeable that I spend the afternoon with him so he could tell me, himself, about his parents and what he was like as a little boy, on up through the years to becoming an idol. Some reports said, "The Presleys were considered 'poor white trash,' always living in shanties on the border of 'Nigger Town' outside Tupelo." Were the Presleys really that poor? Certainly they never were even remotely "white trash." Other reports said Mrs. Presley "tippled" and that it was alcohol that made her ill so often. Yet here was Elvis, who didn't drink or smoke, while the serenity shining on the faces of Elvis and Gladys and Vern bespoke the lies of such rumors—as I was to find out.

I had previously seen Elvis' parents from a distance. They were a handsome couple, outstanding in appearance—and seemed to be the kind of soft-spoken, wholesome, unpretentious people you instinctively felt by their demeanor were honest and god-fearing. They were unusually affectionate and loving with their only child—

7

their son Elvis. Gladys Presley was a small plump woman with large brown pansy eyes and dark soft waving hair. Her dress was modest, simple, and immaculate. She was a lovely woman and with her infectious smile and laughter, vivacious among her own kin. She was forty-one and had been known as a real Southern beauty as a young girl when she married tall handsome Vernon Presley. They didn't try to hide the complete devotion and caring between them.

The studio biography on Elvis was one short page, a few dates and credits—and nothing else.

"It will be two years before I see you again," I said. "A column item this morning said you're marrying a Memphis girl, Anita Wood."

"Yep, I'm getting married," he teased, "to the U.S. Army."

Elvis is a person of interchangeable moods. Everyone wondered how he felt about leaving it all—all the success of being a new movie star, plus the accumulation and the money, making millions in cold cash. Now it had come to a halt!

"What do you think? Honestly I'm glad I'm going in. Every able-bodied American boy should go into the service. And I'm an able-bodied American boy—so why not? In fact, I think it will be a relief!"

"Elvis means," a studio executive offered, overhearing our conversation, "that in the Army he will have a little more freedom. As a civilian he has practically none. He is a prisoner of his fans. I've worked with all of the big stars, but I've never seen anything like it—the way people congregate in a flash if they think they can get a look at Elvis. On location in New Orleans and everywhere Elvis goes, he has to be guarded by security police to keep the crowds away. The hotel elevator operators had to be instructed not to take anyone to nor stop at Elvis' floor without an official pass. Finally we had to have security guards posted at the elevator and the stairways on Elvis' floor. Elvis has to be imprisoned. Even so, girls came out of the walls, the cracks in the floors, and through the windows. It was unbelievable, the pandemonium that went on all hours of the day and night. We had to sneak Elvis in and out of the hotel to work, and there was so much squealing and cheering for Elvis at every turn, that we had to put up loud-speakers and tell the crowd that if they didn't stop it, we'd have to go back to Hollywood. Poor Army. Wonder if the Army will put up with hundreds of squealing, screaming, jumping girls day and night trying to reach Elvis. It's a hysterical adulation—that would drive anyone but Elvis Presley completely nuts!"

"I love the fans," Elvis interceded calmly. "I love pretty girls. When they come running to me, I want to run to them, not away. I hope they don't blame me when Army regulations force me to look straight ahead on duty. I want them to understand I'm not ignoring them."

Someone with a pocket radio turned on the latest new song hit. "I wish I were Elvis Presley's Sarg in the Army," with its threats of KP and busted guitars. Elvis merely grinned. "I've never been accustomed to things real easy. I know it looks like I came up overnight. Not so! I can tell you it was a lot of hard work. I've done plenty of it. I worked as a common laborer, up at three every morning to work in a defense plant; I drove a truck for Crown Electric in Memphis, the same time I was going to high school. I'd get out at three-thirty and be on the job at six-thirty for $12.50 a week ushering in a movie house. Luckily I don't need much sleep. I've got plenty of nervous energy." I had noticed it—Elvis' toe is always tapping. He just can't sit still.

"If I make it hard for me in the Army, the only one it's going to be hard on is me."

"The odd thing will be to get up and start running before breakfast. Breakfast is the one meal I count on. But you work up a good appetite before breakfast!"

"I don't have a 'one special girl'," Elvis said later. "I'm not in love, and I'm glad because I wouldn't want to be in love and get married like lots of fellows and have to leave my wife. I don't even have one special girl to write home to," he added thoughtfully. Then, "I haven't written a letter in eight years. I don't have time. I use the telephone instead."

9

"I'd like to say I'll write to you, but I won't promise. If I promise, I keep my word. I don't want to say that, knowing how I'm not a letter writer."

Yes, he would miss all of the fellows who were known as his "Memphis Mafia," Southern boys he'd gone to school with, his cousin, and the half dozen who surrounded him, sharing the work and the good times. Yes, Elvis admitted it could be very lonely at the top if you didn't have close friends like his chums, "who are on salary" and his parents.

"I'll miss my buddies, but naturally, you can't go through life depending on friends. You have to depend on yourself. I hope to make new friends in the Army."

For a long time, we talked about his earliest remembrances, his boyhood and his way up to becoming an idol. Elvis gave me plenty of time. He spoke of things he had never wanted to see in print. But now he was leaving, he might not come back to a career. People are fickle. Notoriously, the public forgets. Out of sight, out of mind! As people stopped to say goodbye, Elvis replied, "Don't forget me." It seemed it was not lightly said, and now in conversation, it seemed as if Elvis wanted to tie up all the loose ends before he left.

Elvis Presley was born January 8, 1935, in East Tupelo, Mississippi, a rural town of less than 6,000 population (at the time) and a few miles from Memphis. There was a fish hatchery, a cotton mill, textile plants, a Carnation milk plant, a cotton seed oil mill, a fertilizer plant, and various stores. East Tupelo was "the wrong side of the tracks" where the very poor, both white and black, existed in the main as sharecroppers, living in clap-board houses and shanties. The only gathering places for recreation were the grocery store, the school, and the First Assembly of God Church.

Elvis first saw the light of day in one of these shanties, a "shotgun" two-room house built on stilts to protect it from flooding during the rainy season, with an outhouse and a hand water pump at the back door.

The Presleys had a small porch rather than the usual stoop. The two-by-four porch was big enough for three chairs where Gladys and Vernon could sit out on summer evenings.

It was during the Depression and Vernon worked long hours with his hoe, farming cotton and corn for shares to eke out a meager existence. He was a tall handsome man of twenty-one with waving hair and broad shoulders when he married the most beautiful girl in town, Gladys Smith. America's sweetheart, Mary Pickford's real name was known to be Gladys Smith, and the townspeople said Gladys had such beautiful big brown eyes—like Mary Pickford—that if she'd go to Hollywood she could well be a movie star. Gladys, one of a large family, was a sewing-machine operator in one of the garment companies, and when she was dating Vernon Presley, whose also-large family lived down the road, not even a movie producer, had one come along, could have persuaded her to risk leaving Vernon for all the movie-star contracts Hollywood might offer. None did, and Gladys married Vernon, who borrowed the money to build their little house. Within a year, the girl with the beautiful brown eyes, camellia white complexion, infectious laughter, and a firm belief in God and prayer had long stopped her expertise at the roller rink—she was expecting her first baby.

Gladys had a gold mine of courage and encouragement for her husband Vernon who could find no way to take her to a hospital in town when her time came.

"The Presleys were an extremely handsome pair, if only they had money," their neighbors would say. "They have the looks of real fine folk."

Working at any kind of odd job she could get, and during the season in the factory, she helped add to the family income. But it was never quite sufficient to cover more than the table expenses for food and almost no new baby clothes.

Gladys' mother and neighbors offered to midwife at the birth. They were not a little concerned as Gladys' day of pain and trial approached. From appearances it looked as though Gladys was going to have twins! "Looks like two watermelons in there," the men folk would say to Vernon. Vernon was not taking it lightly.

11

He worried about his wife's condition. He tried any means of making a few extra dollars. If only he could get her to a hospital! There, babies could be born proper. His fears were allayed by his kin who assured him, "No one goes to the hospital to have a baby, except rich folk." Most of the Presley women had given birth in their own beds at home.

When the labor pains set in, several women rushed to the Presley home to assist. A wash boiler of hot water was bubbling on the stove in readiness. Vernon knelt down in prayer. The preacher of the First Assembly Church of God, where the Presleys were regular members, offered special prayers for her. All would be well.

All was not well, for Gladys' muffled screams could be heard through the neighborhood as she fought to give birth. There were two babies, twins all right. Both were boys. As she said later, "If I'd only been in a hospital, Jesse Garon could have been saved." As it was, he died in birth and Elvis Aron survived. "I always think of what just having a little money could have done for us," Gladys would say later. She still cried softly to herself years after in remembering the loss of Elvis' twin. "That's why Elvis is so dear to us. I also knew that I would never be able to have any more babies. He would be our only one."

"Years later when we had money and I could go to a proper doctor and to the hospital, they told me that if I had had the care medical science afforded then, I could have had more children. But we were poor in money and rich in love."

"I was so grateful for Elvis and especially knowing he was to be our only child, I guess we three kept closer than most."

The Presleys had no money for movies or any other form of entertainment, except that at church. "We went almost every night to church and always on Sunday," Gladys Presley recalled. "Elvis was such a good little boy, kind and considerate right from the start. When he'd see me crying sometimes, for I had misery in my body long after his birth, he would hug my knees and say, 'Mama, someday I'll buy you everything and make you laugh and smile!' I'd stop crying and smile for him. He was such a little boy, just two, when he first talked that way to me. He was such an affectionate little boy, so full of love. Some of our kinfolk would say, 'Gladys, you're spoiling that boy. Don't mother him so much or he'll grow up to be a mama's boy.' "

"One day Elvis asked me, 'What is a mama's boy?' I told him that meant he was good and he must always mind his mama. And he must make her happy. That satisfied him. He brought me a bouquet of dandelions. I loved flowers and he would help me try to grow a few from slips I'd get from other people's plants. Sometimes they'd grow and sometimes we didn't have enough water for them. Some of the plants would wither and die. Elvis would comfort me, 'Don't worry, Mama, someday I'll buy you a whole rose garden full of flowers.' And he did."

The Presleys loved to sing, as do most people in the Deep South. Singing is a form of recreation that doesn't cost money. They would sit on their porches and sing gospel songs. Sometimes it would sound like a whole singing festival with the neighbors, some white and some black, all harmonizing till sundown on their front steps. It became a regular roundelay of music.

"We went to church where I loved to hear the choir. My mother once told me that when I was less than two years old, I slid off her lap in church and crawled up on the platform. I stood there singing with the choir even though I couldn't say the words. I could always carry a tune. I loved music. I had an ear for it, an ear for tone. If anyone flats or sharps a note, even though I can't read music, I feel it. It goes right through me like a knife."

"Mother began teaching me little songs at home. After supper and the dishes were done, Daddy and Mother and I would sing and harmonize together. It was our way of enjoyment. Pretty soon the neighbors would insist that we get up and sing in church what we sang at home. Next we had long strings of engagements singing at church parties, revivals, and conventions. We

13

never thought of pay; it was all a part of the Lord's work and doing some good.

"We were prayerful people. I remember in school the teacher asked for someone to pray. I was the only one to hold up my hand. I was shy and a little scared, but Mother had instilled in me—that you do what's right. And when you're called on, stand up and be counted."

"My mama taught me a lot of songs from a little old Western folk song book she had bought. I used to sit by the radio and listen, too, and sing along. I'd play phonograph records over and over. That's the way I learned a lot of songs. Then I'd get to fooling around, giving my own interpretation and expressing the songs with my own reaction and feelings."

"My daddy could play a banjo, and he'd keep threatening to buy me a guitar someday so we could accompany ourselves. But there was never that much money around loose.

"I saw a guitar one time in a store window for $12.50. I'd like to have bought it, but I might just as well have tried to buy the City Hall. It took every cent to keep us eating and my mother was out working at all kinds of odd jobs, even a scrubwoman job in a hospital, so hard, that's why her health broke down when she was so young. I decided I'd have to do something big—real big to give my mama the things she deserved. She was so beautiful, and she never complained. But I could see her getting so tired and ill. Maybe if I could get that geetar and sing like those record singers in Nashville, I could earn money to make my mama's life easier—and better."

As Elvis grew, he and his parents were singing together. Their appearances, singing special songs in church, were augmented by singing at social affairs and sometimes even at camp meetings and revivals near and outside Memphis. In grade school Elvis' singing became known. Mrs. J. C. Grimes, one of his fifth-grade teachers, recalls that she first became acquainted with Elvis when she asked the children who would say a prayer

14

to open class. Elvis raised his hand. "He not only gave a beautiful little prayer, but when we had songs to illustrate Elvis sang them for the class."

Mrs. Grimes told the principal, Mr. Cole, of Elvis' talents. Several months later Mr. Cole sent Elvis home with a note asking his mother if he could enter a school music contest at the Alabama-Mississippi Fair. The Presleys caught a ride to the Fair and waited anxiously for Elvis' turn in the contest. It seemed that Elvis was never going to get on, but before the contest closed, Elvis was finally introduced. He sang "Old Shep." The applause for the Presley boy was deafening. All of 5,000 or 6,000 people were standing around listening. Gladys said happily, "They gave Elvis the prize. It was a big night in our lives. We went home and celebrated. I made Elvis his favorite apple pie for dinner. It was all a big, big thing. The Presley folks and all of our kin talked about Elvis winning that prize."

Elvis never hung around with a gang of kids after school. He was off at the closing bell to get home to his ma. Twice he sang in the school's assembly. He never seemed to think he was good enough, and he only did so to please his teachers. He never made pals with outsiders. He was usually with his cousins. His mama was strict.

Elvis told me, "I reached an age where I started rebelling. It seemed like since I was an only child, Mother was always right there with me. I always had to let her know where I was and what I was doing. I'd get angry, being tight reined—which was a natural thing—especially when I wanted to go with my cousins someplace and she wouldn't let me. I was fifteen before I ever went away from home without accounting to my Mama where I was and what I was doing and where I was going. Later on, I realized that she was right and that she was only protecting me and keeping me from getting into any trouble."

"When I grew out of that fourteen-year-old period, I realized what a great friend she was, as well as my mama. I could call her at any time of the night from

15

anywhere and wake her up and she was always there to talk to me, to help me. There will never be anyone in the whole world to me like my mother."

"Mama always let me bring my cousins in for a snack and we'd play. Other kids' mothers would shoo us away. But not Mama. She never minded our noise."

"I just want to know where you are, Elvis," she'd say. "Your friends can always play here."

Was it all timing and superior showmanship that made him become a multimillion-dollar personality? Could he have planned it?

"I never had the remotest idea of a career," Elvis says. "I didn't plan it. When I was twelve I thought it would be great some day driving truck and I like truck driving. If all of this should end now, I could always go back driving truck and like it."

"The way it all really began was the Christmas I wanted a bicycle. My daddy wasn't working and couldn't afford one. Almost no one was working because the big Depression was on. We didn't have much of anything but love, and that was real and very plentiful."

"But I wanted a bike to get me a paper route. Daddy couldn't afford one, but he made up his mind to scrape enough money together to get me a guitar. I learned to play it sitting in front of the radio picking the strings to go along with the music and songs that way. I practiced with phonograph records the same way."

"Later Daddy found a job in Memphis and we moved. Later I got a job as an usher in Loew's State Theater. My $14-a-week seemed like a million. I'll never feel that I had more money than then. For it was the first. Almost equally important to me was getting to see pictures. The movies opened up a whole new world. Getting my folks in to see them for free on slow nights was even better. Just to see my mother and daddy sitting and enjoying themselves in a movie, with maybe some popcorn and a candy bar—well, nothing could have been better. You have to know how it is to be so poor, to never be able to go to movies or to have things you want, to know how really wonderful it is to see and have a few things, like going to a movie, even."

"I heard about an opening for a job driving truck for $35 a week for the Crown Electric Company. I took that money home and handed it to Mama every Saturday night. She needed it. I never thought of spending it. I liked driving truck because I was crazy about cars, and driving one to me was a luxury."

"When Mother's birthday came around I decided to make her a record. I'd heard about how you could for a couple of dollars. I knew what she'd like me to sing for her. I went to the Sun Record Company in Memphis and paid them $4 and cut 'That's All Right, Mama' to surprise her."

"Mr. Sam Phillips, the president of Sun Records, had heard my record when I went in to pick it up. He asked for my address and said someday maybe he might call me. It was a year later when he called and we made the same record again only with music and I sang 'Blue Moon of Kentucky' on the back. I sang it white country and black blues and Mr. Phillips gave me a contract. That was in 1954."

"I didn't figure I was any good. Mr. Phillips gave the record to station WHBQ where Dewey Phillips, a disc jockey, featured records by black blues singers. I had Mama tune our radio in to WHBQ, but I was too scared to stay and hear it. I went straight to a movie so I couldn't hear folks laughing at me, me pretending to be a somebody."

"I was really hiding in that movie scared. But when I got home, Mama grabbed me and hugged and kissed me—she was so excited and happy. She said disc jockey Dewey Phillips had so many telephone calls and even telegrams about my record that he had to play it repeatedly. Well, it sold 7,000 in Memphis. I made several more, but they didn't seem to be good enough. I didn't make big time or set the world on fire. I thought it was just a one-time thing, and I concentrated

17

on driving truck. But I'd sing around at places and on local programs when they'd ask me. Mama wanted me to. I knew it pleased her so I'd sing. And soon I was getting as much as ten dollars for my singing."

CHAPTER THREE

Elvis Jilted by His First Love at Age 17

ELVIS WAS INVENTIVE as a boy. Things he didn't have he'd imagine and make-do with whatever was at hand. "When I was nine I fell in love with cars. I'd play automobile for hours, sitting in a broken chair outside in the yard, pretending it was a real fast sports speedster. When my daddy played the banjo, I would use a broomstick and play along with him, fingering the wooden pole as though it were a real guitar. Like any boy I was full of life and wanted things. But I learned even at four years not to express it. I learned that things cost money and that sharecroppers didn't have money. I didn't like to see the sadness creep into my mama's eyes when I talked about toys and guns, bicycles, footballs I'd seen and wanted so much on different Christmases.

"I didn't know that one Christmas the basket of goodies came from a charity organization. My parents were proud and industrious, they worked hard and they were independent." (Gladys said later they accepted the Christmas basket so "Elvis could have some of the goodies we had no money to buy.")

Vernon was not only trying to grow cotton on the strip of sharecropper land, but he was working as day laborer and WPA carpenter whenever the work was possible. The cotton afforded them little more than the land to live on.

"I was nine when we went to Memphis to see our

relatives, and I discovered a bathroom inside of a house! I was amazed!"

"Real water running out of taps indoors! My mama said, 'Many folk have running water and take their baths in tubs in a bathroom inside their houses, Elvis. It's just the poor in this country who keep to the outdoor outhouses and who have to bathe in washtubs.'"

One of Mrs. Presley's trials with Elvis was that he liked to go to the swimming hole with the boys. He resented afterward having to fill the washtub with hot water and take a good scrub-down with soap in the kitchen. After that he had to empty the tub, clean it, and hang it up outside on the back wall.

For several years it was a constant argument between them; Elvis had been swimming, he was already clean. He "didn't need no hot bath." But Gladys persisted. One day Elvis slipped on the soap he had carelessly left lying on the floor while he emptied his tub. He wrenched his ankle. "Mama," he said, when he got up off the floor, "I'm going to grow up and get you not one indoor bathtub, but at least six!" He kept his promise, although at ten years of age he didn't exactly know how he was going to come by the big money for such luxuries. (She was one day to have seven bathrooms at Graceland.)

Elvis' neighboring playmates were both blacks and whites. The blacks sang jazz and the blues, and the whites sang country music. Elvis began improvising his own singing, which was a blend of both. With his vitality and restless energy, he would move with the music, sometimes dancing along with his singing. "It's natural, you move the way you sing," he explained. The kids would clap and Elvis would get going and really get his "motor turned on high!"

"Elvis could be a great cutup and a real show, when he wanted to be," one of his former black playmates, now in music in Nashville, recalls. "Elvis could be gospel serious and religious like a preacher in church when he was gospel singing, too, if he took the mind! Elvis was a real actor. But when he'd start swinging those gospel hymns, his mama didn't like it. She

19

looked real shocked. When she heard him, she'd stop him right now and then. 'You've got to have reverence for God, son,' she'd say. Elvis would explain to her, 'I have reverence for God, mama, it's just the music, it makes me feel this way. You know I never sing this way nor swing in church!' "

"Elvis sure loved his ma, but he'd argue with her when we'd be out on his front steps playing and singing and dreaming big dreams. I remember often her saying, 'Son, the water's hot, it's time for your bath before you go to bed.' Elvis would say, 'Aw, Mama, I don't need no bath. I'm clean as a whistle, honest I am. Smell my neck—I've been swimming in the creek up to an hour ago, I just got myself dry!' "

"But Elvis' mama, she was firm. And I guess that's why he was such a real gentleman. He didn't have to make no effort to be good. He just had good decency in him. But even when he was doing good, he'd sometimes laugh with that good-natured mockery shining in his eyes. It always said, 'Now don't think I am a goodie or I'm better than you are.' Sometimes Elvis seemed a little shy about his good manners, but he always had them, even when he was joking. One thing Elvis never put us blacks down nor turned a joke to hurt anyone else. Usually the joke would turn out to be on him. He liked to laugh and joke when he was with his own friends, but let a stranger come in and Elvis didn't cotton to him right off. He never trusted anyone right off. When he did you knew he was a friend for life! Just being around Elvis made folks feel good. He had such a nice happy friendliness about him. Elvis was never a smart aleck. But don't bear me no mind—to putting my name down with what I'm telling you. If you talk about Elvis behind his back—you're washed up with him!"

Poverty ruled the Deep South. When an outbreak of a contagious disease started in their area, Gladys was scared. "I'm so afraid, Vernon. What if Elvis gets T.B. and we can't get any doctor? What will we do? Let's move into Memphis, where maybe we can both get work and live a little more like human beings. It can't be worse than it is here." Mainly Gladys wanted to be near medical aid. She couldn't stand the thought of Elvis getting sick and losing him. A neighbor's boy had died overnight with diphtheria, because there was no doctor in the country. Doctors in Memphis wouldn't come out for poor folks outside the city. "We can't lose Elvis like we did Jesse Garon," Gladys would cry softly in the night to Vernon. Vernon loved Elvis as much as Gladys. He went off to Memphis to see what could be done. Luckily he found a job in a tool company, and the Presleys moved into one room on Poplar Avenue. It was an old mansion that had been made into one-room apartments with hot plates and a bath down the hall to accommodate several families. Of the poor, of course. Later, a social worker found the Presleys a new home, a two-bedroom apartment in a new Federal Housing development, the Lauderdale Courts. Then, Vernon was working for a paint company and Gladys worked in a curtain factory, while Elvis went to Humes High School. Red West, to become one of "The Memphis Mafia," was one of his school pals. Elvis played football and baseball. After school the kids gathered on the grass in front of Elvis' home and he'd sing and play for them until Gladys called him in for supper.

Next Gladys found a job serving coffee in a cafeteria. Elvis scouted around for odd jobs, one was cutting lawns. He would knock on doors and offer to cut the lawn for ten cents. If the man of the house answered, Elvis usually got the job. He learned strategy early. He would wait on his lawn-cutting rounds to time his arrival with the man who would be getting home and didn't want to bother to cut his lawn.

At Humes High School, George Hamilton (who would also become the film star) had a brother, Bill. Bill remembers Elvis as a student there. "Elvis played a couple of times at school assembly. But Elvis was on the shy side. He was always neat and clean. He had a hankering for clothes store-bought, and when the family income allowed him to go into a store and buy a ready-made shirt and jeans he was right proud to wear them. There was a place down on Beale Street that catered to country music men. They carried white, yellow, pink, blue suits and fancy shirts. When Elvis had money he started buying his clothes there. His preference was a pink jacket with black pants. He also wore his hair in a pompadour, with a duck tail and long sideburns. In contrast everyone else wore crew cuts. He was different—but no one made cracks because he was always ready with his fists. And good. The kids loved his style of singing. But he wasn't conceited—he was shy like he didn't think he was good. He never hung around after school but promptly went home."

Standing on her feet all day in the cafeteria was hard on Gladys. It worried Elvis. "Soon's I can get a paying job after school, Mama, you can quit that coffee job," he told her. "Mama liked pretty things, not for herself, but for our home. She planted white rosebush slips under our windows and they grew. We were proud of those white roses." The neighbors respected the Presleys as very decent, kind, clean-living people with a thoughtful, nice son.

Elvis experienced his first serious attraction to a girl in high school. Her family lived in the same apartment house as the Presleys. Elvis got into the habit of stopping to see her the first thing when he came home from school and before he started on his job-hunting routines. Gladys soon became aware of her son's first attraction and told Vernon, "I think Elvis is really in love." Vernon smiled, "He's only a kid—it's kid stuff."

"Elvis is so young, but he takes things seriously, deep inside," Gladys pondered. "I don't want him to get hurt. I don't think the girl is old enough to settle down. Elvis is too young, but he's never been serious about a girl before!"

Vernon laughed. "Leave them alone. They're young."

Elvis was a strapping six-footer at 175 pounds. "He had," the coach announced, "great makings and could certainly become a football star." The first skirmish fouled Elvis up, and he came home with some bad cuts, bruises, and a few slightly bent if not broken bones. Gladys insisted he quit. "But I'm a big man, I can't quit," Elvis argued. Mama was firm. Vernon was ill, and she was at that time the sole support until her husband could get on his feet again. "I can't stand the worry, son," Gladys cried. Elvis complied. No more football. Everyone agreed Elvis clearly worshipped his mother.

Elvis told me that at this time he aimed to become a policeman when he graduated from high school. He'd join the force when he was 21, he planned. For the now he was driving trucks.

Gladys Presley liked the girl Elvis was so in love with. It looked like an early marriage. "I'd love to have grandchildren," Gladys told her friends.

By now Elvis was eighteen. He had graduated from Humes and his career was springboarding. From the occasional ten dollars a night for singing engagements, great interest in his first recordings for Sun Records plus a steady job driving trucks kept him busy. Elvis wanted a musical career and he went after it with the backing of a guitar player, Scotty Moore, and Bill Black, a bass player. They formed a group, began playing the honky-tonk spots right up to the top: Nashville's "Grand Ole Opry" and Shreveport's "Louisiana Hayride."

Elvis began playing fairs and one-night stands all over the South, and when he was twenty he signed up for management by and was traveling with The Colonel. Elvis was now gone from home so much Mrs. Presley worried when she noticed another boy calling on Elvis' girl. One night she saw them kissing goodnight. She didn't want to see her son hurt, but the first thing she knew, without interfering or warning Elvis, the girl had chosen the other fellow.

"You never saw a sadder fellow than Elvis was for a long long time," a neighbor remembers. "His mama knew Elvis was hurt real bad, and she tried to comfort him. Elvis' always-ready smile seemed to have vanished. You felt sorry for him, because he was carrying a big torch.

"Elvis would keep practicing with his guitar and singing when he was home now, and he didn't go out or date other girls. Elvis just kept to himself very sad-like.

23

And then all of a sudden he was almost never home. And the Presleys up and moved away."

She added, "I saw Elvis later on in Memphis, and he was real sociable and as nice as he could be—as he always was," she allowed graciously. "I asked him if he still felt badly about losing out with the girl and he just smiled and said, 'She was a very nice girl.' That was all. You could not tell whether he was still torching, like he was for so long. But I guess not by now. He was young enough to get over it."

CHAPTER FOUR

The Colonel and His Foot-Long Hot Dogs and Elvis

COLONEL THOMAS ANDREW Parker, who would one day become Elvis' ebullient, cigar-smoking, incredible-deal-swinging mentor, was in his mid-thirties when Elvis was born. The title of "Colonel" was an honorary one, conferred on him by governors of several southern states. He was known for ballyhooing fairs, carnivals, and country music singers, booking shows, circuses, and undertaking other methods of earning a living. As a smart, husky, balding, fast-talking wheeler and dealer who looked like a rube, The Colonel had also established a reputation for downright horse sense. This, coupled with his shrewd ballbearing blue eyes and carnival-midway-pitch tactics, would get him every last cent from whomever or whatever he was after. The Colonel and Elvis didn't meet until twenty years later in 1955. By then Colonel Parker was an affluent and impressive person in the country music business.

The Colonel neither denies nor confirms that he was born June 26, 1910, in West Virginia in a carnival traveling the south. His parents were performers. Orphaned as a small boy, Tom Parker was taken in hand by an uncle who owned the pony circus. Tom continued the carnival circuit. He was known for his enterprising tricks. It a show's admission was fifty cents, he would put up a sign, "$1.00. Admission free with every paid ticket," or "$1.00 admission. If not satisfied, half your money will be refunded." This kind of con worked.

Elvis Presley was a baby in diapers when Colonel Tom reportedly invented the foot-long hot dog. While running a frankfurter concession in a circus midway, it was said he stuck a bit of hotdog in each end of a bun. He filled the middle with onions. If 'a sucker' complained, the amiable jolly-faced six-foot Parker is said to have pointed to the ground, where stale bits of hot dog were displayed, as though dropped. "Run along, son. You dropped your meat!" His booming voice, wide smile, and a pat on the shoulder would allay any question in a hot dog consumer's mind that he had been conned.

Tom Parker knew what it was to go broke, to be hungry. He learned how to live by his wits. He became an idea man and press agent who thought up all sorts of hokum and the public ate it up. He married a widow with a son and they bought a home in Tampa, Florida, where the circuses had winter quarters.

The private life of The Colonel is speculative. He lives in his hideaway home in Palm Springs with Mrs. Parker. Mrs. Parker is almost a mystery in that she is never seen publicly. Those who have seen her claim she is a refined small gray-haired lady who dresses well but unpretentiously and with a certain air of refinement. She is not outgoing nor a showman like her husband, who may even have exceeded even P. T. Barnum's exploits, to make him a legend in the world of show business.

In the right mood, The Colonel has revealed that as a little boy he started out to be enterprising. He became an expert candy-apple-dipper and ice-shaver for snow cones. He learned to operate the merry-go-round. When he was in his teens he became a barker on the midway, and put together his own pony and monkey act. Becom-

25

ing a general manager of the midway, he was considered a most successful young man in the circus world—a real showman. It is said that during one off-season, he became a dogcatcher in Tampa, Florida. He gave away hundreds of homeless puppies to the kids rather than see them doomed to death in dog pounds. He is known to like children.

In the thirties Colonel Parker, while a press agent, became interested in western and country music signers. He managed such top stars as Gene Austin, Eddy Arnold, and Hank Snow. Many an aspiring young singer aimed to get The Colonel to oversee his career. With shrewd, uncanny know-how he seldom took on anyone who wasn't going to make it big. One thing was understood, The Colonel was captain of any ship he ran, and he ran it tight—his word was law. Any singer he signed had to buckle down to The Colonel's say-so careerwise.

In spite of his jovial manner and his appearance of a country-bumpkin rube, he early became known as the shrewdest bargainer in the South. "If you don't drop dead of a heart attack at some of his way-out propositions on money, you sign his contracts and make money," one impresario in Memphis said. "He demands and gets unheard-of sums." By his hard business tactics and his offers of "double or nothing" contracts with a toss of the coin, he became recognized as the top manager in the country western music field.

Along came Senator Dudley J. LeBlanc of Lafayette, Louisiana, with his wonderful elixir Hadacol. With Hadacol came a tremendous advertising campaign in every media. Colonel Tom Parker, it was widely reported, helped round up a caravan of entertainers to sell the miracle medicine which swept the country for several years. The Colonel denies he was in the Hadacol campaign.

It was the middle fifties when he learned that RCA Victor was on the lookout for a new performer. The Colonel always had his eyes and ears peeled open for opportunities to make money. When he heard about the record Elvis Presley had cut at Sun Records for his

26

mother, he asked to hear it. He was impressed and met young Presley.

Elvis by this time had acquired a sort of manager and was going no place exactly. Elvis had good looks, his guitar, and a lot of talent which The Colonel noted —if well exploited—could be money-making. He had Elvis sing and play. However, he saw with delight the way Elvis moved.

"I discovered the big secret that would send Elvis to the pinnacle of success," The Colonel said. But he never allowed as to what the secret was except to say, "Female entertainers have been using it for years to turn audiences on. I just had Elvis do it in reverse."

Actually, it appears Elvis' shimmying, shaking bump-and-grind-gyrations were a form of striptease which The Colonel added to Elvis' natural movements that would sweep the youth of this country with a frenzy of excitement and elation! And it was Elvis' records that turned hundreds of radio stations nation- and worldwide into rock-music stations.

Elvis tells it: "A long while after I cut that record I got a call from The Colonel, Tom Parker. He said he had heard my record and that I needed a business manager. He said I'd make more money than by trucking."

"He signed me along with guitarist Scotty Moore and bass player Bill Black. We played a hillbilly act around the country, driving from town to town, wherever The Colonel got us bookings. I was called The Hillbilly Cat. We were booked to play for the Western Disc Jockey's Association convention in Tennessee. It seems Mr. Steve Sholes of RCA Victor's specialties department had heard my first record, 'That's All Right, Mama,' and he asked around and recognized me. He went to Sun Records, who still had me signed to that first contract, and, well, they got to The Colonel and me and we talked it over. I had a chance to sign with RCA Victor."

The story is that Steve Sholes, recognizing Elvis' unique style both with ballads and hymns and his natural range and voice, was convinced by Colonel Parker. He agreed to pay Sun Records the unprecedented sum of about $35,000 to buy his contract and unreleased recordings. He also gave Elvis a bonus of $5,000; unheard-of wealth to Elvis.

"I went right out and bought Mama a Cadillac. A pink one," Elvis says. "That was her dream when she was scrubbing floors and cleaning up at the hospital where she was working. She often saw a fine lady drive up in a big Cadillac. She told me about her. Mama is never one to want or ask for anything for herself. I knew how thrilled a car like that would make her. Besides she is the finest lady God ever put on earth. I didn't know for sure how long we could afford to keep it, but I knew one thing—she was going to have it."

Elvis went to New York to try out for Arthur Godfrey's T.V. Talent Show. He wasn't accepted, and this was a big comedown for the youth who thought at last he was going up, up, up. The Colonel told him not to worry. "We'll fix it so New York shows will be asking for you. And at top money, too!"

RCA Victor pressed all five of Sun's unreleased Elvis records under the RCA Victor label. They caught on like wildfire. The teenagers loved them. Elvis was set to appear on Jackie Gleason's Show with Tommy and Jimmy Dorsey. He sang "Heartbreak Hotel," which overnight became the number-one record all over the country. Immediately his other records also became hits. He was big and was booked on the Milton Berle television show in Hollywood. His free-wheeling, swinging, gyrating, twisting, uninhibited style of movement with the beat and his singing acclaimed him the new big record star of the day. He was king of this new medium he had introduced—but the critics blasted him.

"I call it 'rock 'n' roll.' You rock and roll with the music," Elvis would explain to the deaf ears of the unfriendly news media.

From then on Elvis was The Colonel's boy, and vice versa. Everything became "Elvis and The Colonel." Colonel Parker continued his fantastic enterprise to promote Elvis to top worldwide success. He paraded elephants with Elvis ads displayed on their flanks. He hired midgets to parade as an Elvis Presley Fan Club.

28

He made deals with merchants to get articles tagged with Elvis' name. He guided his recordings and his life. He encouraged Elvis to wear fad clothes. Elvis, who had never had money to buy all the shirts and sweaters he wanted, now had them by the dozens and silver and gold lamé suits tailored for him. With his hair long and effected sideburns, Elvis began the rage of wearing bell-bottom pants and open-throat shirts. He used Brilliantine on his hair to slick it down. Soon a whole nation of young men was wearing fancy shirts, bell-bottom pants and long sideburns with hair slicked back. And the girls had discovered a new idol, who was to upset all records of idol worship established by the late Valentino, Sheik of the 20's and 30's.

Elvis Presley also overnight found himself becoming a prisoner of national and international adulation and fame. He couldn't venture forth without being mobbed, without having girls and women fight to reach him, to pull and tear off his clothes—hoping to get something of his as a souvenir. Whenever he ate in a restaurant, even the waitresses would fight for a crust or crumb that Elvis left on his plate. Why? Because his hands, Elvis' hands, the hands of their idol, had touched it. The barber shops carefully swept up the clippings from Elvis' black locks for safekeeping. They had standing offers of thousands of dollars for single strands of his hair for love charms.

All of this pandemonium did not get financially out of hand, for Colonel Parker was working full time setting order from chaos—and with it the dollars were steadily rolling into Elvis' bank accounts.

"We had bought a beat-up old green 1937 Pontiac when we moved to Memphis, my Daddy and me," Elvis said. "My Daddy and I used to work at it all the time to keep it going. But now Mama not only had the pink Cadillac, but we began to have real money. And the next thing we did was buy a nice house. Playing the fairs and one-night stands, I began bringing home so many souvenirs, and so many presents began pouring in that we didn't have any place to keep them all, even in the new big house we'd just moved into. The first thing after the cars—I bought us a good new home. Then it seemed like we were outgrowing it and it seemed so strange, for we had always lived in two rooms or three at the most. And now with all of my guitars and outfits for our shows on the road, everything was overflowing. We had no space."

"I had seen a big church on the highway outside Memphis, a beautiful building. When I saw it was for sale, I promised myself that when I got the money I would buy it for Mama. It was Graceland."

CHAPTER FIVE

P.T.A. Bans Elvis' Gyrations as Vulgar Menace to Youth

THE "ELVIS AND The Colonel" decade started up in 1955 like a hurricane!

Elvis' overnight popularity, with ever-increasing and almost incredible amounts of money demanded by The Colonel that were paid Elvis, caused a tumult of public controversy. Elvis Presley was vibrating into the news, the homes, the senses of the great American public! Like nobody else in years, he hit national curiosity and imagination! Who is this Elvis Presley, people were asking? Millions of people all over the world began buying his records. Elvis was the country boy who had been touched by instant magic. He was now high-powered, racy, sexy, with extraordinary potential to earn millions of dollars.

The Mafia, alert to money-making record kings, decided to dip into the country music field. They decided to dip into a piece of "the Presley action." They'd had no trouble buying percentages of new singers. With their controls in the pop music world and juke boxes they could make or break young singers. "How about this new freak Elvis?"

Colonel Parker wasn't selling Elvis in any percentages. "Cut up my boy? I should say not!" He ignored the Mafia's offers and later on their warnings. No one was going to muscle in on his boy. Elvis was becoming so sensationally big world wide, "the dark-suit boys" decided not to press the action. The powerful Mafia, for once, was forced by the sheer spotlight of Elvis' popularity to lay off!

Elvis not only set the music world on fire, he shook up the whole record business. Soon even the most staid but bewildered conservatives were forced to admit that Elvis Presley was changing the whole shape of American pop music. His influence on the personal and entertainment tastes of teenagers grew with lightning speed. It opened the door for almost every new teenage craze that has since zoomed to popularity in the ensuing years. Nothing and no one like Elvis had happened in a decade.

Elvis made an appearance on the Ed Sullivan TV Show. Sullivan had been indignant at the Colonel's price, but he wanted the top ratings Elvis brought. The camera panned to Elvis' waistline and carefully avoided showing his swinging, gyrating hips. (He had already been labeled with the dubious title "Elvis the Pelvis.") But he was to return on the Sullivan show again. Each trip, The Colonel upped Elvis' price tens of thousands of dollars.

Elvis was signed for Las Vegas by Sammy Lewis, the enterprising producer at the New Frontier Hotel. This was Elvis' first appearance in a plush Vegas nightclub, and his only one until 1969. Lewis signed Elvis for two weeks at $7,500.00 weekly. Sheckey Greene was second on the bill. A sign of Elvis' figure, fifty-feet high, was put out in front in blazing lights. But Danny Thomas and other well-known entertainers easily outdrew Elvis, the newcomer, who was not then quite ripe for Las Vegas' sophisticated older audiences.

Elvis spent his time between shows in the local movie house seeing western films. He would see the same western bill over and over again, recalls Mr. Lewis. Elvis also had a penchant for the peanut butter and banana sandwiches that he would have sent up by the dozen to his room. It was also noted that Elvis neither smoked nor drank hard liquor but was fond of cold milk and ice cream sodas. Mr. Lewis, discovering that Elvis was to start his first film in Hollywood, offered Elvis a third week. The Colonel said no. Others said Sheckey Greene was the bigger attraction, but footage of Elvis on stage with a bevy of dancing girls behind him was filmed by The Colonel for a future movie. The Vegas chorus girls dug Elvis and coteried around him on sight.

To keep him from too much mauling, a group of hometown Memphis boys traveled with him. They were always on hand. When Elvis came through the hotel gambling casinos, and by chance was unnoticed, the boys, prodded by The Colonel, would stand off to the side and start yelling, "There goes Elvis Presley!" This created a commotion which Elvis smilingly accepted as part of his job, and he'd sign autographs.

Timing is everything. Unfortunately it was not until two weeks after his Las Vegas engagement that his new hit records resulted in his picture and story in a big national magazine. People began to realize *who* "Elvis the Pelvis" was and became more fully aware of his impact.

His effect on teenage girls grew alarmingly out of hand. Soon vicars and ministers and PTA groups began to voice disgust and great alarm at Elvis' gyrating actions on stage. They denounced him as vulgar! Girls went into hysteria or shock or both on sight of Elvis— they swooned listening to his records. The gyrations of the 'King of Swoon' had the teenagers glassy-eyed with ecstasy. While parents were protesting Elvis' show as lewd, the teenage girls were saying, "Elvis' voice makes me shiver down to my toes." Or, "I feel suddenly nice and warm inside, when I play Elvis' records."

Irate fathers felt differently. When the beloved thirteen-year-old daughter of a powerful New Jersey mobster took sleeping pills, her adoring father found her death note to Elvis. After the doctor was able to restore his daughter, the father heard her cry, " I love Elvis and he will never marry me!" The mob man was set to

32

give the word "to nail Elvis," when he learned, and his daughter readily confessed, that she had never had a physical encounter with the singer. She was a victim of the national hysteria of girls who wanted to die for the love of Elvis!

"Who is this fuckin', pukin' ham strung pig singer?" the father demanded. The report on Elvis came back within an hour: Elvis was the worldwide hero of teenagers; hands off!

The New Jersey mobster was only one of hundreds of protesting males; parents, brothers, husbands, and boyfriends who wanted to get Elvis killed, due to their women folk's love-lorn hysteria. In some cases this often verged on suicide. The best they could do, they found, was to urge the churches and the wives and mothers to get rid of Elvis! Ban him as a national scourge. Their protests and bans at the time threatened Elvis' demise!

"Elvis Presley is sexually setting young American womanhood on fire," declared ministers. They rose in their pulpits all over America demanding that Elvis be banned. Elvis was accused of actually corrupting thousands of young girls by "exciting them physically and emotionally in the wrong way."

Fan clubs for Elvis at the same time were organized throughout the country with membership cards. The instructions to Elvis Fan Club members read: "To be members in good standing each week you must send out five postcards to a disc jockey in your vicinity, and follow it up with ten phone calls a week to the radio stations, demanding Elvis' records." Girls formed Elvis Presley clubs of their own which met at their various homes for Elvis-record sessions. They would scream and cry at every record with over-wrought emotions.

Boys at first began to tease the girls who were avid Elvis fans. Soon young men were trying to imitate Elvis by singing and wiggling, while department stores stocked cheap guitars and bell-bottom pants that proved fast sellers. Young men began wearing long sideburns, à la Presley. Schoolteachers told their classes that Elvis Presley was hurting the teenage generation, with his

33

erotic behavior in public. His sexy gyrations were said to be disgraceful. He was introducing to this young generation a new uninhibited sexual freedom which was declared unhealthy and demoralizing. Boys with long hair and sideburns were always the ones, it was declared, who started trouble in the cafeterias and the classrooms.

Elvis' imitators were decried as "awful hoodlums!" Some of the boys were accused of setting their long hair in finger waves like Elvis. Elvis was reported going to beauty shops to get his pompadour set.

In Los Angeles, when Elvis appeared for two nights at the Pan Pacific Auditorium, thousands of girls were turned away. The place was packed solid and tickets sold at three-to-five dollars with a dollar for the program. A large contingent of boys imitating Elvis' dress style was on hand.

At the start, a rock 'n' roll band preceded Elvis. When the star, Elvis himself, walked on stage, everyone began to shout, stamp, jump, scream, and shriek. Extra police were called in to stop the bedlam. They had to stand by helplessly! Who can shut up three thousand screaming teenagers!

Elvis began to play his guitar. Whatever he had said into the microphone couldn't be heard over the cheers and screaming ovation being accorded to the idol. Elvis strummed his guitar and talked and no one could hear that either. You could see Elvis was singing, but no one could hear a word.

Elvis finally grabbed one of the mikes, holding it, and he began petting it as though it were a girl or a teddy bear. The latter had now become, he said, his passion. He had long won teddy bears by pitching balls into holders at the fairs! Now he collected teddy bears and never traveled anywhere, even in a car or on a plane, without his big teddy bear for a companion. This of course was The Colonel's idea. Whether Elvis, who was actually on the shy side, was embarrassed or not, he never faltered in carrying out The Colonel's programming.

With the mike in hand, Elvis began his shimmy wiggles. His whole body was moving from head-to-toe in a

34

sexy frenzy. At times he pulled at his clothes as though he wanted to be free of them. Some of the girls fell on the floor as if they were having a fit. Some girls kicked and lashed out their arms. Some grabbed their faces and dug their nails into the flesh. Some closed their eyes and pulled their hair out by the roots. Everyone reacted, caught up in a wild maddening love-in.

Colonel Parker's shape was seen behind the curtain pushing out a statue of a big dog—the RCA Victor record dog. Elvis who was singing 'Hound Dog,' began to sing to the dog. He gyrated to the floor and appeared to be making love to the dog as if it were a girl. Elvis moved toward the dog and he rolled over and over. He pushed the dog, and it almost fell off the stage but Colonel Parker pushed it back at Elvis. The fervor of his fans had reached fever pitch.

Elvis kept singing and rolling on the floor. Everyone seemed to go mad. A fourteen-year-old girl began snarling and biting her own arm. Others were rolling in the aisles in convulsions.

Finally Elvis went off stage, and hundreds of girls rushed up, stomping the security guards. Using their handkerchiefs, they rubbed the floor where Elvis had stood. One grabbed the mike and made love to it. Some girls and some fellows rolled on the floor like they had seen Elvis do. Policemen had to drag them off by force as they screamed and cried incoherently.

The next morning's newspaper banner headlined, "Elvis performance disgraceful, lewd and disgusting." The police and the vice squad came the second night to make arrests. Elvis, however, had toned down his act. Everyone who'd seen the previous night's show, kept saying, "But you should have seen Elvis last night."

Teenage fans throughout the country made an uproar. They began to fear for their idol Elvis. They didn't want him to be banned or to lose him. "Please don't take Elvis from us," they'd write in thousands of letters to newspapers and to the ministers who were crusading against him.

Among those aghast at the Presley performance and

one of the most vociferous anti-Presley columnists was Hedda Hopper. She spent many columns trying to kill Elvis and The Colonel, decrying them as "the most obscene vulgar influence on young America today!" Years later Miss Hopper had the good sense, she said, to realize that the Twist which she was trying to master one night at a Hollywood nightclub, was actually "the gyration that would never have become accepted as a part of Americana if Elvis Presley had not prepared us for it."

Elvis, brought up as a strict church-going, God-fearing young man, had many qualms obeying The Colonel's showy sensation-seeking tactics in setting him up as a world-wide sex symbol. Gladys and Vernon Presley, reading in their hometown paper that their son was "demoralizing the youth of America," that he was " 'Sir Swivel Hips,' a vulgar unworthy idol of the young," were appalled. Elvis consoled them and explained it was all a show to get him known. They must not worry. Trust The Colonel, who knew what he was doing. "I trust The Colonel," Elvis said. That was good enough, or had to be, for Gladys and Vernon. "The Colonel is really like a daddy to me when I'm away from home," Elvis said. "He has to make me controversial to get me going. We haven't done anything bad." The blue noses thought otherwise.

The Colonel, a good judge at appraising character, had known that Elvis had something else as basic as his obvious sex appeal that drew young women to him like a magnet. He had a quality inside of him that made girls and women alike know that he was a good person: that all of this razz-ma-tazz was a sensational springboard to get him on the glory road to fame. Actually by instinct, no matter what he did, how he acted, you knew what he was—that basically Elvis had integrity, honor and good character. You knew that no matter what he was called to do on stage, that he was a nice religious person beyond reproach, who would never change. That made him worthy of being an idealistic idol to believe in and praise, which was accepted and acknowledged by his fans.

The Colonel had in mind a combination Valentino-Gable in Elvis. He had to start the ball rolling big, and sex is the best ready-seller in any market. While Elvis was being voted the promising country western artist of his time, ironically the press everywhere was blasting him with personal criticism. "Unfit Hero for Youth," said even the Communist press, which took pot shots at Presley when young West German teenagers formed Presley fan clubs. The East German teenagers formed a Presley Ban. *The Young World,* a Communist newspaper, declared the singer was a "weapon in the American psychological war. His secret function is to recruit youth with unclear political views."

The Evening Independent in St. Petersburg, Florida, in the summer of 1956, editorialized on its front pages that Elvis was the Pied Piper of rock 'n' roll, "a swivel hipped, leg-lashing entertainment bomb who blasted the downtown area into chaos all day yesterday. Screaming fainting teenagers lined the streets early to catch a glimpse of Elvis, a rock billy gyrating singer whose sexy sultry style has caused a revolution!" Some proclaimed, "We must protect our daughters from the Elvis Presley exposure."

Elvis' single records followed hit after hit. "I Want You, I Need You, I Love You," "Hound Dog," "Love Me Tender," "Too Much," "All Shook Up," "Loving You," "Jailhouse Rock," "Hard-Headed Woman," "I Got Stung," "A Fool Such as I," "A Big Hunk of Love," "Elvis' Volume One," "Elvis' Volume Two," and "When Elvis Sings Christmas Songs."

"I live with my conscience," Elvis declared. "That's what's important. That and my faith in God. It hasn't been all easy," he admitted, "But I keep my faith in God, and I want to keep on, so my Mama and my Daddy and my folks will never be poor or hungry again. No one knows how poor and hungry we've been, and how it is when you're sick and there's no money to get a doctor or to get some medicine from the drug store. Or to get even bare necessities without taking food out of your mouth to do it—because there's not

37

enough money for both! My Mama has worked so hard, I want to make it all up to her every way I can."

Elvis and The Colonel cooled the sexy dynamics of his act. The following year Elvis, who was winner of all honors of the teenagers' popularity polls, now discovered when the count came in, he had dropped to fourth place. The press headlined, "Perry Como, the baritone barber of Cannonsburg, Pennsylvania, shaved the sideburns off Elvis Presley to win a flock of honors in the Annual poll. Elvis' appeal to the bobbysoxers' poll, however, beat out Sinatra from third place in the voting." This gave Elvis a lot to think about. Would his popularity hold or vanish? He knew he had a service hitch in the army coming up in his immediate future. Would it all end then?

Happily at this time Elvis could lay away his gold lamé suits and teddy bears—Hal Wallis, one of motion pictures' most respected and artistic producers, was sitting at home watching television. When he saw Elvis on the Jackie Gleason show, the celebrated starmaker immediately called Elvis for screen tests.

Elvis was signed to a seven-year contract. His first film however, was a loan-out for another producer for *Love Me Tender*. Forgotten were all the 'Ban Elvis' campaigns as Elvis Presley was acclaimed a big new star and the sex symbol of this generation. That was how Elvis Presley's career was launched.

Elvis had done a lot of growing up by the time he was making his first movie in Hollywood. His parents came out to be with him and to see a movie studio. Elvis lived in a rented house. The Presleys soon returned to Graceland in Memphis, the beautiful mansion Elvis had by now acquired for them. Elvis was aware that Frank Sinatra had once experienced this same kind of fan adulation. And long before him, Valentino. No fad or no such adulation Elvis believed could be enduring. He shaved his sideburns. He began dressing more circumspectly, and he appeared to be less sensational.

He might have easily defended his gyrations against the tirades on his vulgar dancing by calling attention to the 'Black Bottom,' 'The Shimmy,' or 'The Tango,' and other sexy dance crazes of an earlier era. They were described at the time as vulgar and naughty. Certainly any clear-thinking person would not read super-sex into a good rolling rocking rock 'n' roll, which actually is only a little more than a 'swing your partner' version of folk dancing. Elvis, however, had never attempted to defend himself or his gyrations.

The Colonel allowed no interviews with Elvis. The press had to pay admission tickets to see him perform. The Colonel said what they wrote was their own business. Elvis said it was all a good wholesome outlet for emotional energy. It had none of the adult impact of the slow moonlight ballroom cheek-to-cheek body-pressed-to-body waltzing and fox-trotting or the undulating rhythms of the rhumba—but he never propounded this theory publicly. "Never complain, never explain," became his behavior pattern.

Either way Elvis' gyrations made speculative happy reading in the press and made his name bigger. It induced a greater curiosity about what he was really like as a human being.

Since reporters couldn't get interviews with either Elvis or The Colonel, they went to his home grounds in Memphis, Tennessee. They learned from his close-mouthed home folk that Elvis had extremely good manners, unfailing courtesy, and a gracious generosity to his family and friends in sharing his success and his earnings. There was an unpublicized, unknown-to-the-world Elvis Presley Youth Foundation in Memphis for the poor and underprivileged and he was raising money for it. In fact his contributions had begun at a figure of $50,000 donations twice a year.

When 12,000 people who've known you right along crowd into the state fairgrounds in your hometown to see you, and when they purchase the clap trap two-room house where you were born as a memorial shrine to you, in the first year of your blazing success around the world, you're indeed an unprecedented hero.

Can a boy so admired by his very own be so wrong?

Elvis, it was learned, called his mother every night no matter where he was. When he wasn't making a movie in Hollywood or wasn't on tour, he was home at Graceland living with his folks.

In Hollywood studios, people expected Elvis to be downright repulsive according to the publicized image that had preceded him. Instead they were amazed to discover Elvis Presley to be a highly regular, decent, intelligent and even modest young man. Everyone wound up liking Elvis. The reports on his conduct as a person were all good. People couldn't understand how he could remain so unspoiled with his tremendous success and adulation. Hollywood realized how unfair it all was to be prejudiced about a person they'd never met.

The Colonel, however, continued the mystery cloak of privacy and the Garbo technique surrounding his boy so that Elvis would continue to be a highly controversial subject of interest.

"Elvis never said 'Damn' or used any four-letter word at the studio," set workers said. All sets carried the sign, "Closed to all Visitors." The press had to snatch a word or an opinion willy-nilly to latch onto anything about the real Elvis.

To everyone's astonishment, Elvis retained the habit of saying 'Sir' and 'Ma'am' and 'Thank you' consistently to any and everyone. He seemed in person more like a Boy Scout than the world's new hot torrid male sex symbol!

CHAPTER SIX

Vegas Chorus Girl Tells Her Intimate Romance with Elvis

FOLLOWING HIS OWN instincts, Elvis relies on his own interpretive vocal and physical phrasing, which comes spontaneously and naturally. He doesn't ask for opinions. It is noted that Elvis does not rock 'n' roll all his songs; it depends on his feeling for each song at the time. So far he hasn't made the error of treating any one song unhappily. Surrounded by the usual yes people and backslappers and with everyone saying, "You're the greatest, Elvis," or, "That's just marvelous, just great!"—Elvis relies on his own judgment.

At times Elvis will ask a girl friend privately how she relates to something he has newly recorded. Or he will sing a snatch of verse to get her reaction.

"I used to always ask my mama. I sure missed her when I couldn't talk some of these songs over with her. She was always right. She had the feel. 'Sing the way you feel right from the heart, Elvis,' she would say. That's what I do."

Elvis, in spite of the lavish extravagant praise and some of the unwarranted criticisms, has maintained his own thing. He has and keeps on doing his own thing and successfully: "I don't want to get complicated. I want to keep myself and my singing as simple as possible. That way I enjoy it, and I hope other people do."

At the beginning of Elvis' newfound career with The Colonel, he bought his parents a new $40,000 house on a fashionable residential drive in Memphis. He had a swimming pool installed. One room was filled with the stuffed animals that fans had sent him as presents from all over the world. Elvis was finding that he was collecting so many gifts on his tour that in spite of the new large home, the Presleys soon had a problem—lack of space for all of Elvis' increasing gear and souvenirs. Crowds also began collecting around the house. Cars were driving and stopping to take a look at the place where Elvis Presley lived. Soon the private residential street was as busy as a downtown section in Memphis. It would require a traffic light; neighbors began complaining. A committee asked to buy the house so they could have peace and quiet again. Elvis suggested perhaps that he should buy the homes of his neighbors.

This all resulted in Elvis negotiating for Graceland. He purchased the beautiful estate that had been used for a church for the sum of $100,000. He had a high iron fence built around the property with a figure of himself playing his guitar featured on the front gates. The crowds now collected in greater numbers. In a short time the highway was dotted with gas stations and hotdog stands. Enterprising merchants saw the advantage of cashing in on the Presley popularity.

Everyday at four o'clock Gladys Presley would walk down to the gate and talk with Elvis' fans. She would spend an hour or two with them, answering their questions about her boy. Sometimes she would pose for snapshots.

In the beginning, Gladys Presley would happily invite some of the girls to come inside and take a brief tour of the grounds and the house itself. She was so proud of their new home with its mirrored walls, winding staircase, organ, grand piano, lush drapes, plush carpeting, and beautiful furnishings. She was proud to show her model kitchen and her new china and glassware. Sometimes she'd open her chest of silver with place settings for a hundred.

"Elvis gave me this last Christmas," she said happily.

"The other night Elvis called me from Hollywood," she confided. "He had seen Kim Novak in a mink coat. Elvis asked me if I wanted a mink coat for my birthday. Imagine, a mink coat," Gladys Presley smiled proudly. "I told Elvis no, where would I wear a mink coat here in the South. I'd be embarrassed. I don't know anyone here who has one. 'We're not movie stars,' I told my son."

Gladys Presley had worked very hard with decorators doing all of the furnishing herself. She and Elvis had pored over colors, materials, swatches, and plans to have it just so. His gold records were framed in the white pine-paneled library. By now they numbered 31. Elvis' bedroom was mirrored and draped with red velvet, contrasting the gold and white decor. He had a huge kingsize bed.

Elvis was out of town most of the time now making a movie in Hollywood. Usually his parents went along with him. They first stayed at the Hollywood Knickerbocker Hotel on Ivar Avenue on Hollywood Boulevard. Since Elvis had so many kin and people with him, the hotel assigned him the entire eleventh floor. The following year Elvis stayed at the Beverly Wilshire Hotel, where the hotel management complained of the many fans who hung around the lobby and entrances at all hours of the day, congesting the doorways. Elvis had to be taken out in an ambulance to avoid the mobs of girls. It was decided he had better take a private home as his next Hollywood residence.

Many young women came into Elvis' life. He enjoyed the company of girls. While he was pleasant and said to be sweet and thoughtful, he didn't get seriously involved with any one special girl during his career's first big swing upward.

"Suddenly I am reading all about my love life in print," he exclaimed with dismay. "It isn't even true, most of it!" This was 1956. "I have been so busy keeping up with the schedules The Colonel sets up for me, I haven't had much time to date girls. But I manage," he winked.

Barbara Hearn was a girl in Memphis he'd known for some time. He liked her. In the beginning Elvis used the big green family car. When overnight he got into money, he went car-happy. There were six cars either in the garage which held three, or on the driveway or out front—all for the Presley family.

Elvis' new popularity soon made him a virtual prisoner. One night when he had returned to Memphis, he called Barbara Hearn to explain to her that there were so many people out in front of his place he couldn't get out. "I can't hurt their feelings by driving out without stopping," he explained. "Mama has cooked a nice dinner and I am wondering if you'd mind coming here to Graceland and having dinner with us? Please bring your mother if she'll come too."

That became a habit with Elvis, to invite his girl friends to visit him at home. It became increasingly difficult for him to get by the mobs of fans that congregated and waited for hours, wherever he might be.

Barbara knew Elvis when he was still driving truck. She was as excited about his new career as he and his mama and daddy. Elvis loved to play pool. He was a

43

whiz, said Barbara. They often played at Elvis' small pool table.

Elvis would be fine until nine or ten in the evening, when the crowds had thinned out in front, then the restless energetic Elvis would sneak out his big white Lincoln and cruise around the town.

Making his first two movies in Hollywood, Elvis began meeting and dating starlets. He began dating Natalie Wood.

From childhood his Mama had always told him to bring his friends home to play. Now that he was a young man, Gladys still encouraged Elvis to bring his friends home. Anyone Elvis met and dated in Hollywood was welcome.

Usually a plane ticket was provided, and either Elvis flew with them or met them at the airport. Or Vernon Presley met them. Gladys was always gracious and made the girls' visits enjoyable.

Natalie Wood had hoped to keep her week's stay with Elvis at Graceland a secret. Elvis and Natalie's scoot around the city on his motorcycle came to the attention of a local photographer, however. He tracked them down. Pictures of Natalie and Elvis hit newspapers all over the world. It was hinted that they were engaged.

In bewilderment, Elvis said, "I can't understand. If I even date a girl one time or two times, I read we are engaged. When a girl friend comes to Memphis to pay my mama and daddy and me a visit at our home, I read we're getting married when there's been no such idea of anything like that at all."

Judy Spreckles gave Elvis a friendship ring, a black star sapphire which Elvis wore on his little finger with great pleasure. Judy was one of many Hollywood starlets, actresses, and young socialites who visited Elvis in Memphis.

Most of the girls on their return were asked to describe their visits to Elvis' home. Few did. The girls generally conceded that Elvis was traveling around so much, and that with an army hitch ahead of him, it would be ridiculous for him to get serious with any one girl. It seemed Elvis usually gave a girl a big rush, invited her home to meet his parents, and next month there would be another girl to enjoy his company. Affectionate by nature, he appealed to girls right and left. All sang his praises, grateful to be singled for even a short interval as his date.

Yvonne Lime was just twenty-one and a budding young actress when she met Elvis on his second movie in Hollywood, *Loving You.* They began dating, going for drives and late movies around Hollywood during the weekends. On Monday when Elvis was back at the studio as Mr. Big Movie Star, he asked if she'd like to pay him a visit in Memphis. Her mother approved and Yvonne had a wonderful week.

"We stayed in his old home—the new big home Graceland was still in the process of being furnished," she said. "Elvis said the family wouldn't move in until it was all completed. He seemed to worry that his mother was working too hard getting it ready. He kept telling her she should take it easy, that if they didn't move in next week, it could be next month. 'Don't work so hard and worry so much, Mama,' Elvis would tell her."

Even in Memphis, as a hometown boy Elvis was mobbed everywhere they went. They drove about in his big cars. Elvis took her on the back of his motorcycle. They sipped sodas at the local drugstore. They visited some of his school friends. Yvonne reported that she went with Elvis to get a haircut. (Even in Memphis, the barber was carefully sweeping up the trimmings of Elvis' locks that had been promised to fans.) They attended a high school dance and they went to church together.

Elvis was a night person, who liked to stay up late and go to bed at dawn. His mother Gladys was an early riser. Often Yvonne would go downstairs and visit with Gladys in the kitchen, before Elvis was up.

Yvonne returned from Memphis, and it was weeks before she saw or heard from Elvis again. Then unexpectedly he was calling her on the telephone. They yakked and planned a picnic at the beach. Yvonne said she and her girl friends from Glendale would bring the food. Elvis arranged for cars, and over three dozen kids formed a caravan to the beach, but it rained. The group finally had to return to the hotel where Elvis was staying. Elvis had told them in the downpour they could picnic in his hotel suite.

At the hotel they couldn't get past the elevator man. They also couldn't reach Elvis' suite—the telephone operator had strict orders not to put any calls through to that floor for Elvis. In desperation the kids ganged up at a corner outside the hotel and they began to yell for Elvis. He stuck his head out, saw the situation and sent one of his Memphis boys down to squire them all upstairs.

Everyone sat around and watched TV and munched sandwiches, until someone suggested that Elvis play his guitar and sing.

"You know something, they are all at the studio," he said. "Where can we buy one?" Someone remembered that Music City in Hollywood was open all day Sunday until midnight. Soon the whole gang was en route to Music City to buy a guitar so Elvis could sing.

Some girls found dating Elvis thrilling just being that close to him. Some actually found it rather boring. Elvis couldn't take a girl to dinner for the two of them alone. They'd get mobbed. It was too complicated and turbulent for Elvis to walk a girl into a restaurant or even a movie. Soon he never went out without his Memphis cousins and friends who worked for him, ran interference and played guard when necessary.

A girl dating Elvis usually found herself driving around for hours with him in his car, stopping when possible at some small nondescript hamburger stand for a sandwich and a coke. Even this was not always satisfactory, for Elvis would be recognized. The owners and others would gather around and talk and ask for autographs.

People would ask Elvis to explain his bumps and grinds. Good-naturedly he'd try to explain. "I just go with the music, naturally," he'd say. "The music goes round and round and I go round with it."

46

The Presley name was great bait for Elvis' Memphis boys, who became known as his "Memphis Mafia." "It goes great with dames," said one. "I tell them I work for Elvis, and would they like to come up to a party at Elvis' place? No girl ever says no. In fact they are eager to come along and bring a girl friend for me."

Elvis had eyes for the gorgeous chorus beauties in Las Vegas. And everyone had an eye for Elvis. Kathy Gabriel, Kitty Dolan, and Sandy Preston were among those he dated. Elvis would rent a Cadillac and motorcycle in Las Vegas, buy the girls a helmet, and go for spins on the highways.

Kitty Dolan, a gorgeous brunette, had eyes and a face like Elvis' mama, Gladys Presley. Elvis invited Kitty to visit him at Graceland. Kitty talked to this writer about it at the time. It was now 1958.

"It was amusing the way I met Elvis," Kitty said. "I was singing at the Tropicana Hotel in Las Vegas. When I came off the show, and was walking through the lobby, my eyes were attracted to a group. The group was composed of every pretty girl in the show and out of it. And they were flocked around Elvis Presley, whom I instantly recognized."

"The girls were making a complete fuss over Elvis. I walked over and looked for a second. And I laughed tongue-in-cheek. I wouldn't let myself do a thing like that. The girls were sitting on the floor at his feet holding onto him anywhere they could. From the back they put their arms around his neck and a couple were trying to balance on his lap. It was too, too, too!"

"As I looked at this display of idol worship, Elvis' attention was drawn to me. He caught my expression completely. I smiled like, 'You're too, too, too, Honey Chile.' He got the message."

"Those girls had a lot of nerve, and Elvis said later, 'You struck me as a girl who was different, who couldn't care less.'"

"I caught every detail and as I walked away, one of Elvis' boys—there are usually three or four of his pals who hang around him, and I believe a couple of them are on his payroll to help him—ran after me."

" 'Elvis would like to meet you,' the boy said."

"I replied, 'You tell Mr. Presley to speak for himself, John Alden.' "

"I thought that would get some reaction, and I kept on walking but very slowly. My intuition told me that Elvis had started walking slowly the same direction, to catch up with me by accident."

"When we both had walked slowly enough—long enough, we turned and smiled at each other. Elvis began stuttering an introduction, and I told him, 'We met forty-five minutes ago. We know each other already.' "

"Elvis looked relieved that he didn't have to make a big issue of introducing himself. I put him at ease, and I smiled. 'The girls sure make a big thing out of you, and a fool of themselves. But eat it up, Baby, while you can get it!' "

" 'How about a date?' " he asked as we walked to my car which was parked outside."

"Of course I was thrilled, but I said, 'you can call me tomorrow.' I gave him my telephone number."

"Now if it weren't for Elvis Presley, I can say I could never be induced to get on a motorcycle. But the next morning he telephoned and asked if I'd like to go for a ride with him."

"Elvis was racing along, and I was sitting on behind, a little scared and sticking to him like glue. Some of the cops were so thrilled to recognize Elvis that they rode along with us as an escort. When we were going fast, I said, 'If you were not you, you'd get tickets.' "

"I saw a lot of Elvis during his week's stay vacationing in Las Vegas. Elvis said to the others, 'One thing about Kitty. You can't put one over on her. She knew I was going with other girls like crazy. She knows.' And, 'I love her long black hair. It is wonderful.' "

"The other girls in the show were so jealous that I was the real date with Elvis. But I didn't care. Elvis was sweet and I loved being with him."

"One day we were out riding and it began to get cold. Elvis said, 'Here,' and he took off his shirt and put it over my shoulders. It is a gray and white striped shirt, and when we got back, Elvis said, 'You look

48

cute. Keep it.' Inside, the label says, 'Designed especially for you.' When I would wear it, some of the catty girls would say, 'What you doing with that shirt?' And some of the nicer ones would say, 'Isn't it like having Elvis' arms around your shoulders?' "

"Elvis called me about the time I had finished my engagement in Las Vegas. He was starting his last picture, *King Creole,* for Hal Wallis at Paramount, before the Army. He was staying at the Beverly Wilshire and often, since he couldn't walk out on the street without being mobbed, he'd invite his friends up to his temporary home. There would always be records and food and pop for everyone, and we'd all sit around and talk, sing, and listen to records. Often I'd help Elvis with his script and I'd play the characters opposite him while he memorized the lines."

"Sometimes Elvis would take out a cigar, but I think it was for a lark for I don't think he really liked it. It was probably one someone gave him because Elvis doesn't smoke or drink. And he doesn't chew gum. Only occasionally he'd go for a piece of candy. At the Presley home near the base he had a big glass jar of hard candies, and he'd take a piece now and then. I noticed, however, after his mother's death, he was not eating like he had. He'd take food and leave about half of it."

"It was Valentine's Day, and Elvis had invited me for dinner with him. It was sent upstairs and served in the elegant dining room of the penthouse atop his hotel. I didn't expect a Valentine. But secretly Elvis sent downstairs and had a kid bring back the biggest Valentine box of Louis Sherry candy they had. It was lavender and gold and I keep the metal box for things."

"I don't know how to tell the fun we had that night without it looking a little ridiculous. But we sat on the floor eating candy and watching television. And I'd say, 'Elvis, try this piece.' He'd bite into it and throw it back with, 'I don't like this, try this one.' We were throwing pieces of candy back and forth, and I guess we looked loco but we were having such fun."

"Elvis invited me to go to Frank Sennes' Moulin Rouge to see Sammy Davis, Jr. Elvis said, 'This will be my third time. I learn so much from watching him.'

"There were so many fans standing around the hotel. They were wise if a studio car with a chauffeur arrived, so I told Elvis I would call for him. I knew we'd never make it if he called for me and walked through the lobby of my hotel. I had a white Cadillac convertible with violins painted on the doors that I had bought from George Liberace. First I telephoned (telling him to meet me) blocks away—poor Elvis, the price of fame. He went down the freight elevator and through the kitchen to the garage where two of the other boys called a taxi for Elvis to go two blocks to my car. When he got out there were squealing fans, and the two boys rushed in front of Elvis first. Then Elvis was in the middle and they ran till Elvis was shoved into my car. We drove away from the running fans who tried to get in the car."

"At the Moulin Rouge we met Elvis' producer, Hal Wallis, and Charles O'Curran, who joined us for dinner. Elvis loved the show, but the word had gone around and people were coming up for autographs all the time. Sammy's finale was a takeoff on and his impression of Elvis."

"Elvis said, 'Imagine him putting me on the finale of his show! This guy is the most versatile, the most talented.' "

"We went backstage to avoid the mob out front waiting for Elvis, and Sammy walked us out to my car. Sammy thought it was Elvis' car, because he said, 'Oh, this is the new one! I haven't seen this one before.' Elvis squeezed my arm and we laughed, and kept the secret."

"Elvis is such a gentleman. He has a noble way about him. He never says an unkind thing about anyone. The only time I ever saw him angry was when someone made a disparaging remark about another person. Elvis took hold of that one's arm firmly and said, 'Don't you say that. He's my friend. It's only what you've heard. You should be careful about repeating thinks unkind about people you don't know.' "

"One time I asked him about all the girls who were supposed to be in his life. Elvis replied in a very gentlemanly way to the mention of the different names, 'Yes, I know her,' or, 'I liked her.' Or 'I did go out with her.' It is one of his virtues to be honest. When people, even close friends would say, 'Write to me from overseas,' Elvis would smile and say, 'I haven't written a letter in eight years. Don't count on it.' "

"In this business of being in the limelight, Elvis had trained himself not to take what he read and heard about himself too seriously. Even with the adulation of fans, I saw Elvis laughing a little at times inside himself when they would follow him because he never thought this would happen to him."

"One lady writer however did hurt him, and what she wrote about him hurt not only Elvis but his mother. Because it hurt her, it hurt him even more. She wrote quite a column panning his act as vulgar when he appeared at the Pan Pacific Auditorium."

" 'I don't mean to be vulgar, and I am not,' Elvis declared.

"One night at the Moulin Rouge, seated right across from us, and facing Elvis, was the woman who so hurt him—all during the evening she never looked at Elvis. 'She won't face me, she won't look me straight in the eye,' Elvis observed wonderingly. As soon as the show was over she (Hedda Hopper) jumped up and ran up the aisle, avoiding Elvis completely.

"That was the only time he was hurt personally, and with the reviews for his acting in *King Creole* for Hal Wallis, I didn't think he would ever face that kind of panning again."

"Elvis said to me in talking about his career, 'In the other two pictures, I felt like a singer trying to be a ham. But in this one I'm not uncomfortable. I enjoyed it. I felt that I was really acting.' "

51

CHAPTER SEVEN

Elvis Trades His Blue Suede Shoes
for Combat Boots

ELVIS IN 1953, had registered with his draft board. When he was eighteen, there were no fireworks, for his ducktail haircut, sideburns and tight pants and personality had yet to explode upon an unsuspecting world, not to mention Uncle Sam's.

Elvis wasn't too shaken up when he received his draft notice. A year had passed from the time he had passed his preliminary physical. It was then that the military became aware fully and somewhat alarmed of what the army would be in for when a young multi-millionaire movie and record idol became a G.I.! Special conferences were called at the Pentagon in Washington to discuss the merits and the problems to be anticipated when Elvis Presley would trade in his famous blue suede shoes for combat boots and army gear. A definite strategy was called for to handle the famous G.I.

Even before the Memphis Draft Board notified Elvis to report for induction, newspapers and columnists were giving exclusives on Elvis' future assignments in the service. The world of Elvis was told not to cry— he would be allowed to make regular television appearances and he would continue making records. All of which proved to be unfounded rumor.

An inkling of the hubbub to follow actually began in January, 1957, when Elvis was summoned for his pre-induction examination. He was just 22. Due to all of the speculation and reports the local draft board kept Elvis expertly top secret. He was notified by telephone one night to report for physical the next morning. Somehow the word leaked out, and when

Elvis Presley arrived in one of his white Cadillacs at Kennedy Veterans Hospital's examining station, he was greeted by Colonel Parker and hundreds of reporters, fans, TV cameras, and radio equipment. Waiting in the car for Elvis was Dorothy Harmony, a blonde singer and dancer from Las Vegas, who had been visiting him at Graceland. The army, in its eagerness to treat Elvis like everyone else, did not object to the photographers at first. "They've got a job to do," said an officer in command. He only objected when he discovered Elvis blushing to the roots of his dark hair stripped for physical and trying to politely fend off a photographer from snapping him in the nude.

Elvis walked out, passing Grade A. His I.Q. was reported later as average. The Elvis world had expected it to be pure genius!

"No, fellows, no pictures please with the young lady," he pleaded as he drove Miss Harmony to the airport.

It was announced that Elvis Presley would, like Vic Damone and other singing stars before him, be assigned to Special Services. Therefore Elvis' hair would not be sacrificed for a regulation army butch cut. Thousands of letters of appreciation for this information clogged the mails of the Pentagon.

This bulletin, however, which so delighted Elvis fans, enraged many mothers of G.I.s enough to write their Congressmen. Republican Senator Clifford Case forwarded such letters of indignation from mothers, asking why *Elvis* should be given a different VIP kind of treatment over their sons, directly to Army Secretary Wilber Brucker and forwarded it to Brigadier General J. E. Bastion, Jr. Word was issued that Elvis would receive his basic training at Fort Chaffee, Arkansas. And he would have to sacrifice his locks along with all of the other draftees.

By now strategy conferences came to amount to states of emergency as daily new Elvis crises plagued the big brass. The problem of how to handle Elvis Presley, said to be "the Teenagers' Delinquent Delight," became acutely real. Thousands of letters tied up the government mails from Presley supporters, and quite a few came from dissenters. State Representative H. Nick Johnson of Harlan, Kentucky, a Purple Heart veteran of World War II, on reading that Elvis had been granted a deferment to complete a film in Hollywood, resigned from his draft board. "If a making of a movie in Hollywood is a criterion for deferment, then the Sputnik and the Mutnik Age isn't as serious as represented. I can't conscientiously ask any mountain boy to serve the same country unless afforded the same treatment as Presley." This denouncement brought thousands of letters to Uncle Sam from fathers, mothers, wives, sisters, brothers, and children who had lost a member of their family in World War II.

More meetings were called at the Pentagon on "Problem Elvis." It became classified in several filing cases as "Operation Elvis" as the mail grew. Branches of the American Legion sent wires against such preferred treatment. Selective Service Director Lewis Hershey in Washington, D.C., swamped with telephone calls and wires, had to employ extra help. The army base switchboards within a radius of five hundred miles of Memphis were swamped with calls of inquiry asking if Elvis had been secretly inducted there?

It was no longer a matter of conjecture whether Elvis could take the army, but rather could the Army take Elvis? And how could he be treated just like the average American G.I.? While all of this pandemonium was snowballing into a cold war of the Elvis World vs. the Army, Elvis had yet to be inducted.

The news media kept the Elvis story in the headlines, by interrogating not only military heroes but stars and experts on the issue of Elvis—pro and con. Word from the Pentagon finally ruled: "Do not antagonize the press, but stop making any statements whatsoever on Elvis Presley."

By this time Hal Wallis had completed production plans for Elvis' third film, *King Creole*. He was ready to start when Elvis' draft notice arrived. Elvis was very reluctant to ask for a short deferment to complete the

54

picture. He certainly now wanted no favors and no special attention paid him. When it was pointed out that the studio would lose a lot of money invested in the scheduled picture, Elvis reluctantly asked for a 90-day deferment. It was immediately granted happily.

"Millions of other guys have been drafted, and I don't want to be different in the army from anyone else," Elvis insisted. "I don't care what branch of the service I'm in, I'll do my best. But I don't want to be placed in a soft spot or in special services as an entertainer," he announced. "I want to earn my way, earn respect. I don't want any outside influences to make it hard for me."

On the windup of *King Creole* Elvis said philosophically of the army, "I look forward to it as a great experience. If they make it tough for me, it won't be due to anything I do. The Army can do anything it wants with me."

Back in Memphis for his two weeks home before induction, Gladys Presley held open house for all of Elvis' friends. Hams were baking in the kitchen ovens and cakes and pies as she and Grandmammy Presley cooked Elvis' favorite foods—lots of pork chops, mashed potatoes, gravy, and apple pie—and plenty for everyone. Elvis always had lots of hungry friends. Elvis rented the local roller-skating rink after hours for a week at $70 a night, to start his parties at midnight. Graceland became fantastic with beautiful starlets from Hollywood and Las Vegas, displaying their charms on the verandas and in and out of Elvis' fancy four Cadillacs. Elvis had originally purchased the pink one with his first money for Mama. Then he bought a purple one, a gold one, and a white one. As his taste became more conservative, so did the color of his cars. His four Cadillacs were all white now.

Elvis had long found himself constantly beset by hecklers who wanted to fight, and he had never backed away. So The Colonel had Elvis take up judo in self-defense. His rapid progress in those manly arts of self-defense were publicized to thwart the jealous males who hankered to tangle with "Elvis the Pelvis."

During these last days at Graceland, Elvis enjoyed his friends. Calls came daily from California, girl friends who wanted to come to Memphis and pay Elvis a visit before his induction. Elvis always supplied the plane tickets and met them at the airport. Among these was blue-eyed Venetia Stevenson, the actress-daughter of the film star Anna Lee Venetia would ask her younger sister Caroline to sit by her telephone if she was momentarily called out of her apartment to "listen for a long-distance call from Memphis. If it comes, say I'll be back in twenty minutes."

Caroline had it all made up what she would say when Elvis called because her voice and her elder sister's were so much alike. The call didn't come through, however, until a day when Venetia was at home to answer. Venetia flew to Memphis to spend a few days with Elvis and his parents. She rode with him on his motorcycle. She said his parents were the nicest and so was Elvis.

Each girl seemed to sense after a visit at home with Elvis that it would not develop into a serious romance. They were not given that kind of encouragement either by Elvis or his mother.

Anita Wood was a Memphis girl, a pretty, dainty, sometime blonde whom Elvis had seen on their local TV station. They met and became good friends. For two years it had been long conceded that Anita Wood was his "best girl" in Memphis.

Elvis, who loves movies, also rented local movie houses after hours for his own theater parties. They would start at midnight and go on until morning, running his favorite films. Afterward Elvis and his friends, all kid-like, would fast-drive the town, pulling up in their caravan of cars at the first breakfast spot and pour in famished. As often they would also pile into the kitchen at Graceland where Gladys Presley would cook up flapjacks and hominy grits all night long.

Always people were ringing the front gate bell and pouring into the house to see Elvis. More and more reporters and photographers from all over the country were swarming about Graceland. Elvis didn't seem to mind. He was always cooperative, pleasant, and cheerful. There was no evidence here of The Colonel or his well-known Hollywood restrictions about seeing Elvis.

The night before Elvis was to report to his draft board, he took Anita Wood to a movie. He had given her a $500 cocktail ring. Now he gave her a car. It was a year old, not exactly new, but he said she needed one, and he wanted her to have it. She was overjoyed.

Anita was thrilled to be "Elvis' No. 1 girl." She had danced cheek-to-cheek with Elvis at the big school auditorium dance honoring the hometown boy who had made good. She loved sharing all of the excitement.

Anita admitted that she had been terribly impressed at first, dating Elvis Presley, the big idol. He had bought her extravagant presents; bottles of perfume, chocolates, and big teddy bears, but more, she found that he was "the kindest, sweetest, nicest, and most sensitive person in the world." She adored him and decided she wasn't really yet good enough for him. "He is so genuine, so real, so serious, so mature, and such fun."

Now that he was leaving for the army, Anita told Elvis she didn't want any more expensive gifts from him. But there was one thing she would like to keep her company—a little dog.

Nine months later when Elvis was a G.I. in Europe he called Anita long distance to say Merry Christmas. A toy French poodle arrived special delivery that same day for Anita Wood. It bore a big Christmas card that read, "Merry Christmas, Anita—Elvis."

Gladys Presley wasn't feeling so well. Elvis said to her, "Mama, is there anything wrong?" Her skin was yellowish and she seemed to tire easily. Often he would find her sitting at her work in the kitchen. She admitted she didn't feel quite herself, but perhaps it was because of the worry of Elvis going to the Army.

Elvis and his mother were great friends. They'd often sit up all night talking to each other in the kitchen when Elvis came home from a tour or Hollywood or even a date. Gladys called her son "Baby" affectionately, and now Elvis called her "Baby," too. He wanted to buy her everything, but Gladys did not care for fancy clothes. She was plump and preferred simple attire. Elvis bought her things like a special massage lounge chair and everything he could find for the house —Graceland was hers. Soon Gladys was taking the beautiful knick-knacks to the attic. "You've given me enough to open a gift store," she gently remonstrated. And when they'd talk Gladys would be making Elvis' favorite, bacon and tomatoes or mashed banana and peanut butter sandwiches, and they'd sit and eat. There was never a night when Elvis was away that he didn't call her for a long goodnight visit; when he missed the roses in full bloom at Graceland, she'd mail him some. With the new puppies, the horses, the donkeys and chickens and ducks, there was always a running report on the daily happenings at Graceland. Christmas was the big day.

Gladys and Elvis talked over the marvelous times in Hollywood while he was filming. She had even had a small part in one of his pictures. Then that wonderful summer of 1956 when "you performed for your very own in Tupelo, the entire proceeds went to the City for the start of The Elvis Presley Youth Foundation for Under-privileged Children." At the Alabama-Mississippi State Fair, Governor Ballard had presented Elvis with a gold key to the city. Elvis and his mother had so much to talk about. So much happiness they now shared. Always Elvis was asking, "Mama, isn't there something you want?" For Christmas he had given her a carving set. He hadn't known about mink coats and diamond bracelets—things like that—nor did Gladys. Gladys never really wanted anything for herself, just for Elvis and Graceland.

It was March 24, 1958. Elvis got to bed at 4:30 A.M. and his father Vernon called him at 5:30 to get up to go to his draft board. Gladys Presley was up, too. No one had had more than an hour's sleep. At 6:30 the Presleys were driving out of Graceland to the draft board with Elvis at the wheel.

Judy Spreckles, sugar millions heiress, had come from Hollywood to be on hand.

"If you think I'm nervous you're right," Elvis smiled at the swarms of photographers and reporters. After the oath of army allegiance, Elvis and the others were taken by army bus to the depot. The army had arranged for full press coverage of Elvis' induction. He was constantly answering questions, making statements, posing for pictures, and making recorded taped interviews and TV appearances. Finally during a short lull, Elvis, the great idol, curled up on a bench and in sheer exhaustion took a short nap.

Lamarr Fike, one of the boys in Elvis' entourage of helpers, had reported with Elvis that morning. Lamarr, weighing in at 270, was rejected, but he went along anyway, living off base to be on hand in case Elvis needed him.

At the draft board were the press—TV, radio, and news reporters. Some were from as far as West Berlin, London, Montreal, and New York—and as always hundreds of fans. Colonel Parker added to the color by personally handing out endless balloons advertising, "See Elvis in *King Creole*." It was like a carnival, except that Elvis was dead serious. Tired from being up all night, Elvis said, "The army will sure be different. These fellows get up when I'm usually going to bed." Promptly at 7 A.M., Elvis and fourteen other draftees were on a bus for the Kennedy Hospital induction center. Elvis was constantly questioned and besieged by the press.

Elvis became U.S. 53310761. He was handed a batch of telegrams and letters, including one from the Governor of Tennessee which read, "You have shown that you are an American citizen first, a Tennessee volunteer, and a young man willing to serve his country when called upon to do so." Signed, Governor Frank Clement. The Colonel prodded Elvis to read more from affluent people but Elvis declined. When The Colonel insisted, Elvis for the first and only time, became impatient. "It is me going in, and what happens will be to me. Not you."

While waiting for the army bus which was to transport the men to nearby Ft. Chaffee, Arkansas, Elvis asked permission to call Anita Wood. She drove up in her new car and gave Elvis a goodbye kiss.

Elvis was chosen as the leader of the new inductees. He was assigned to do roll call and make out papers and see the time schedule was kept. His first day in the army entailed responsibilities.

The Greyhound bus with Elvis and his compatriots set out for Arkansas. So did a hundred or more cars filled with fans and press. The bus kept to its regulation speeds, but the enthused fans and press raced and criss crossed the bus to gain vantage points to say hello and wave directly to Elvis aboard. It was miles of parade. When the bus stopped for the company to alight at a restaurant for chow, the army almost lost Elvis. The mobs awaiting him pushed forward and Elvis almost became a casualty in the folding doors of the bus.

"You're in the army for sure now," one of his fellow inductees said to Elvis as the bus rolled along. "I saw you when you played those two shows at the Southern Armory last summer. Man, that was something to remember," said another. "My sister had 'Elvis' tattooed for keeps on her bare legs. Some of her friends . . . well, they had 'Elvis' shirts, bracelets, stockings, garters, hats, and flags. Mom had me go along with my sister to see that no harm came to her. Man, when your white Caddy arrived at the stage door, the word blew the auditorium. I thought I was going to be stomped with all those kids yelling and screaming. Did you know there were one hundred ushers and a hundred police that night there to protect you from all those crazy women that love you."

Elvis smiled, yes, he remembered.

"Who was that feller that came onstage before you did, and he took a bow and said he knew Jimmy Dean personally—then he ran off? Nobody never knew who he was," another boy said.

"Oh, that was Nick Adams, an actor friend from Hollywood," Elvis enlightened him.

Elvis remembered it all well. There had been the first half of the show and then the second half when he came on. There had been all of those civic officials and The Colonel backstage, then they went out on stage to receive plaques for boosting Elvis' career, always plugging his records. Everyone had sung "God Bless America and God Bless Elvis."

He smiled as he dozed in his seat on the bus, remembering that pure gold-leaf suit and gold shoes that had cost almost $5,000—it had been torn half off of him. He'd been paid $30,000 for that day's work. Would it ever happen to him again?

"What happened to you that night, Elvis?" the boy behind him in the bus asked. "You didn't wiggle your fanny as much as you had before. I hear the police got after you so you had to cool it." Indeed Elvis had agreed to confine his virile exuberance and sway sideways instead of any back-and-front forward movements that usually accompanied his singing. And the kids, could they hear him? They were all screaming and squealing so. Elvis recalled how he usually signed off with "Thanks, everybody, you bring a lump to my billfold," (meaning all of the money that he was getting). Then how the girls had run up on the stage after he'd left and wiped the dust where he had stood and tried to swallow it, to get "a taste of Elvis inside," they'd said.

It was a hysteria and it would probably never happen again. But he had been able to live through it all and assure his Mama and his Daddy a life of security ahead. His Daddy could retire at 39, and they'd never have to worry about money as long as they lived. His only fear was always that someone crowding and mobbing to touch him would get hurt. He'd had so many fights picked with him when he ventured out alone, dropped into a bar for a soda or even an ice cream parlor. But for so long someone was always picking a fight with him. He had flattened a few, but now that he had learned karate, that was all behind him and he hoped everyone knew it. He knew he must never lose his temper, or he might kill someone.

It was still a nightmare to think that people had actually been killed over Elvis Presley. Two girls had gotten into an argument over an autographed photo of Elvis—whether it was his real signature or a stamped one. One girl had pushed the other into a swimming pool during the argument, then ran off, leaving the girl, not able to swim, to drown. There had been DeeJays fired and even arrested for burning Elvis' "White Christmas" records in the public squares at Nashville and in Seattle and Portland. The fifteen-year-old daughter of a city official in Redwood City, California, was bludgeoned to death with a baseball bat by her brother in a heated argument over Elvis.

"That's all gone, all behind me now," Elvis thought as he jumped out of the bus, which had now entered Fort Chaffee, Arkansas, to report at the initial receiving point. It was close to midnight, and the men were all tired. But there were hundreds of teenage fans waiting along with the ever-present media.

A photographer called out, "Give us a salute, Captain Elvis!" Elvis walked quietly on with the men. Several teenage girls attempted to follow him. They attempted to climb the post's fences. "We just want to sleep outside of Elvis' tent or wherever he'll sleep," they insisted. "We are his honor guards." When they were turned away, some of them jeered the army and Uncle Sam for kidnaping "The King of the Whole World, Elvis Presley."

Photographers were constantly being rejected from hiding places around the base. Twice hidden television cameras were discovered. At times reporters were found hiding under his bed in the barracks.

Elvis was now just a serial number, but Congressmen had a field day using Elvis Presley as a sure way to get into the news headlines. One introduced a bill saying, "The reason 18-year-olds should not be allowed to vote is Elvis Presley, who appeals to the low I.Q. of hoodlums." The Teddy Boys in London had ripped a movie house where an Elvis picture was playing to shreds in the frenzy of the Presley gyrations and rock 'n' roll. This was all reported in international headlines. The melee did not daunt The Colonel who relished all of this controversy over his boy. "That keeps him alive, keeps people talking Elvis!" the Colonel declared. The reporters got so out of hand in keeping the Elvis story going that one printed Elvis took dope. The Colonel issued a statement: "My boy doesn't use any stimulants. He needs soothing syrup."

Elvis established himself quickly as a solid citizen and good soldier. "I just want to be treated like everyone else," he insisted. And he was, but fans continued to plague Fort Hood, where Elvis was stationed for basic training with letters which added up to seven mail bags a week. Songwriters got on the bandwagon and wrote special songs for Elvis in the army and what his top sergeant did, etc.

Millions of record and movie fans had acclaimed Elvis, but the army, which trains G.I.s like Private Presley, revealed the real honest down-to-earth truth. Elvis took plenty of razzing from his fellow G.I.s: "How about the loan of a couple of million, El?" "Hey, El, want to give us some phone numbers of your Hollywood babes?" "Sure, this army isn't killing you, El." And "How can you sleep without your teddy bears, Elvis?"

"When 'Elvis the Pelvis' first arrived here at Fort Hood, we fellows aimed to give him the works! But brother, he proved to be a regular guy who can take it," the private report from one of Elvis' army buddies verified. "He is so damn decent and hard-working," he said. "We all fell in line with respect. I don't know one guy in the outfit who doesn't like Elvis. Now I can understand some of the women's enthusiasm which, until I got to know him, I checked off as pure wild femme infatuation, on the looney-bin side!"

Being in the army was not exactly an ideal way of living. Certainly, not when you're a film idol like Elvis with a garage full of Cadillacs and a white custom-built Continental; not when you have a big home with inch-thick purple carpets and a king-size black bed, and you can make a million or so a year on camera and records.

Unlike some film heroes, Elvis did not incite a private war with the army. He carried the same slice of responsibility with him into the service that he had in civilian life. He accepted and adjusted well.

"Do I miss my buddies and my friends? Naturally, but you can't go through life depending on friends. You have to depend on yourself. In the army, I'm making new friends," said Elvis.

"I am flexible," Elvis said. "I expect to conform. I've never become accustomed to things really easy. If I make it hard, the only one it's going to be hard on is me. I certainly don't mind hard work. I've done plenty of it before this. I worked as a common laborer, up at three every morning and in a defense plant. I drove a truck in Memphis for an electrical company. When I was in high school, I'd get out at three-thirty and be on the job at six-thirty, ushering for $12.50 a week. I'd be up at dawn every morning. It's nothing new to me."

"The oddity," he admitted, "is to get up and start running before breakfast. Breakfast is the one meal I count on. But the army isn't so rough. My folks had it rough. We lived in a housing project, and we were used to a hard life."

The army, his fans kept on worrying out loud in print, can make it rough—real rough—for anyone. And for a movie star—brother! Glenn Ford, Red Skelton, and any number could but didn't tell Elvis that they were kept on latrine duty for weeks and were assigned other degrading tasks to prove they were not privileged. The army is interested, a general once said, in mechanical manned units. Men who obey orders without question and are no longer individual personalities. Elvis, it was feared, would be subjected to much unfair treatment and find the going really rough. His fan clubs constantly voiced their worries—one fan-club president called the base, declaring, "If the army mistreats Elvis, we'll fix the army. We know how!" She didn't elaborate on how. One group organized "The Ladies in Waiting." Object: to ask disc jockeys to play Elvis Presley records for the duration.

Elvis' records were sellouts from "Heartbreak Hotel" to "All Shook Up" to his straight ballads sung in Rockabilly rhythm. The Christmas album that had been banned the year before with great publicity by some radio stations was now a complete sellout.

Elvis was put on the spot regarding his rock 'n' roll. "Every generation goes through a new era of music," he kept on patiently explaining. "It is young, alive, and fun. You can't stop it."

Then tragedy struck Elvis in the middle of his basic training and no one could help him—only God!

CHAPTER EIGHT

Elvis' Last Days with His Mother; Her Death

ELVIS, SHORTLY AFTER being sent to Fort Hood, Texas, rented a house for his parents, and they came to be near him. They could see him on the weekends when he could come home nights to sleep. Gladys Presley was obviously not well at all. She managed to keep her pain to herself. She wouldn't show it. She cooked dinners, assisted by Grandmammy Presley. "Don't worry Elvis about me," she told the Presleys. "He has enough on his mind getting along so new in the army." She had a prescription she used. She made Vernon promise he wouldn't let Elvis know how badly she felt.

Elvis came home and brought his new friends to meet her, along with Elvis' friends piling in from Memphis—Open House as usual.

Not taking the easy way out in the army, as an entertainer for the G.I.s, finally had a profound effect on the boys in the service as well as the public in general. Elvis' behavior and his willingness to do all duties assigned him without a gripe or single complaint made him a model G.I. The huge mailbags of packages of cookies, cakes, pies, and other goodies, baked and sent to Elvis by his thousands of fans, were shared by their recipient with his fellow G.I.s. This also added greatly to Elvis' image with the men.

However, the news media made daily contact with the base for reports on Elvis, which tied up an information officer day and night. The mail came in such numbers that it also required special men to handle it. How could Elvis Presley be handled like any average G.I. was still the major question at the Pentagon.

Within a few days after her arrival at the temporary Presley home at Kileen, Gladys Presley had a real bad spell. She had to go back to Memphis to her doctor right away. Gladys was scared. Elvis, undergoing the transition of million-dollar movie idol to G.I. Joe was confronted with a new fear and worry. He couldn't go with his mother. The day the Presleys left for Memphis Elvis was often noted going into the base chapel where he would kneel in prayer for long periods of time.

Mrs. Presley and her husband, now in Memphis, went to see their family doctor. He ordered her hospitalized for tests. Her illness was yellow jaundice, hepatitis. The disease had seriously attacked her liver and four specialists were called in.

Elvis was calling frantically at night from the base for reports. But the full seriousness of his mother's condition was withheld from him.

In three days, Elvis' commanding officer at Fort Hood received a request for emergency leave for Elvis due to his mother's severe illness.

Elvis had a fear of flying from the time a plane had set down in a semi-crash with him as a passenger. Even though he and the passengers had escaped without injury, it was his policy from then on to take the train or drive a car. He had also made his mother a solemn promise not to fly. This time, however, he took the first plane and rushed to the hospital. Elvis looked pale and worn when he brushed by thousands of fans keeping vigil outside the hospital. He rushed to his mother's room.

When Elvis came out of the hospital, there were undisguised tears in his eyes. To the questions he said quietly, "Mama is not doing well, at all. Not at all." Elvis spent the next day in his mother's room. He held her hand and she would manage a wan smile. The doctors felt greatly encouraged, for Elvis' strength and nearness had given Gladys new strength to fight the dread malady that was to claim her life. As Elvis left her room, he noted for the first time hundreds of floral offerings that his fans had sent to his mother. He was happy and proud that they all knew his Mama and loved her so much.

Confiding to me later, Elvis spoke of his mother dying. He said, "When I got leave to go home, she seemed to get better right away. She recognized me immediately. Mother hadn't been feeling well, and when I put her and Daddy on the train for Memphis to go home to see her doctor, I thought, 'Mama really doesn't look well.' Mother was put in the hospital immediately.

"Two days later they called and asked that I be given an emergency leave. Mama has always made me promise not to fly, but I flew to Memphis. When I walked into her room she tried to raise up, and she tried to put her weak dear arms around me. She said, 'Oh, my son, my son.' I guess she knew how sick she was, but we didn't."

"Four specialists had been called in by our doctor. They were doing everything they could. I thought, thank God we have money for doctors and a hospital now. When I was growing up Mama was always afraid one of us would get sick and we would have no money to get us well. It would be like when she lost Jesse Garon, my twin."

"That night, later, I was told to go home and get some sleep. A little after three in the morning I got a call to come quickly to the hospital! I got there and as I walked into Mother's room, I heard my father scream and break into sobs."

" 'It's too late, son. She's gone,' he said. I couldn't believe it. I flung myself over the bed and I tried to hold on to her. I couldn't let her go. I have never really let her go. She's here in my heart. She always will be with me."

Thousands of telegrams and floral offerings poured into Memphis for Elvis. Colonel Parker flew to Memphis. Anita Wood, preparing to make a television appearance in New York, took the next plane to Memphis to be with Elvis. Cliff Gleaves, one of Elvis' best friends, was in Florida appearing at a night club. He arranged leave to get to Elvis. Wires came from Frank Sinatra, Sammy Davis, Jr., Dean Martin, Rick Nelson, and almost every big name in show business, all expressing their concern for Elvis' sorrow and loss.

Thousands of fans, men and women, girls and boys, stood outside Graceland. Finally about noon, Elvis and his father came outside. They sat sobbing on the front steps. There was a great hush that came over the crowd, standing outside the gates in front of them. They remained for hours in respectful silence.

"She, Mama, was all we lived for," Elvis said. "She was the most wonderful mother anyone could ever have. She was so young to die—only 42. She was always so kind and good."

Elvis' father put his arms around Elvis and they both cried unashamedly. "She's gone, she's not coming back," Vernon said. "Everything is gone."

His mother's funeral would be small and private, Elvis decided. It could be held there in the home that Gladys loved—Graceland.

Colonel Parker, however, advised against the home funeral. Elvis' fans were pouring into Memphis on every bus, train, and plane to extend their sympathy, hotels were jammed. Fans were going door-to-door asking to rent a room for the two nights until Mrs. Presley's funeral. The townspeople complied. Even some of the biggest homes opened their doors to take in the Presley fans and give them shelter.

Colonel Parker arranged that the funeral be held in a downtown chapel, and that the public be allowed to pass by her casket and pay their last respects. Over 1,500 people did so, right up until the time of service.

Elvis arrived in a big limousine with his father. Both were limp with grief and red-eyed from crying. They had to be helped from the car into the private entrance of the funeral home. Elvis sat with his relatives in the mourners' room which was screened by a thin curtain from the view of the rest of the chapel.

"The most important job a woman can do is to be a good wife and a good mother," eulogized Rev. James E. Hamill, pastor of the First Assembly of God Church that the Presleys attended.

"Elvis was given comfort in the belief," said the Reverend, "that these people have a firm belief in God. They know there is a life in the hereafter. They know they will see her again." The Blackwood Brothers sang several of Gladys Presley's favorite hymns during the service, including by Elvis' request, her favorite, "Rock of Ages."

After the final prayer at the graveside, Elvis leaned on the casket and sobbed, "Oh God, everything I have is gone. Goodbye, darling, goodbye. I loved you so much, so much." He was assisted back to the car with his father. Almost three-score policemen had been recruited, and they held back the crowds and onlookers.

The army sent not only flowers, but Elvis' fellow G.I.s sent personal notes and condolences. Elvis was granted a few days' extension on his leave so he could be with his father. The two men remained in the seclusion of the walls of Graceland, where lights burned all night long. Neither was seen out.

Elvis said over and over his mother's favorite maxim, which he had heard her say since babyhood when life was at times by sheer poverty almost unbearable, "Things will get better." It helped him. It continues as his favorite morale booster and sustainer when times are rough.

All the girls Elvis knew sent condolences; some tried to get him on the telephone. For the first time Elvis wasn't receiving or returning calls.

Kitty Dolan, the Las Vegas showgirl Elvis had dated,

said, "I wanted to talk to Elvis, to tell him how sorry I was. I wanted to help share his grief."

"I couldn't reach Elvis, but I reached Colonel Parker. The Colonel told me that Elvis was heartbroken, in a state of shock, wasn't eating, and wasn't talking with anyone. I sent a wire to Elvis in care of Colonel Parker to deliver to Elvis personally, for there were thousands of wires coming in from all parts of the world. I wanted to be sure he got mine.

"It was three weeks after the funeral that Elvis called me. 'If you'd like to come down to Kileen next week, I have a weekend pass, and Honey, we could see each other. I'll wire a ticket,' he said. But as he talked, he seemed a little vague for Elvis, though he did not mention his grief.

"I flew to Dallas where Elvis' father, Vernon Presley, met me at the plane. 'I am so glad that you could come,' Mr. Presley greeted me. 'But to tell you the truth, I expected to see some made-up glamorous blonde from Hollywood.' Turning to Lamarr Fike, who with Elvis' cousin Gene, was always around with Elvis, Mr. Presley smiling, remarked, 'Now here's a girl with natural beauty.'"

"We drove in Elvis' white Cadillac to the house they had rented from Judge Crawford in Kileen. It had five bedrooms and Elvis' mother had done the cooking, with the help of one maid to care for the house. Elvis had loved his mother's cooking, and they had been very happy together there even though they were away from their home in Memphis. Elvis' Grandmammy Presley, a tall, stately, lovely woman welcomed me with that special kind of Southern hospitality. She said, 'You must be Kitty. Elvis tells us about you. This is your home, and anything you want is yours. We are so glad that you could come and give him some comfort.'"

"Since I had been on the plane all night I decided to take a nap until Elvis came home from the base. I was given the master bedroom that had been used by his father and mother. His father was now staying with Elvis in his room."

70

"I was combing my hair before the mirror when, without knocking, in walked Elvis. I dropped the brush and he grabbed me up in his arms and kissed me. He looked so great in his uniform, and his helmet was still on his head. We kept laughing and hugging; we were so happy to see each other."

" 'Come, let me see what they did to your hair.' I said, finally breaking away from his arms to take a good look and see what the army had done to Elvis. 'What did they do to your curls?' "

"Elvis wasn't about to take off his helmet, but I insisted. When he did, I said, 'I like it!'

" 'So do I,' he said. 'I'm going to keep it this way.'

"Elvis didn't want to talk about the funeral. Then his Grandmammy came in, and she said, 'My baby has been so upset. I want you to have fun, and be happy and gay during your visit.' "

"That night we sat down to dinner with Elvis at one end of the table and his father at the other. Then his grandmother. There was a platter of bacon cooked crisp and one of pork chops, thin and crisp, with a big platter of white bread for sandwich making, with lettuce and tomatoes and all the trimmings, and a big platter of Southern baked beans. This was topped off with a delicious pie his Grandmammy had baked."

"Elvis looked at me with a shy little smile and said, 'I hope you like our Southern cooking.' I said, 'You've been eating this way ever since I knew you.' I recalled when Elvis was making *King Creole* and was staying in the lavish nine-room penthouse suite atop the Beverly Wilshire Hotel. He'd order platters of bacon and white bread to make sandwiches, and we'd all sit, Elvis and his chums and me, at the big table in the mirrored dining room, making sandwiches and drinking Pepsis. It was always the same order for Elvis. He loves bacon sandwiches. Sometimes Elvis would order the Beverly Wilshire ice cream pie with chocolate sauce and eat as many as three helpings. I'd say, 'Elvis, you'll explode!' He'd laugh, 'I only do this once in a blue moon.' Elvis remembered and we talked and laughed about it."

"After dinner some of Elvis' local friends dropped in for a jam session. Elvis had two electric guitars, and he'd rented a piano and an organ for the house. Elvis had become real great on the guitar. Before he was the wiggling Elvis and now he was a fine musician. He'd been practicing. He sang 'Hound Dog' with two different sets of lyrics that were very funny, and the guys would chime in. Elvis and I sang the duets—as we used to do."

"We had a lot of fun and we danced and all. Then Elvis began singing—lots of songs—songs I've never heard him sing. Songs like "Because God Made You Mine," "I Love You Truly," "One Alone," and even very softly half to himself "Rock of Ages"—that had been his mother's favorite and had been sung at her funeral."

"Neither Elvis nor I knew a note of the music. We sang strictly by feeling. Elvis also plays a terrific piano —boogie, classic, popular, and with some real wild chords all his own—and all by ear. He also beats the drums like a pro."

"At 2 A.M., we said good night. When he kissed me, I said with a little laugh, 'What is this with you and Anita Wood? I've been reading all the stories.' Elvis smiled and said, 'She has a good press agent.' And then he kissed me again, and I forgot about any other girl."

"Elvis is just like any other boy, and he is just as different. I met him because he is famous, in Las Vegas—the showplace of the world. I would have been attracted to him if he had been a cowpoke, but I don't think a cowpoke would have his personality. He is so sincere, so genuine. He doesn't say anything to flatter a girl. He is completely honest."

"The next day was his day off, and we talked about everything, including his life in the army. 'I like it. It is great for me,' Elvis said. He was crazy about his officers and the other men. 'But,' he observed honestly, 'It's a funny thing. All of a sudden I'm in the army camp. I'm just another guy. No pretty shirts, nothing special—K.P., chow duty, drill, work—just like everyone else. The day before I was up there being someone, making money. Now I am one of the guys watching TV when I get the chance—watching the other guys who are still up there. You don't begrudge them, but you feel empty inside, because you are not performing too!"

" 'For the first time I began reading the fan magazines. Me reading a fan magazine! I'm reading about how all the guys in Hollywood get a start. But,' he said emphatically, 'I'm glad that I'm in the army doing the job every young American boy should be doing. All I hope is that I'm doing a good job.' "

"Elvis has guts. I have seen him sick, and he'd never say anything, but keep going on doing his job. On the set of *King Creole,* he got a big gash in his arm in a fight scene. He went right on working. He wouldn't say anything. Finally they bandaged it up. He looked sick, but he knew he only had five days to finish the picture before induction, so he did his best."

"We saw movies and went for drives and we played records. Elvis doesn't like to play his own records. You have to sneak them in on the player. He wants to hear others, but he'll sing for you readily."

"I asked him if he received my wire, and he said, 'Yes I did. I read all the telegrams—thousands of them!' "

"That night we were talking and the subject of marriage came up. Lamarr said, 'It will surprise me if Elvis gets married before he is 50! He's a career man.' I said that I know better. I think Elvis will marry young. He has a lot of love in him. He is loving and affectionate and in turn, he needs love and affection."

"The next morning Elvis drove me to the airport in the white Cadillac. As we drove we began talking about his going to be stationed in Germany in the week following. 'I've never been to Europe,' Elvis said. And turning to his father, he said gently, 'You know, Daddy, she's a tender little thing, this one.' "

"At the airport, everyone was gaga over Elvis. We stood there as the motor of the plane was warming up

73

preparing for flight, saying last things, like 'Take care of yourself, dear, please.' "

"I kissed him goodbye, and I remembered the fresh clean smell of him. He didn't use colognes or even a hair tonic because Elvis is just himself. And that's pretty wonderful."

CHAPTER NINE

Razzings: "I'm in the Army Now"

ELVIS WAS ONLY one of 10,000 young buck privates in basic training at Fort Hood, Texas. In the Second Armored Division, he was scheduled for duty with the Third Amored Division in Germany. Movie stars, record idols, and various and sundry celebrities had it tough with the regular men in the army. That was another reason for their being assigned to Special Services as entertainers.

Elvis, realizing the position he was in, decided he was going to be a regular G.I., a good soldier, with no privileges, nothing special. He was going to prove to the world, and his fans and himself, that he could take it. Fame and money hadn't made him soft. Elvis had received all kinds of warnings from show business men who'd preceded him. Elvis was soon to discover that not only his own men, but men from other outfits started making pin-up pictures from the movie magazines of Elvis to razz him. Bing Crosby's son Gary had told Elvis that "the only way to get along in this man's army is to pull your fatigue cap so low you're hard to recognize full face," or to blot out his name tag and try to appear a blob so that no one would pay any attention. Others advised Elvis to always get in the background like the third row center, never up front.

At the start there was plenty of tension and razzing. Newspapers and the colored covers of magazines of

Elvis were clipped and posted in the barracks. Sometimes obscene words were lettered near them. It was a trial, but Elvis never panicked or lost his temper, no matter how he was baited those first few days.

If the boys would ask Elvis to sing, he seldom did. He'd say, "I'm just an army serial number like anyone else here. Mine is Number 53310761." The men took his measure, evaluated Elvis, and decided he was an okay guy.

The word went around in the officers' quarters that the reason Elvis didn't sing was due to his manager Colonel Parker. The Colonel was reported saying, "If the army wants Elvis to sing, they will have to pay him like everyone else!" There were conferences called by the upper brass to discuss whether Elvis should be moved up to Special Services like Eddie Fisher, Vic Damone, Tony Martin, Steve Lawrence, before him. Pros and cons. Talk that Elvis would be a great morale booster as a singer petered out—he was against it. Elvis said he didn't want anything soft; he wanted just to be a good soldier. Finally it was decided not to pressure him with a transfer. To leave him alone. Perhaps that would be the better advertisement for the army, that Elvis Presley was doing his thing like any other patriotic young American male.

Since Elvis was a controversial figure, there were critics and those who still gave him plenty of guff, but no one heard it from Elvis. In time he earned the respect of most of the men, with the exception of two or three who still alluded to him as "Elvis the Pelvis."

After Elvis' mother's death, there was no more name-calling or mention of "Elvis the Pelvis." A couple of buck privates close to Elvis settled that score with their fists. Elvis was not told about it. The new rule was: "Elvis has the right to respect as much as any other man in this man's army, man." That was how it was to be. Elvis had rightly earned that respect.

Elvis was to leave for Germany on September 22, 1958. This he had known when he said his last good-bye to Graceland after his mother's death.

"Mama and Daddy were coming to Germany to be

with me," he disclosed while sitting on the front steps of Graceland on the last afternoon of his emergency leave. Elvis had returned on his motorcycle from the cemetery to say another farewell at his mother's new grave. Tomorrow he'd be back at Fort Hood.

"Mama nor Daddy nor I had ever been to Europe," Elvis said. "We looked forward to it, being together. When my service hitch would be over, we'd planned to go to London, and Mama always wanted to see Paris and the Eiffel Tower. I don't want to see them without her. Maybe I never will."

The Presley living room inside the house was full of girls. There were pretty girls, town girls, girls from everywhere. Some of them were crying. All looked sad. They were there to say their final goodbyes to Elvis. Some were members of the many Elvis Presley fan clubs. A new girl arrived, and Elvis' father, Vernon, stepped forward to greet her. Elvis jumped up from the steps and extended his hand. She introduced herself. "I'm Anna Fleming. I'm here from Detroit. I was here for your mother's funeral."

"Yes, I know," Elvis acknowledged, greeting her with a warm handshake. "Thank you for your flowers and the letter. I read it," he added.

The girl asked if she might go inside the house. Elvis escorted her, and opened the big door with the true hospitality that the South is noted for.

The girls had come from all corners of the world. They were nice-looking and seemed well-mannered.

Some had come by bus to Memphis to say goodbye to Elvis. There had been hundreds who had been content to stand outside the Presley gate and just look. One girl from Paris had flown over on borrowed money against her salary as a secretary, to say goodbye to Elvis. She had the hope that if he were to be stationed in Germany, they could meet in Paris. Or she would come to Berlin to see him. Most of the young women were torn up with their own emotions, and they talked amongst themselves how they felt.

Eight young women had come from Brooklyn by bus earlier for Gladys Presley's funeral. Even though they had their own money, Elvis had sent his father to pay their motel bills. Elvis always took care of any expenses of any young ladies visiting him.

A seventeen-year-old said, "Elvis doesn't throw us out or try to avoid us. We're his friends and he proves that he is the best friend a girl ever had."

Elaine Owen revealed that she and two other girls had even gone down to Kileen to visit Elvis. "His mama was there then. It was just before she died. She invited us in the house and she made us so welcome. She let us wait until Elvis came home for supper from the base. Then she and Elvis invited us to sit down and have some dinner with him. She had made a big ham. She had a pot of baked beans, a cake, and ice cream.

"Later Elvis and the boys had a jam session. A couple of his cousins, who worked for him, were there, too. No one knows how he can play the piano. He even had us join in and sing with him. That's how thoughtful he is, how gracious, and how kind and lovable. If anything happens to Elvis, God help the army!"

One little girl sat there, her eyes glistening with tears. "I'll never love anyone but Elvis," she said.

Vernon Presley went to her. He put a fatherly hand on her shoulder, displaying some of the warmth and affection that is so natural in Elvis. He said, "You are a pretty little girl. You are intelligent and bright, you will meet a boy you will love and marry someday and have your own children and your own life."

She replied, "If anything happens to Elvis I can't go on living. I know I don't mean anything to him, but a good friend, but he's everything to me. He's all I want, all I have. I'm prepared, however, for the day when he gets married to some nice girl. I know the girl he marries will be my friend, too. I trust his judgment."

"Some girls will be so heartbroken they won't want to live" another girl said. "The army to us is war, a bomb—the end. Some of us have complete hysterics just thinking about it. But Elvis just laughs and tells us everything is great, and he's mighty proud to get a chance to serve."

77

"Yes, I date boys," a redhead said. "No one can compare with Elvis, however. He's the most. Some of us come here with the blessings of our parents, and others just come. But we all adore him, even worship him, as our ideal."

It was obvious that they did, and that Elvis thought them all wonderful and appreciated their affection. Elvis, so full of affection himself, was manfully covering his own bereavement smiling and being cheerful with his fans.

Thousands of them were standing outside his house at all hours. Some people would consider this a nuisance and an invasion of privacy but Elvis said, "When I didn't need them, they were there, loyal and wonderful. And now that I am out of it for a long time, and I need them, they are there, loyal and wonderful. Mama used to spend hours with them. She was delighted to show them through our house, until my baby—" Elvis' eyes brimmed with sudden tears, "Until my darling baby—my mama—got to feeling so tired, too ill, and she never let us know how bad she felt."

Elvis walked down to the gate aware that it would be his last time for two years or maybe forever. They were all ages and both sexes. Little kids began pushing papers and pencils up to him for autographs. Elvis signed them one and all.

Some of the fans had beautiful albums and scrapbooks filled with Elvis pictures and clippings. Some cost a couple of hundred dollars or so, all in color and with Kodachromes of Elvis. "Isn't that something!" he smiled. He didn't want to say more because he didn't want to hurt any of the others whose books were less elaborate.

There were young men who asked Elvis to autograph their shirt sleeves. There were cocktail waitresses who wanted their aprons autographed. Elvis laughed, "Let's be sure we get the front, the right side."

The fans asked about his records. Would any new ones be released? Elvis replied, "Yes, I've rolled some

78

new discs. They're on the demonstration records, and they'll be out. One's 'A Fool Such as I,' he laughed.

"Did you get the cookies I sent to you at Fort Hood?" one girl asked.

Elvis said, "I sure did, and were they good. They went in two minutes!" Another asked how many cookies he received. Elvis said, "Well, about seven or eight hundred packages a week with two to four dozen in each one. All the fellows appreciate them. If they'd been just for me, well, I'd have been eating my way into diabetes." Elvis also received candy and homemade pies and cakes and fruit fresh from the farms.

"All the fellows share their boxes from home," Elvis explained.

One of the fans introduced herself as a member of Elvis' fan club from New York. She'd flown down for his mother's funeral. She said, "All of your fan club presidents flew down here, Elvis."

"I knew your mother well," another young woman told him. "One day about a year ago I got a chance to catch her eye when she came out on the porch here at Graceland. She invited me to come in and see your beautiful home with all of its mirrors and the organ and the piano and the fabulous stairway, well, everything. She was such a sweet lady. She said to me, 'This is all my son. What other boy would love his parents so much. I'll take you outside so you can see the car he bought me with his very first big money—a pink Cadillac!' She was cooking Southern baked beans in the oven of the beautiful kitchen and a ham. She said she was expecting you in from Hollywood on the night train."

Elvis listened and tears came to his eyes, but he held them back. "Thank you," he said. He was, it was evident, still in a state of shock, and his grief was too new to permit him to discuss his mother and his loss of her.

"My father will be in Germany with me," he said. "We'll get a chance to see each other weekends when I get a pass."

A woman fan who might have been Elvis' mother

79

said, "I want to apologize to you. I enjoy your talent now that I understand it. I confess in the beginning I thought all of that wiggling was a little vulgar. But now that I understand more about music and you, I realize that the music just takes over and runs through your blood and your body goes along. I used to forbid my teenage daughter Louise to play your records. But now I know better and I wanted you to know."

Elvis squeezed her hand with gratitude. He was still blinking back tears.

"I realize," the woman added, "that there's nothing wrong with just healthy jitterbug and swing. It's a good way of enjoying yourself and letting off all of that youthful energy and steam. In my day, back in the twenties, we had cheek-to-cheek dancing, and moonlight waltzes, and danced almost in the dark. That was nothing less than petting on the floor. I guess each generation has to pounce on the next a little."

As Elvis turned to leave, a young girl reached up and threw her arms around him and kissed him. He smiled good-naturedly and said, "Thank you, honey." This often happened and Elvis was not offended. He didn't kiss them back, but he didn't push them away. Usually their kisses landed on his cheek. People who were seen handling his admirers acknowledge that he does everything with the greatest of taste and ease.

Most of the people were taking motion pictures and snaps and Elvis obligingly posed for everyone. "Thank you," he'd say. He was so pleasant and polite to everyone. While he was not humble exactly, he was also not self-important. Miraculously Elvis remained nice and regular and completely unspoiled, in spite of being an idol—as much a miracle as the fame and money.

"What do you think of the stories in the fan magazines about you, Elvis?" one of the fellows asked.

Elvis said, "You know something? Before I was in the service, I never had time to look at fan magazines. Now I find myself reading all of them. Not always to read about myself but to see what the other kids are doing. How they are making out."

"Something else," he added, "I read my fan mail.

Before I never had time, I was always working. But now when it's mail call, I read it."

Some seven thousand letters arrived weekly to Elvis at the army post. They were sacked and held for Elvis. The trouble often was that none of the letters from his personal pals and close friends got through. "It is hard to get mail direct," Elvis admitted. "But we work it out. So please keep writing."

CHAPTER TEN

Frauleins in Germany Take Over; "First-Rate Soldier" Elvis

ELVIS PRESLEY BOARDED the troop train from Fort Hood to the Brooklyn Army Terminal in New York. It was hot, stuffy, crowded, but there were no gripes, said his fellow G.I.s of Elvis, although there were plenty from some of the men on that long three-day ride.

Eight weeks of basic had proved the quality of the men. Elvis had scored high. He had become assistant squad leader, he proved to be a sharpshooter marksman with a pistol, was rated an expert in tank gunnery. Elvis was a first-rate soldier, according to his officer, in fact some went higher and said he was a model soldier. But always there were those who'd insist, "Aw c'mon now, he can't be that good. Nobody can." But Elvis was. An officer observed that during his eight weeks basic, Elvis proved to be deliberate rather than fast. But he always accomplished what he had to do. "Elvis has a mind which is orderly and systematic. He also has a certain inborn dignity that gives him a bearing that demands respect. He is one of the most dependable men who has come under me for training. He was born to lead. Most of the men soon sensed this and they accepted Elvis' promotions without question.

"The only time I have known of Elvis Presley to anger was when regrettably one of our men came back to base drunk. He muttered a 'son-of-a-bitch' as he passed Elvis! Elvis swung him around lightning fast, 'You weren't speaking of my mother were you, sir?' he demanded. The drunk G.I. actually cowered and apologized on the spot.

"The word went around fast, never make any aspersions that could even slightly refer to Elvis Presley's mother or you were a dead one."

"I watched Elvis fight against depression since his return from his mother's funeral. It is there, but he hides it well!"

The army issued a press release when Elvis left on the troop train for New York to board the troop ship General Randall. "Private Presley showed outstanding leadership training from the start and a fine attitude toward his service obligations," it said.

While the other men could relax on their arrival at the Brooklyn Terminal, Elvis was already scheduled for a press conference. Two hundred press were waiting for him. His buddies gave good reports: "Elvis is hard working, kind and considerate"; others said, "He's real lonely inside in spite of his smiles." Another: "He may be the world's sex symbol but he never uses a four-letter word or tells off-color jokes. He is a real gentleman!"

Despite his mother's recent death still so new, and naturally being tired from the long train ride sitting up nights (no sleepers or staterooms), Elvis still appeared smiling and friendly at the conference. He said he hoped to be a good soldier. He laughed with the reporters, and he only struck a serious note when someone thoughtlessly asked without taste: "Do you still miss your mama, Elvis?"

"I always will," he replied. His voice was choked full of emotion, but he managed self control. Then to everyone's surprise, he paid his mother a beautiful tribute. It was so sincere and so heartfelt, that when he'd finished the few brief words he had to say, everyone cheered.

Elvis then turned on a brighter, less sober mood. He was somewhat witty.

"Elvis, what type of girl do you like?" came the question.

"Female," replied Elvis.

Rumors were hot that Elvis Presley was planning to be married, and who, or rather, which girl was the lucky one, was the question. Always the beauty on his arm was a new one, and until now all of that world-wide speculation as to whether the "army could take Elvis," or whether "Elvis could take the army," had cooled. Elvis was now no longer a teenager's juvenile delinquent. He was a fine, upstanding young man, agreed one and all.

"Me getting married?" Elvis reflected. "I haven't heard about it." Elvis, with his six feet of sinewy lean-ness and his twenty-two years, asserted that unmistak-able virility that smashed through his personality, even in uniform. It lighted his eyes with a distinct challenge when his interest was quickened by a compliment or question or any attraction that would instantly reflect his mood. Elvis was a composite of many moods, it was discovered. But Elvis could sustain or cover them with self-discipline.

He was twelve pounds leaner, and the Elvis fans and the press agreed that he had never been more hand-some. Women wept openly. There were even tears in the eyes of some of the men spectators. Elvis had come through basic, a champion.

Elvis was asked if he'd see Paris. "I hope to. I'd like to meet Brigitte Bardot," he said. (Later Miss Bardot, on reading this report, said she didn't want to meet Elvis. When Elvis was told, he was very gentle-manly about the turndown. "I admire her. She is one of several nice people I'd like to meet.")

The Colonel was at the interview helping out, but there was not much he could do or offer his boy now. Not for two years in terms of personal handling, but there was plenty he could and would do while Elvis was gone. The Colonel would be doing plenty of wheeling and dealing to keep his popularity and his career up there on top.

The General Randall sailed and the army brass sighed a sigh of real relief. The Pentagon had finally decided that as a great morale builder Elvis should be in Special Services. What a drawing power! The army could well use it. But Elvis' own request relinquished any glamor the army wanted to invest in Presley. So the order on "Operation Elvis" was filed, to let him be, as he requested, just a regular G.I. Now it was the turn of army overseas command in Germany.

Almost five hundred girls had scaled the high barbed-wire fences at the Bremerhaven docks the night before the General Randall docked on the morning of October 1, 1958. Police lines couldn't hold back the German frauleins whose numbers increased to thousands to see Elvis. Most of them had flowers, and as Elvis marched by they threw posies at his feet. This caused a crisis when an officer slipped on them. "This is a military operation strictly," the harassed officer said, "even with Presley here!"

Elvis was assigned a jeep, and became a driver for his platoon sergeant. Living off base after hours was no special privilege. Under the military regulations any G.I. could do so. Elvis first lived in a luxury hotel, before taking a three-story house on Goethestrasse in Bad Nauheim, near Friedberg. The cars and crowds of people and fans gathered there day and night as they had done at Graceland, U.S.A.

An East German Communist paper wrote long editorials on the U.S. Army's soldier Presley; it decried "those persons plotting the atomic war are the ones making a fuss about Presley. They are the youths dumb enough to go and become Presley fans, so they are dumb enough to fight a war." Elvis' records were banned in Communist countries, but they sold regularly into thousands on the black market.

To all of this when asked, Elvis replied, "Those Commies are real squares, don't you agree?"

As time passed, Elvis bought a few cars. He drove to the base in his Mercedes, arriving at 5 A.M. to avoid fans or any other hindrances that might make him late. All day he chauffeured the sergeant in a jeep and then drove himself home in his Mercedes.

Mama had been the shining star of his whole world. She was the one he could count on to talk over his troubles with, to ask and to be advised. She applauded him and adored him. She was the one who had no mercenary reasons and who would never betray him. How could he go on without her? Perhaps his love for his mother was beyond the normal love of mother and son, but she was his all—his confidant!

It was Gladys who inspired him and encouraged him when the going was so brutal, so rough, when he was disclaimed, when he was ridiculed. It was Mama who made him believe that he could be a great star! Those people making fun of him, yelling and jeering and calling him "Elvis the Pelvis," resounding in his ear into nightmares, would go, his mother reaffirmed. They would accept him, once they understood what he was really doing. All pioneers had to go through ridicule and being misunderstood, she counseled. Gladys would subordinate herself in every way for Elvis, and her happiness was his happiness and his convenience. For his sake, as the human being she loved, who was part of her, she had given her every thought, her strength, and her life.

Now Elvis had no one to turn to, to call in the middle of the night when things were so out of hand and everything was going wrong; when the conflict of decisions and uncertainties were tearing him apart—Was he great? Was he ridiculous as he sometimes read? Would it all stop? And now that he had left it for two years, wasn't it all over?

Gladys Presley had always said, "Son, as long as you do what you feel is right and you have a clear conscience and you love God and Jesus, you are right. You will be protected. Don't let the others bother you. Feel love, give love, and love comes to you."

Was Gladys Presley ever outraged over the sometimes unfair, unjust, bad publicity Elvis drew? And when the preachers of the nation whipped into a frenzy, lashed out at Elvis in scorching tones? Gladys would hide her tears: "Why are they trying to crucify my son?" she'd say to her own family. But to Elvis she remained strong, his own Rock of Gibraltar. "Ignore it. Colonel Parker knows what he's doing, son," she'd tell Elvis. "They don't understand now but they will. Tomorrow will be better as it has always been for us," she'd remind him.

"Keep your faith in God first and then yourself. You know your Mama and your Daddy are with you and behind you always. If you ever need me, just call on the telephone and I'll come running."

Only once was Gladys Presley outraged visibly. That was, Elvis recalled, "when Mama and my Daddy came down to see me do a show in Florida. Afterward, I was coming out the stage door and my clothes were ripped off of me. Mama was real upset. 'That was your very best new suit, Elvis,' she cried. I told her, 'Now Mama, please don't pay any mind, because that was all part of the business.'

"Mama told me later after she'd thought about it all that she felt it would be better for me to get cheaper suits to wear when I was out working where the public could rip them off of me."

In Germany, Elvis was promoted to Private First Class. By 1959, his rank was raised to Specialist Fourth Class. The army realized now that Elvis had been wise to go in and earn the respect of the men by being a regular. Had he been Elvis Presley, singer, they could have made his life unbearable. He had well earned his respect.

Thousands of fans wrote to Elvis in Germany. Contests were rigged by the press worldwide to determine if his popularity were slipping away by his absence. Elvis' popularity not only continued, it even grew during his army stint. Huge mailbags arrived at the German base weekly with hundreds of thousands of letters from all parts of the world addressed to Elvis Presley. No one took his place or even came close, as had generally been expected. The fan-letter count averaged 10,000 a week.

Elvis, his father, and his Grandmammy Presley had taken a house with a garden and trees in Bad Nauheim. Elvis drove off the base at 5:30 P.M. for home and he spent his weekends there. He was lonely, for he long distanced Anita Wood often in Memphis. Venetia Stevenson flew over to Germany to see him. From time to time Elvis would meet a German girl he liked, and they'd date. There was a stenographer, Margret Buergen, and an actress, Vera Tchechowa. Whenever either girl appeared on Elvis' arm, the photographers made big money taking snaps and sending them out for worldwide release.

Elvis' popularity was so great that his autographs were selling in Frankfurt to high bidders; Bad Nauheim promoted as "The city where Elvis lives." Business doubled and visitors came to drive by his rented home, much like they did outside of Memphis to see Graceland.

CHAPTER ELEVEN

Elvis Rock 'n' Roll—New Product of Fifties Embraces Entire World

ELVIS PRESLEY PROVED to be the new product of the Fabulous Fifties, with hundreds of imitators. General Dwight D. Eisenhower was President of the United States. The Elvis period also ushered in Ed Sullivan, Howdy Doody, Sid Caesar, Bill Haley, James Dean, and Marilyn Monroe.

Marilyn too inspired imitators attempting to be the delicious dumb blonde, but only Jayne Mansfield succeeded as runnerup in the race to become "Sex Goddess."

The Ford Company introduced the Edsel, which didn't click. Pat Boone on TV and movies made a gimmick of his spotless white buck shoes. He was the All-American boy, and overnight became Elvis' biggest contender while Elvis was in the service those two years. To American girls, life became one long Pat Boone movie. Elvis' ducktail and Valentino pants gave way to the white bucks and sharp haircuts a-la-Boone. Rick Nelson and his guitar, more genteel, and Bobby Darin zeroed in as top teenage record stars. The Gabor Girls, Zsa Zsa and Eva, tired of domesticity and bored with cleaning their diamonds, went to work in the movies and on TV. Sister Magda married a millionaire, and Mama Gabor with a glamorous Manhattan wedding married a titled gentleman from Europe. Errol Flynn raised eyebrows dating fifteen-year-old Beverly Aadland as his constant companion.

Girls became "chicks" and the boys, "guys." The girls wore their hair in ponytails, and some pinned on curls and falls. There was the Sputnik and Korea and Lawrence Welk's Champagne Lady, Alice Lon, with her many lace petticoats twirling with the maestro. There was the "$64,000 Question" and the problem of Cuba. Status symbol was a mink stole, and women's skirts went longer. Elvis cost the government $500,000 a year in lost tax while he was in the service.

The challenge: Would Elvis fans forget him while he was away? The Presley fans demonstrated their loyalty like no others ever known. They formed clubs, wrote, telegramed, and badgered radio stations to play Elvis records; put out Elvis magazines, and never let their enthusiasm weaken, even when they had no more personal cooperation from Elvis and The Colonel than perhaps some photos of Elvis. They made up imaginary stories about Elvis and worshiped him from afar. They expected no reward other than to keep "The King" on top. Colonel Parker was wheeling and deal-

ing in every direction to keep his boy's popularity
zooming in spite of his inability to produce his boy in
the flesh! RCA Victor released periodically a new Elvis
record, from several he had recorded in advance for
this very purpose. And by that time Elvis' enlistment
was over, and the record sales on the Elvis Presley
discs had reached 50,000,102.

An international crisis flashed in headlines all over
the world when Elvis had tonsilitis! His temperature
and his illness were minutely reported as far as they
could be guessed or ascertained. When he recovered
sufficiently to take a weekend furlough in Paris, he was
mobbed. Elvis' popularity and fame in Europe equaled
that in America.

In the army, his superior officers were saying that
Elvis was a fine soldier, one to be proud of. Statesmen
pointed with pride to Elvis, a young American from a
free democratic country, who assumed his responsibilities and adjusted well. Elvis was marvelous propa-
ganda for the army, even if the Colonel did not allow
him to sing one note, free or otherwise, during his
service hitch.

On Elvis' birthday, January 8, 1959, Dick Clark
dedicated his popular American Bandstand TV program to Elvis Presley in Germany. He telephoned Elvis
there to announce he had been voted the Best Singer
of the Year and that his record was the Best Record of
the Year. Elvis' voice was choked with emotion coming
over the trans-Atlantic wires. He couldn't believe all
this had happened and was still happening to him
while he was gone for all those months. The image of
Elvis, the lonely boy suddenly bereft of his mother, his
career, and swept into the army perhaps to endure the
razzing of the G.I.s, was a poignant one that pulled at
the heartstrings of all America. That Elvis emerged a
model soldier made everyone feel personally responsible, in a way, with the concern and morale boosting
they'd given the singer so much of the public had
initially misjudged. Now that Bobby Darin and Rick
Nelson and a hundred more boys were twanging guitars
as they sang and gyrated to popular approval, they

realized it was all a trend of the times, and they also felt twinges of guilt in their former accusations of Elvis.

There had been reports of the fifteen-year-old daughter of a commanding officer stationed in Germany in the Air Force, named Priscilla Beaulieu, who adored Elvis. No one took the romance rumors seriously, however. On various occasions Elvis was reported and sometimes photographed by some candid camera on a date with various girls. He himself said he had no serious romance.

But the romance of Vernon Presley with a blonde glamorous young divorcée with three sons, Mrs. Davada Dee Stanley, was considered alarming at first. No one reconciled the thought of anyone taking Elvis' mother's place. And would Elvis?

Dee had three small boys. She had made friends with Mrs. Minnie Presley, Elvis' grandmother who was keeping house for Elvis and Vernon in Germany. Grandmammy Minnie's birthday was June 17th. By coincidence so was Dee's. The two women with mutual interests stemming from the same birth sign, became friends. And love again found Vernon Presley.

But Colonel Parker was never worried about his boy Elvis.

"Who's your big love, Elvis?" the press and fans would ask whenever Elvis arrived home. He'd stop to to talk to the more than a hundred who were always waiting for him outside, and no matter the hour—all hours!

"No one," he replied good-naturedly, then stopped to pose for pictures for some of the teenagers.

"Come on, Elvis, play ball. Who is she?"

"Yeah, tell us," a brash young reporter demanded. "Let's see your wallet, Elvis. Who do you carry?"

For a moment Elvis stood silently. Seemingly he was debating whether to show his wallet or tell the reporter it was none of his business. But the reticent simplicity and kindness he has retained throughout his life to date caused him to pull out his wallet.

"I carry my best girl with me," he said smilingly, almost mischievously. "Here's the only girl I carry with me," and he opened his wallet. "My mother," he said proudly. And sure enough she was the only female in his wallet. "I'm married to the army for the duration," he quipped.

One of Elvis' army buddies had accompanied him home one night. They went into the big house. Due to constancy of the swarming crowds outside, they used the back door to exit on their frequent trips into town.

Elvis had dropped a few pounds, he said, but he had toughened up. He had added a lot of muscle. He still had a good healthy tan. Physically he felt better and mentally he felt more alert.

Some of the crowds swarming outside of Elvis' home were men. They liked to see Elvis' expensive automobiles. Elvis admitted he was a car nut. When he could understand their German and they, Elvis' English, they'd go over points of respect for the qualities of the Presley automobiles.

Continuous calls "collect" from various girls in the States were for Elvis. It was apparent that Elvis spent part of his free time on the telephone in the hallway. As at Graceland in the States, the Presleys' German home rocked with visitors, pretty girls, boys, and Vernon and Grandmammy Presley, who were always on hand to extend genuine Southern hospitality.

Elvis slept in the third-floor bedroom to avoid all of the noise and the constant ringing of the telephone. "I have to get up so early," he'd explain to a visitor. "I still find such early rising hard to get used to."

As for the army, Elvis concluded that if he didn't have work to go back to in the States he'd enjoy a career in the army! "But," he added, "once you get show business in your blood, there's no business like it."

"I'm not a loser," Elvis told a friend. "I've got lots of determination. I got the point across I could do a job in the army. Now I've got to do a job getting back to work when I get home."

Being philosophical, Elvis told one friend that "when rock 'n' roll goes, I'll think of something else to do. I love music. I always have," he added.

When Elvis was promoted to Specialist Fourth Class

he was paid $122 a month. "That's real money," he said, feeling the sweat he'd used to earn it.

Elvis got a chance to visit Munich where a night-club cutie at the Moulin Rouge appeared on stage wearing nothing but an Elvis record. She tried to inveigle Elvis to join her in a song, but he was actually embarrassed at her nudity although he laughed and tried not to show it.

"Elvis Presley's In Paris" headlined front pages of every newspaper in Paris when Elvis spent two days there. Pictures of him at the Lido and Follies Bergere with bevies of beauties surrounding him made front pages all over the world.

By the late summer of 1959, Elvis had his father Vernon, who had cracked up one of his cars, return to the States to get Graceland ready for his return. Elvis called Vernon the "Hot Rodder" after the accident which fortunately Vernon escaped with only very slight injuries.

At this time, Hal Wallis arrived in Germany to see Elvis about his next picture for him, *G.I. Blues*. Mr. Wallis reported his visit with Elvis to this writer on his return.

"I've sure been getting a lot of experience and local color to play this part in your picture, *G.I. Blues*," greeted Elvis with his usual sense of humor. "And I'm sure anxious to see the script."

"I'd like to give you one, but I didn't bring you a script," Mr. Wallis told him. "You'd probably memorize it, and we might make some changes between now and when you start shooting in Hollywood." Actually, I didn't take Elvis a script because I remembered when I first signed Elvis for pictures, I didn't have a script ready for him at the time, and he went to Fox to make *Love Me Tender*. The studio sent him a script in Memphis, and Elvis arrived with every line of his part and everyone else's parts memorized. If he could memorize an entire script when he was on a heavy schedule of personal appearances, TV, and recording dates, I felt sure he'd do it on his free time after army hours. I didn't want him to put himself to such a task, although knowing Elvis' restless mind, he'd probably have enjoyed it.

" 'I'm sure anxious to get back to work,' Elvis continued, 'and you are here—actually here in Germany—with the cameras and the crew all set to go for background in the picture. That is really great," Elvis repeated.

"Then I had to disappoint Elvis all over again and watch the excitement in his eyes fade to a thoughtful mood that hid any letdown he may have felt," Mr. Wallis reported.

" 'You won't be before the cameras over here,' I said, 'I understand that this is your own decision, too.' "

" 'Yes, of course. I guess I just forgot for the moment,' Elvis sighed. 'It's because I'm so anxious to get back to work.' "

"While anyone in the army can do whatever they like on their own time, I had decided in the beginning that Elvis would not appear in any scenes we'd shoot in Germany. I didn't want him to take the risk of being embarrassed by putting him in front of a camera, with the possibility of some taking exception that he was being privileged to work as a movie star while he was still in the service. This is one of the daily problems that Elvis faced as a G.I., making sure that he did not receive any special attention or privileges. He himself didn't make a case out of it, but he was very careful to go along living a normal life, as quietly as possible, as a soldier. That's why he was successful in the army and won the liking and respect of his buddies."

" 'Man, how I'd like to be working in front of those cameras,' Elvis repeated with boyish enthusiasm cropping out. 'I've often wondered if I've forgotten everything I learned, and how it will be again. Man, how I'd like to try it again. I can't believe it—you're all here, the whole crew!' Then, 'It's just like it was yesterday at Paramount, and it's almost two years.' "

"Elvis was reacting to my announcement that I had brought director, Mickey Moore, assistant director on Elvis' last picture, *King Creole,* and my art director, first cameraman, and company unit manager with me to Germany to start Elvis' new picture. I had filled in the rest of the crew, I told him, and we had forty, all set to shoot locations when I went out to see Elvis."

" 'I'm sure glad to see you,' Elvis had greeted me when I had first arrived at his house which is outside of Frankfurt in Baden Mannheim. Elvis was living in a modest house, a cottage with a fenced-in back yard rather than the huge castle he was reported to be living in. Soldiers were all permitted to live off base if they so desired and many others lived in similar places. Elvis' house was unpretentious stucco and when I arrived Elvis opened the door. 'Colonel Parker wrote me you were coming, and man, it is good to see you, sir,' he said warmly. He was playing records at the time but not his records. 'Some new imports from the United States—Bobby Darin and Ricky Nelson's new hits,' he said. There's not an atom of jealousy in Elvis. While he had consistently worried that his fans might forget him, he was a great booster of the boys with talent, who had come up as the top waxers of rock 'n' roll during his army stint.

" 'You know Lamarr Fike and Bob West of course,' Elvis said, indicating the two boys who were with Elvis in Hollywood and who were with him in Germany. We exchanged greetings. Then Elvis said, 'Come on out into the kitchen and we'll have a coke.' We sat down at the table and I was delighted at the new Elvis. He was in uniform, since he'd just come back home from field maneuvers. He'd matured and while he still naturally retained his youthful quality of charm and was basically the same, he was also noticeably sleek and physically as hard as nails. Too, the Presley with the ducktail haircut and sideburns was gone, for he would wear the same G.I. haircut in the picture in his part as a G.I.

"Elvis wanted to hear all about his new picture, however, and I told him that we were taking some exciting locations, shooting all of the exteriors in the locale of his army activities. We'd shot in Frankfurt,

Weisbaden, Idsten, Friedberg, and along the Rhine River. We were set and ultimately shot the tank corps in action but never with Elvis. We used plenty of G.I.s but again, not Elvis. This seemed unfair, but I would not take a chance of any criticism being directed toward him with this picture."

" 'Are you shooting in color?' he asked. I told him that I was and that the weather was perfect.' "

" 'Now that the two years are up, it all doesn't seem so long,' Elvis said, 'But man, in the beginning I counted the days—thirty and thirty-one to each month and 365 to a year—like that,' he laughed. 'Then it seemed forever.' "

"Elvis' face saddened when I again expressed my condolence in the loss of his mother. 'You'll remember, Elvis,' I recalled, 'that we had both your mother and your father in a scene of your picture. You remember they were visiting you on the set that last day of the shooting, and we asked them to sit in the audience as players? We have some good footage, and you can have it as a clip when you return.' "

"Elvis' appreciation, which is so ready and so genuine, lighted his eyes. He swallowed hard. 'I still miss her,' he said. 'I guess I'll never get over losing her.' He was quiet for a while and then he said as though half to himself, 'The first place I am going to head for when I get back is to her grave. We have flowers sent regularly, but I want to take them myself. I'd like to spend some time there, at least a day, before I hit out for Hollywood.' "

"I could well understand Elvis' feelings. We sat and talked for a while longer. Then we went outside for a while to get a breath of air and sit on the grass. The boys took some snapshots of us. When it began to get dark, I arose to go."

" 'Maybe we could have dinner together if you can spare the time,' Elvis said. I told him to call me the following week at my hotel."

"In the interim we began shooting the picture, and I must admit I felt a little regret that Elvis couldn't have been with us, if only as a spectator. But his army duty kept him elsewhere. His officers and army friends, however, were anxious to talk with me."

" 'Elvis is a fine boy, and he does his job well,' one said. 'He certainly avoids any favoritism, and he bends over backward to do his job one hundred percent!' "

"Another of his officers observed, 'The army has sure changed Elvis. We got hold of an old movie magazine with a pre-army story about Elvis. It sure made him out to be a belly-rolling vulgar type of singer who had a bad, if popular, influence with the American teenagers. But today he sure has changed. He is a perfect gentleman, in fact he is always polite. No one has ever heard him say a vulgar word or tell an off-color story.' I could have told him that he had found a very wrong story based on a very wrong conception of Elvis. One that has long since been dispelled and erased. He was, and long before he came to Hollywood, a thoroughly nice and well-mannered boy, who had no feeling about ever being vulgar. As he once said, 'I just follow the beat of the music. It's the folk dancing of this generation. The kids understand it. Sometimes I get carried away, but I never think it is vulgar.' I'm sure Elvis has never had vulgar thoughts. He just isn't the type."

" 'Our only trouble,' another officer told me, 'is the girls. They can't leave Elvis alone. We've had to put up roped lines to get him through them at times. Elvis always looks amused, but he never takes advantage of his popularity. He just tries to go on with what he is doing. When he is off duty, I've been amazed at his patience. He'll spend time talking to these kids; some of them are only ten or twelve. They can't speak English, and he can't speak German, but he has the utmost patience with them."

" 'Elvis will get out his little German-English dictionary, and they'll make signs and talk back and forth. The kids worship him. But he sure has an amazing patience with children and such a real liking that he'll be a wonderful father someday.' "

"Another G.I. made this observation on Elvis' romantic status. 'It looks like Elvis is going home single all right. He'll take a fraulein out a few times, and they blow it up big in the papers. But he hasn't gone steady over here with any one girl. He doesn't have much time, and the time he does have he spends pretty much at home with his dad and his grandmother. His grandmother sure can cook. El is always nice about taking some of us home for her real Southern cooking.' "

"Elvis is very prompt and reliable, and he called me a week later as he said he would. 'I can make it tonight to get in for dinner,' he said. We made an engagement to have dinner together that night. Elvis arrived driving his Mercedes Benz, a stock model sedan. We went to a German restaurant, and I must report that it was very unique. There weren't a dozen or so girls popping out of the walls and the ceilings as they did in America when I took Elvis out to dinner. I said to him, 'This is different than it was in New Orleans.' He smiled. In New Orleans, on the location of *King Creole,* I had to hire a special security police to keep the girls off of his hotel floor, and still they seemed to manage to come in through the walls—in every direction."

"Elvis ordered German food. An accordion trio played during dinner, and again I must report that Elvis did not get up and sing. The busboys and the musicians recognized him, and one by one they politely sent a menu over with a request for his autograph. Elvis seems to have a quality that is warm and polite, but one which also commands respect. Today people no longer seem to impose on him even though the very little girls may mob him."

" 'I've been very homesick at times. That's the worst,' Elvis admitted as we ate. 'I've thought again and again, man, if I could only go home for just one day. And wow, the time is almost here to go home. I'm very excited about it.' "

"Elvis also said that he wasn't going steady and that his 'little old heart' was still in one piece. 'But it would be nice to fall in love, after I get my career going again. Not before, because I've got too much work to do first, to have the kind of time to fall in love.' "

"His thoughts kept returning to the picture, his new picture. I told him, 'There'll be parts for two German girls and one Italian girl. And there'll be parts for your G.I. buddies, for you'll be playing yourself, a G.I. in the tank division.' "

" 'Have you cast the girls?' he asked with natural male interest.

" 'No, not yet,' I laughed, 'any suggestions?'

" 'No, I guess not,' Elvis replied thoughtfully, adding half to himself, 'as long as they're pretty.' "

" 'I'll be seeing you,' Elvis said, 'in Hollywood! Man, that sounds good, be seeing you in Hollywood,' he repeated with a flash of a smile. Then he turned and walked towards his car, jumped in, switched on the ignition and roared up the road."

From that minute on, Mr. Wallis said he was besieged, all of the way home by the foreign and the international and the domestic press, for any word of this interview and his visit with Elvis or their plans. Luckily, I caught up with him for this exclusive and promised report on Elvis!

CHAPTER TWELVE

The Colonel Turns Down $100,000 Advance to Write Book on World Idol Elvis

SCHEDULED TO CIVILIAN life from the army on March 24, 1960, The Colonel announced joyfully, "When that little boy of mine, Elvis Aron Presley, comes marching home again to Hollywood, I aim to give him the biggest old welcome home party this town's ever seen!"

To anyone who would listen, the ebullient, flamboyant, and colorful Colonel announced contracts for three movies all set and, "waiting for Elvis to start filming the minute he steps into his civvies! We have offers for more concert tours than we could do in a lifetime.

"There's going to be a new Elvis, brand new," The Colonel further announced. "I don't think he will go back to sideburns or ducktails. He's 25 now, and he has genuine adult appeal. I think he's going to surprise everyone and be more popular and more in demand than ever before!"

En route to Memphis, Elvis acquired stage fright. Would he be awkward in front of a camera? Did he remember the lights, the tricks he had learned before, the techniques he had painstakingly acquired and which had been set aside those two years? Were they forgotten? So many things he had learned, things like how to kiss a girl on camera so he didn't bump her nose or cover her face as when he'd kissed Carolyn Jones in his last film, *King Creole*. Carolyn had taught him the way of a film kiss in that picture.

Yes, it had been a long time since he had been before a camera. "Maybe I'd better stop off in Vegas before I get to Hollywood and get a little tan?" he said to Vernon—and get a glimpse of some of the kids that he'd know in shows. Get a taste of show business back in his blood.

His heart skipped when they drove up to the big gates and he saw Graceland again. There it was, the white old-style Southern mansion with eighteen rooms . . . built atop a landscaped hill, overlooking the whole countryside. A lump stuck in his throat, and his eyes misted as the two men walked up to the door where his mother was now not there to greet him. "C'mon, son." Vernon nudged his arm gently.

Elvis walked into his own room, the King's Room, as Mama had dubbed it. It was still the same—the king-size bed with its white satin tufted bedspread, the bed and dresser, black-and-white trimmed with leather, the dark-blue walls, the white ceiling, the one wall solidly mirrored and the bathroom, orchid-and-pink. The same gold telephone that his mother had chosen. It was all Mama's handiwork, the long hours she had spent planning and decorating the house, so each time he returned to Graceland another room would be ready. It had been too much for her, he thought now. Too much.

Elvis glanced about the big room, all the same as he'd last seen it. As he had remembered it. All in order. His father had seen to that by making an advance visit to Graceland a few months before so it would be in readiness. Graceland was sacred—Elvis' Mama's home.

Then it all came back, hitting Elvis all over again—his mother. His mother had always been there, sitting by him at the window looking out down the long winding path to the outer gate. As he looked he saw them, his friends, the fans all standing outside waiting patiently and hopefully. It was as though he'd never been gone, and always his mother would say, "Maybe you'd better go out now, son. Don't keep them waiting, it's a little chilly perhaps."

How his mother had loved his friends. She'd always invited them to come in. She'd proudly take them through the big house and perhaps stop at the big refrigerator to offer a piece of fresh sweet strawberry pie or a slice of cake. "That was Mom, hospitable, always showing that true wonderful Southern hospitality. She'd been that way until there were so many hundreds gathering at the gate that neither her waning health nor the house could any longer accommodate the welcome tours."

As Elvis looked out at the gate, the phone continued ringing. Sammy Davis, Jr., was on the wire. "Welcome home, man. It'll be great seeing you again." And Milton Berle—Uncle Miltie—who'd given him his first big TV break, and Nick Adams, and Frank Sinatra. Elvis was glad that Nick had his big break now, and that Frank had invited him on his TV spectacular. Through those two years he'd wondered what it would be like when he got back, and now here he was.

There were hundreds of wires, and as Elvis sat there looking out a smile began to appear on his face. He wasn't so lonely anymore. There were the fans, all at the gate, waiting to welcome him home. They'd stayed loyal, just as they'd said they would.

"Welcome home, Elvis," they cheered in unison as he opened the front gate. The tears welled up in his eyes and then because a soldier—well, an ex-soldier—doesn't cry, he began to laugh. Grabbing up the closest moppet, a little honey-blonde aged six, he said, "Say, Honeybelle, is this you? Why you've grown up for sure. You were only four when I left." Fondly he gave her a hug and a kiss on her pink apple cheek. Elvis loved children. He always said that someday when he married he was going to have "at least a dozen." Then he was talking to everyone at once, but individually, singling out the familiar faces he recognized.

Some of the fans had come a long way to see him. They were all ages and both sexes, and there were little tots with their papers and pencils pushing up to ask for autographs. When they began crowding in, in their eagerness, Elvis stopped and said, "Don't hurry. I've got all day. Got nothing else to do." Elvis is one star who never considered his fans a nuisance.

"When's your next album out, Elvis?" he was asked, while some of the kids held up their beautiful albums and scrapbooks, filled with Elvis pictures and clippings, a complete record of his life in the Army. Some of the girls held up handkerchiefs, aprons, and even their skirts to be autographed. And Elvis laughed.

"Did you get the fudge I sent you to Germany?" one girl asked.

"I sure did, honey, and was it good. It went in two minutes. Our outfit sure liked sweets."

"You mean," the girl faltered, "that you gave some of the fudge away?"

"Now, Honey, you didn't want me to eat all of it, and let the other fellows sit there miserably watching?" Elvis asked.

"How many boxes of cookies and candy did you receive?" another asked.

"Some weeks when we were lucky, it seemed like hundreds," Elvis acknowledged. "And other weeks, not so many. All of the fellows appreciated them, and be-

101

lieve me, I did. It was wonderful of all of you making our army life a little sweet."

One of the fans introduced herself as a member of the Elvis Fan Club from Montreal, Canada. She'd also flown down two years before for his mother's funeral. "All twelve Montreal fan club presidents flew down," she said. "We didn't try to see you, Elvis. We knew how badly you felt, so we just stayed away in case any of us were needed."

Elvis blinked his eyes and smiled a silent thanks.

"I loved your mother, Elvis." one girl added. "She once invited me to come in and see your home with all of its mirrors and the organ and the fabulous stairway, and well, everything. I remember she said, 'This is all my son. What other boy would love his parents so much."

"Are you going to sell Graceland?" one fan asked.

"I never want to," Elvis replied. "It is Mother's, and we hope to always keep it. But we'll look for a little ranch house in Hollywood so we'll have a place to stay when I'm out there working. But this is home."

As the door closed behind him on his first day at Graceland, the crowd began to quietly disperse. "He's so pleasant and polite to everyone," some said. "He's just himself, nice and regular, and completely unspoiled."

Had the army changed him? Yes. He was lithe and sinewy and a little older. His sideburns and ducktail haircut were gone forever, he laughed.

It was easy to see why such a wonderfully beautiful relationship and unusual understanding existed between Elvis and his fans. They were friends, real friends.

A little later a car drove up. Pretty, pert, and blonde Anita Wood, excited, ran up the path and the steps and into Graceland. They were good friends, but as Elvis told his pals who were marriage-license bound when his unit broke up: "I had no one steady date to come home to. But I have some wonderful girl friends it will be good to see."

Taking up the thread of Elvis' return, I spoke with

Colonel Parker and learned the astounding fact that Elvis did not keep a diary overseas. The highly reported diary which was to appear in print in a national magazine *(The Post)* to the tune of $250,000 to their knowledge did not exist. "If such a diary had been written and such a sum been paid, we'd certainly have known about it and we don't," said The Colonel.

Of course there was another book in the offing about which Colonel Parker was quite enthusiastic. "I'm writing my own book on Elvis. I've already turned down $100,000 for the book."

Would the new kind of hero worship vanish? Elvis prayed he would be good on the screen, that he wouldn't wake up and find it was all a long dream— unless it would give him Mama back. He'd take her any day to all of this!

CHAPTER THIRTEEN

Frank Sinatra Pays Elvis $125,000 to Welcome Him Home from the Army

THE COLONEL HAD long announced that he was "going to give my boy Elvis the biggest Welcome Home party in the United States on his return from the army!" Surely The Colonel would rope off the streets in Memphis with flags and banners for parades and street dancing and food, and people would be pouring in from all parts of the country for it!

"That wouldn't be fair at all," The Colonel finally decided. "No siree, not at all." He also couldn't see Elvis paying for his own Welcome Home party. Elvis should be paid, for without him there would be no Welcome Home party. The Colonel figured it well. "Can't show no favoritism, that would not be fair! We got to give my boy a party in which everyone in the world can participate!" And just where was even such a showman as The Colonel going to produce such a party as that? Where?

"Why, on television," smiled The Colonel. "I got the best party figured out, and everyone can come and join Elvis by flipping on the dial on their sets. Besides I like to see that soft folding green, that doesn't make any noise abound when Elvis appears. That's a real welcome!"

The nationwide party the Colonel arranged for Elvis tied right into Frank Sinatra's TV show—and let Frank pay the tab. It was called "Frank Sinatra's Welcome Home Party for Elvis Presley," and it beamed on ABC-TV May 8, 1960. The unheard of tab of $125,000 was the privilege Frank was given of hosting the party welcoming Elvis home. The show broke all the ratings—a nation tuned in to see its boy back from the service!

Joey Bishop, on the show and two dressing rooms down from Elvis, tells that it occurred to him that his niece in New Jersey would like an autographed picture of Elvis. Joey asked his man Friday to go down the hall and get one. The man returned and told the stunned Bishop, "The Colonel stands guard in front of Elvis' dressing room. You can't go in. So I had to ask him. He said Elvis would be pleased to give you one for one dollar. That is the charge for an Elvis Presley photo." "Did you tell the Colonel it was for me, Joey Bishop?" "Yes," replied the man, "and the Colonel said, "Well, perhaps in that case it should be ten."

In Hollywood, among the hundreds of girls standing around Paramount and the Beverly Wilshire Hotel day and night in hope of seeing Elvis wave from his big black limousine, some of the more sophisticated divulged they were going to flirt with the Memphis Mafia! "If we get the chance, the only way to get to Elvis is to try to make it with one of his boys." The limousine swept through at such speed—or if Elvis stopped to stick his head out of the window—the boys ignored the girls. Not one claimed to have managed to even exchange a word, let alone ply one to succumb to her charms.

Inside the studio, on the "Closed, Absolutely no Visitors" set filled with boys in G.I. uniforms, anyone could readily spot Elvis, even with his back turned. Is it the breadth of shoulder, the careless wave of his black hair, the easy graceful height of his lean body? I thought. Or is it the sheer magic that Elvis possesses, with a magnetic quality that draws people to him?

Whatever it is, it was Elvis, going to his portable dressing room. He turned at my hello and simultaneously we both began, "It's been two years, one month . . ." and Elvis continued "Two days . . . exactly, since I left this particular sound stage for the army."

"I've taken off eleven pounds and there hasn't been a let up since I got here. I need more sleep, too. I've been recording nights and trying to see everyone and get about. I wanted to see all of my old friends, but soon now we'll be winding up to go home."

"Live permanently out here? Of course not. I only come out here to work. My home is Graceland and Memphis. I know everybody there. All of my friends—well, most of them—that I grew up with and went to school and church with are there. At no time have I ever thought of leaving to make a new home anywhere else. Yes, I've read about it, but it isn't so."

"What about you and Tuesday Weld and Juliet Prowse (Elvis' leading lady in the picture) going to Las Vegas?"

Elvis gave me a long look. "I didn't get to Las Vegas as reported. When I go up there I like to stay a little while at least. May, do you believe everything in print? I've only met Tuesday. There's no big romance —nothing. She's a pretty good kid, but that's all there was."

"Juliet plays my leading lady in this picture. She happened to be in Las Vegas one time, so we took in some of the shows. And Cathy Case, like it says in the columns, everytime I date a girl it is blown up out of all proportion as a big romance. And there is no romance!"

Elvis still wasn't one to discuss his girl friends, but I

managed to ask about the blonde (18-year-old Pat Boyd) he was calling daily at Graceland.

"Oh," Elvis smiled, "she's my secretary. She comes to work at 9 every morning and leaves at 6. She's blonde and beautiful, and she did win a beauty contest. I needed a secretary, and that's the way it is. I am very fond of two or three girls, but no *one*."

"I'm not building a wall around my heart, and I'm not afraid now of getting hurt again, but love just hasn't happened to me. I love kids and I want to marry and have companionship, have one special girl to be interested in. I think about it plenty. I thought about it a lot of the time I was in the army. Each time I take out a girl I naturally secretly wonder if she'll be the one. But it just hasn't happened yet."

"I think every man wants to marry and have his home and family. That's the good way of life. But you can't force it. At no time did I have a serious romance in Germany. I made some nice friends. I enjoy friendship, and I learned enough German to be able to talk and understand when the people would talk slowly. The language wouldn't have been any barrier, if real love had come along. Love, you know, isn't a matter of geography. I have set no age limit, nor made any plans," Elvis elaborated. "I've got to be sure, very sure, when I marry. It will have to be for keeps when I do.

"I'm going on as I am, working hard, and especially right now to get my career going again," he continued. "I have two more pictures to make this year. This one for Mr. Wallis. I am very fortunate to be under contract to a producer like him. Have you ever noticed the hundreds of best-picture awards and trophies presented to Hal Wallis! I'm going to do my best to merit the opportunity I have here to become a good actor. That's uppermost, and Mr. Wallis is giving me every opportunity."

"I'd love to do some P.A.s again," Elvis observed. "I'd really like to get out again and meet the people I've missed while I've been away, see the kids and talk with them. But I don't know when that will be. It looks

106

now like it won't be possible this year, not with the pictures and records."

"It's a little strange getting back, getting used to it all over again after having been away from it for so long. In a way I missed it. In another way," Elvis confided, "I wasn't in a fever to get back to it. I had a way of life for two years, and I became absorbed in it."

Elvis excused himself to return to the cameras. The eyes of every girl, about 16 extras on the set, were riveted on Elvis, hoping for a smile. Individually, he did not disappoint one of them. Elvis would be disappointed himself, if he thought he had failed to stop and say hello to each one. His complete lack of being self-centered, of being considerate to everyone around him is a large part of his personal charm.

"Me keep a diary? A diary in Germany?" he laughed. "Of course not. Priscilla Beaulieu—she's just a little kid." No, he did not know of any national story on his life, for which he was to be paid $250,000 as stated by some highly reputed news sources. "Money is not in itself an important commodity. It is what it can do. For me it is what it can give those I love."

It was clearly, even profoundly told me, that I could have one interview with Elvis on each picture. If I said as much as "Hello" to him, that constituted an interview! Some frustrated columnists reported I boasted that I could see Elvis anytime I wanted!!! That was out-and-out fabrication. I never said it and in my wildest dreams never even imagined it. I strictly followed the rules.

A few days following my regular scheduled interview with Elvis, I returned for an interview with Letecia Roman, one of the feminine leads in the picture. I hoped to high heaven that I'd not run into Elvis. Instead he ran into me!

I managed to murmur the briefest hello and went sailing right on past him, without so much as a handshake, taking myself past him as quickly as possible. About twenty feet away I found an obscure corner and with innate feminine curiosity, took a quick look back in Elvis' direction. He was standing there with a slightly bewildered and puzzled expression on his face. Then he was coming after me, and I thought, "Oh, no!"

"How have you been?" he asked with usual outgoing warmth. I lowered my eyes and didn't reply. I didn't dare! I had been forbidden to speak to Elvis.

"I finally made Las Vegas, went up over the weekend," Elvis offered, his eyes looking at me with wonder and a "what have I done?" look.

"Did you have fun?" It came out before I could help it. Oh, Elvis, go away! Please go away! Don't you know—I can't talk to you—you must not talk with me, I thought. The resentment of my unfair situation burst inside of me with righteous indignation. This was a friendship I treasured, but I was there on my honor not to speak one word to Elvis since I had not been cleared by The Colonel. And The Colonel's word was law!

I remained silent. "You must not talk to Elvis!" rang in my ears. Elvis stood there puzzled for a moment and then quietly he walked away. My heart dropped with a thud of mortification, humiliation. Unbidden tears glistened in my eyes.

"Does Elvis know?" I asked the press agent on the set, "that I am not supposed to talk with him?"

"I don't think so," he replied noncommittally.

"It is so unfair," I stammered, blinking back the misery I was feeling. "Elvis is my friend. I like him, and now what will he think?" What could he think? How could he know, or did he know that to be allowed on his set I had to have a special clearance from Colonel Parker and Producer Hal Wallis combined before I could speak to Elvis. That's the way it was.

Why couldn't I tell Elvis that I had a scheduled interview with Letecia? The publicity executive reminded, "You are invited to this set on the one condition only that you do not speak to Elvis since there is no clearance."

"Then I had better not visit the set at all." But business was business, I was reminded, and personal feelings do not enter into business. A Letecia Roman interview had been set. I had gone feeling perfectly miserable, hoping that I wouldn't see Elvis and that Elvis wouldn't see me. Of course, fate had me walk right into him the first thing!

I sat there wishing I'd never become a reporter in the first place—while trying to watch Juliet Prowse do her dance for the Elvis movie. The men on the set looked bug-eyed watching her sensuous dance with its bumps and grinds—S-E-X in gyrating capital letters. But what girl can watch Miss Prowse, no matter how seductive, when Elvis is in view. I watched Elvis watch Miss Prowse. His eyes seemed more casual than langorous. Girls from all over the world have perhaps tried equally seductive scenes to intrigue him. Obviously this wasn't new to Elvis, as he did not seem to be restraining himself.

Elvis watched her, as again Juliet enchanted with her bumps and grinds to lilting music, and finally she stopped. Elvis called, "Don't chicken!" She laughed and went into another take.

Life and *Time* magazines were also on the set, which had always been continuously closed to all press. The studio executive assured me that they also were under strict orders not to talk to Elvis. My situation was not unique—except I knew Elvis and from time to time was allowed to talk to him.

Letecia and I chatted in her dressing room. While we talked, my eyes were instinctively turned out the door watching Elvis. She laughed, "You like Elvis? But of course, everyone's crazy about him."

At that same second Elvis poked his head inside the door. His face still wore that puzzled amused expression that said, "What have I done to be treated like this?" Elvis, being a man who takes the initiative and a situation in hand, said "Can I come in?"

"Of course," Letecia said. As Elvis sat down, Letecia asked, "Do you know May?" Elvis said, "I hope so." I was silent. Inwardly I screamed, "Why can't I tell Elvis the ridiculous truth! Why had such a condition been imposed on me!" It seemed stupid.

Letecia brought out cigarettes. Both Elvis and I refused. Letecia looked for a match. Elvis said, "Just a minute, I'll get one for you, honey." He leaped out the door and in a few minutes he was back with a match. At the same time he was called back into a scene. As he left, he looked down at me and winked, a friendly little wink. I felt like five cents with embarrassment!

"You like him, I can tell," Letecia was saying cheerfully. "Shall we talk about him instead of me? Of course. Let's see, I first heard of Elvis when I fell in love with his record "Heartbreak Hotel," playing on a radio in Rome. I was learning my English, and I loved that record. I have been educated on the classics and opera, like all true Italians, but Elvis and his rock 'n' roll—it's new and I love it. Five days before I started this picture, I was introduced to Elvis here on the set. We are both shy, and we didn't exchange many words. But we have become friends since.

"Elvis is such a famous idol. We didn't say much of anything. The first day there was a box of red roses for me. The card read, 'I hope you enjoy yourself. Lots of good luck. E. P.' I didn't know who E. P. was. Then someone told me the roses were from Elvis Presley! I couldn't believe it!"

"I thanked him and he said, 'Don't be scared. Just relax and you'll enjoy making pictures. Anything I can do to help, let me know.' He tried to make me comfortable, and he was so friendly, I almost lost my heart.

"Then I began to know Elvis," she continued with her big brown eyes lighting, "seeing the various sides and images of Elvis, working here every day with him in *G.I. Blues*. He tells me he is anxious to go back to Europe. 'I want to go back and sing for everybody over there in the army! I was asked to sing and I couldn't. Now I want to go back and make it up to everyone."

"Elvis never talks about what he does or what he's doing or what he did yesterday or what he's going to do tomorrow. He never mentions his personal friends or life. While he's gay and plays jokes, he has so many sad moments. He never lets you know he's like this, but I see it. Something is worrying him deep down inside, and he tries to cover it up. He is very happy at other times. Then in repose he goes back into his shy-

110

ness, and you wonder what it is that troubles him so deeply. There's a great sadness within him."

"I never thought," she continued, "a personality like this with all his gifts and talents could be so intelligent. But he is. He almost holds it back in spite of all the gifts he has. He doesn't want you to know that he is so talented. He has some sense of modesty that keeps him from displaying himself unless he is on stage or before a camera, but never just before people."

"One day Elvis told me about his mother and how much he loved her—and how it was such a shock when she died. I think he is troubled perhaps about the possibility of someone new trying to take her place. He doesn't discuss it, but someone asked him about his father getting married again and living at Graceland and Elvis said, 'Whatever makes my daddy happy is okay by me.' Elvis told me that when he isn't working he likes to stay up at night and sing and play records and shoot pool at Graceland. He loves his home very much. He always says he bought it for his mother and she furnished it, every little thing. But if there is a stepmother and her three children living there now it will be different. Perhaps this is what is bothering him. Working for everything for his mother and then nothing for her.

"Elvis always has lunch in his dressing room. It is the only way he can have freedom away from people. All of his cousins and friends, about six of them work for him, and he is never left to be lonely. One day Elvis and I got to talking about being only children. I am an only child and so is Elvis."

'Are you spoiled?' he asked me. And I said, 'No! Are you?' and Elvis said, 'No, I'm not!' And he isn't."

"Elvis says he doesn't like parties; in fact, he hates parties. 'I don't like lots of noise, and I don't smoke or drink—and well—there's no fun for me at one. Now I never go to parties, I give them instead!' "

CHAPTER FOURTEEN

My Fateful Kissing Picture with Elvis

TEENAGER PRISCILLA BEAULIEU, the daughter of the Air Force captain in Germany who had become friends with the Presleys, was a great Elvis fan. She had heard much about Graceland, and Elvis, with his usual hospitality, had invited her and her parents for a visit. Priscilla asked to stay on to finish high school in Memphis. Elvis was agreeable. Dee Presley and Grandmammy Presley took over. Elvis thought no more of the round-faced Priscilla with the mop of dark curls than a cute kid. The girls in Hollywood didn't consider her even in the running—and they were all running after Elvis.

Vernon Presley was put in charge of Elvis' money, which was handled by a shrewd accountant. Investments were made in local real estate and municipal bonds, but Vernon shied away from the stock market, preferring the safety of good savings accounts at four percent in the banks.

Elvis rented a private railroad car to take his entourage of Memphis boys with him to Hollywood. Everyone noticed that he was more mature. He went to Sy Devore, Frank Sinatra's tailor, and ordered himself a new and more conservative wardrobe. He took such a great interest in clothes that he even began wearing expensive hats, and Hollywood began taking note that this country boy had become a "sharp" dresser.

Elvis had second thoughts about buying a ranch in California. Instead he leased a pretentious Mediterranean home with a pool and gardens in exclusive Bel Air. His neighbors were the affluent society: millionaires and socialites; Jerry Lewis, Pat Boone, and Greer Garson had homes in a radius of a half mile. If Elvis

112

had felt everyone would be happy to have him as a neighbor, he was soon to be informed that he was considered highly undesirable. Elvis had bought all of his boys new motorcycles. Including himself, there were twelve of them roaring up and down the heretofore serene and quiet winding roads of Bel Air. Complaints poured in. Elvis was not about to give up a sport he has always loved, but how could he appease his neighbors? He realized the racket he was causing. Legally there was nothing anyone could do about it. Elvis, who has an innate sense of good judgment and fair play, shortly solved the problem. Every morning a moving van would deposit the motorcycles at the Bel Air gate on Sunset. Elvis and the boys would drive down the winding road and roar off on their jaunts. The same van would be there to pick up the motorcycles on their return. There was no more motorcycling on the roads of Bel Air.

With Colonel Parker's old ruling still held fast: "No interviews with Elvis," the leading ladies in his life were obliged to take up the ordeal and tell how it was to kiss Elvis, date Elvis, or even know Elvis.

Carolyn Jones, who had worked with him in a picture, made this report to me:

"From all that I had heard about 'Elvis, the Great Lover,' in print, a girl around him was supposed to go around in a metal suit to protect herself."

"At the start of our picture we had a gag going about my (then) husband Aaron Spelling being six-feet-four inches tall and weighing in at 190. On the set Elvis was told, 'Better take it easy with Carolyn, because Aaron is really tough and will tear right into you.'"

"Elvis, at first not realizing it was all a gag, said in all honesty, 'I want you fellows to know, I don't mess around with married women.'"

"Elvis is anything but the extroverted big rough Hillbilly Don Juan. He was gentle and tender, and I was so surprised with our first love scene—he held me like I was a replica of a Dresden Doll."

"It sort of takes the zing out of a kiss when it is done

113

in front of a lot of people, like the producer, director, and all the camera crew. But when we began our first kiss, Elvis whispered to me, 'Carolyn, you know more about this than I do, which side do you put your nose?' "

"Do you mean to say you've never kissed a girl before?" I exclaimed, stopping the scene in astonishment.

" 'Sure,' Elvis said, 'but not much before cameras.' "

"Elvis put his arms around me and drew me to him. 'Man, you're sure soft,' he whispered, politely."

"Our next big love scene was on location in New Orleans on a boat pier. It was very cold, and I had a 103° temperature."

" 'I'm worried about your kisses,' I said to him. 'I'm afraid you'll catch this cold.' "

" 'Don't worry,' Elvis replied nonchalantly before reaching for my lips, 'I never catch anything.' "

"Then he kissed me, and when he let me go, he said, 'Hot lips! Wow!' "

"We were almost lying on the pier together, Elvis and me, for an angled shot, and after every take the wardrobe man, mindful of my bad cold, would run over and throw a coat over me to keep me from taking more cold."

"After several takes, Elvis said, 'Carolyn, I sure am cold. Mind if I borrow a little of that coat to get warm?' So the next time the wardrobe man threw the coat over both of us, which, to the observer, could look quite sexy."

"I'm two years older than Elvis, and being very happily married, there was never any real romantic thing going on between us off screen. My husband was with me on the New Orleans location and it became a pleasant triangle friendship with Elvis, Aaron, and me."

"One day Elvis said to us, 'You know, it sure is a pleasure to see the way you and Aaron are about each other. I hope I'll be as lucky in my marriage.' "

"Elvis said he had loved to buy things for his mother for whom he had such a deep affection and love. Now that she is gone, he is certain to long for a woman's love, the kind you marry."

114

Kitty Dolan, the Las Vegas beauty, had holed up in an apartment in Bel Air with a dozen Elvis autographed and framed photos and all of his records. After Elvis left for Germany, Kitty gained fifty pounds just snacking and playing Elvis records. Before he returned she took them off.

"Kissing Elvis," Kitty disclosed, "is dreamy. Elvis is one of the most sincere boys I have ever met. He lets you know how he feels about you without making up any stories or giving with a line."

"When Elvis kisses you, he makes no promises, no commitments. You take him as he is. He doesn't ask to kiss you, it is a mutual magnetism that naturally draws you to him."

"Romantically Elvis is very gentle. When we were dating, my girl friends would ask, 'What's it like to kiss Elvis?' I must admit, it is beautiful!"

"When Elvis takes you in his arms, he's not a boy, he's a full-grown man. He has a lot of feeling and tenderness, and he has a great need for affection and love."

"Elvis doesn't make it obvious that he expects a kiss. He doesn't make that many overtures. He leaves it up to the girl. With him it's what she wants. He doesn't force himself. He's just sweet and wonderful, and big and strong, and you are drawn to him like a magnet. The girls just can't help themselves. No matter who or what happens, Elvis is always the gentleman."

"Elvis respects the girl fans, and he never pushes them away. It would never occur to him to do so. He gets a big thrill that they adore him, and I honestly believe he adores everyone of them in return."

"The girl who marries Elvis will be very lucky indeed. If she wins his love, which I don't believe Elvis has ever fully given to a girl, she'll have the most wonderfully romantic, exciting husband in the world."

Elvis, meanwhile, was dating new girls in Hollywood. "They keep combining too many new names with mine. It makes me look like I don't have real or true emotions—that I am fickle. That's not me!

"I've had a few heartbreaks as far as girls are con-

115

cerned. In fact I've had quite a few. Some of the girls, I guess, like the idea of publicity, so it is sometimes hard to know whether they are serious about you or just about themselves."

"So in Hollywood, it seems, you don't want to take it serious or you can get hurt good. Two or three times it has happened to me—one of those things. But everything has come out all right. I've just had to say, 'Elvis, hang on to your heart.'"

"Maybe," Elvis said, "it was my fault. Maybe it looks like I play around too much. Actually I don't. It's just that I'm working, and on the move."

"I react like anyone else does to hurt. I start brooding, go to bed early at night, and listen to music instead of going out. Or I'll stay around the crowd and try to be cheerful, so the hurt doesn't show."

"I think people in Hollywood have feelings, too, but many of them are so intent on their careers that they hold their emotions in reserve until success comes."

"Hollywood's like any other town," Elvis continued. "If you know where to go you have a good time. I like mainly to go to movies, and to be with my friends. But I don't hit the glamor spots much unless it is to hear a friend playing there—like Bobby Darin at the Cloister and Milton Berle at the Cocoanut Grove, etc."

As for Hollywood parties, Elvis said, "If I started to go to parties, I'd have to go to all of them," he added modestly. "I do get invited to quite a few." In fact, Mary Pickford, whose guest list for Pickfair is comparable to Buckingham Palace, had asked me to invite Elvis to Pickfair. "That's very nice, and I'd like to go," Elvis said, and then he was quiet for a moment.

"I haven't been to many parties because I have my own parties instead of going to them," he smiled. "There are always people coming to my place out here. We sit and talk and play records and have Cokes and something to eat. I enjoy it. I don't go for big Hollywood parties."

"It's like back home," he continued. "I'm always giving parties. When I first came back, there were always a lot of kids coming by from out of town. I would

116

have liked to invite everyone inside, but that isn't possible because I don't have that kind of room. So I gave a skating party and had a few hundred at a time that way. Or we go over to the fairgrounds and let everyone roam loose and have a good time."

"I feel obligated to see people when they are interested enough to come and see me. I'd let them all come into the house at Graceland if it were possible. I mean," Elvis said, "whether they are people I know or not, they are friends or they wouldn't be coming to see me. But there just isn't that much room. So you can see I like my life just as it is at home, and while I like Hollywood for a stay—it's not permanent for me."

I asked Elvis if having three new noisy young stepbrothers around Graceland was quite a new experience. He laughed, "There are times, and there are times."

Elvis declared he had no idea of marriage for some time to come, "since I haven't met 'the girl' yet."

"I could never go through one of these quick marriages and divorces and all that in the papers. Not for me. When I marry I will be like my Mama and Daddy, who were together for keeps and happy. I love children and someday, naturally, I hope to meet the right girl. But I don't think it will be Hollywood style, just a good plain marriage for no reasons of career or anything impressive except the most important fact that I love her. And that she loves me so much that we want to marry and spend the rest of our lives with each other."

Since Anita Wood was out from Memphis visiting Elvis, I asked if this long-time friendship with the pretty little blonde was serious. "No," he said, "we're just good friends."

"Good friends are always good friends. Real friendship is not a matter of the moment back home—it's for keeps," Elvis concluded with a warm friendly smile.

In the next few weeks Dee Presley announced her pregnancy and shortly afterwards the loss of the expected Presley heir. Elvis expressed his regrets and now observed, "She is a real nice woman."

117

CHAPTER FIFTEEN

Wild in the Country with Elvis

THE REPORTS COMING across seas from Germany were all praise for Elvis as a G.I. Editors for almost every publication queried me for Elvis Presley pieces. But with the stipulation: Make him human. Be objective. A guy who has all the women after him and makes that kind of dough has to have plenty of faults, a super ego, and a few skeletons in his closet. Let's have the low-down since you know him.

They didn't want the truth. There was nothing to find fault in about Elvis. They couldn't believe his shining wholesome character, honesty, integrity, and the real human, kind, compassionate side of his nature. Some suggested he must be gay, a homosexual. Why else did he have all those boys hanging around him, "The Memphis Mafia?" This was such a laugh, and completely ridiculous. The boys worked for Elvis and they all liked girls. So did Elvis! The boys all got married in time to come, raised families, as did Elvis. While starlets about Hollywood often reported the boys taking them to Elvis' place and what went on—a bit of discreet balling with the boys sometimes—but if it happened with Elvis, it was never reported or it was far too sacred. Not one of the girls ever talked about it.

I didn't write the Elvis pieces requested. The press, in general, was uptight already, since they never had open access to Colonel Parker's Elvis. *Life* Magazine, deciding to give Elvis their cover and send a special photographer to shoot it, was turned down. "You can have my boy's picture for the cover for $150,000" was the reported reply from The Colonel. The same reply was given to all of the national major magazines. That is the sole reason why Elvis, in spite of his tremendous popularity, never graced other than movie magazine covers. The Colonel always made certain that his boy got his percentage if anyone was going to make money on his Elvis.

Right along through the years into 1974, when wax museums throughout the world asked for Elvis' personal clothing to garb a wax effigy of the star, The Colonel reportedly warned, "No percentage of the gate's overall." It doesn't matter that every star and press agent tried to get this recognition offering the star's clothes, jewelry, and assistance in the form of free personal appearances, etc. (maybe even offer to pay for the honor), they can't get Elvis—the most in demand of all!

Elvis could have his image smothered with pictures and all kinds of enviable publicity but The Colonel cagily keeps him from and out of it. More remarkable, Elvis and The Colonel have the Internal Revenue make out their taxes. It is said they don't try any of the usual accepted tax shelters and ways to dodge taxes, but pay whatever is asked. Elvis has said, "even so there's plenty left over."

Returning to Hollywood and the day of reporting on his assets, The Colonel happily showed Elvis his earnings, which had gone right along accumulating during his army hitch. Three million dollars had accrued in Elvis' bank account from recording royalties, and now that he was home he had cut his first disc as a civilian, "Stuck on You." RCA couldn't fill the immediate two million advance orders—and the $125,000 Frank Sinatra had just paid for appearing in his TV show (an unheard of 50 percent of the picture profits and all music and record rights reverting to Elvis; 75 percent was Elvis' take, 25 percent was The Colonel's, with the William Morris office taking 10 percent off the top of the movie revenues. The Colonel puts 50 percent of his 25 percent back into the business side of the operation, office expenses, staff, advertising, and exploitation, while Elvis' 75 percent goes straight to the Memphis accountants.

To any producer who'd ask to contract a film with

119

Elvis at a cut price, The Colonel would hike the price. Once a deal was made, The Colonel said, "We don't have approval on scripts—only money. If we'd start telling people what to do, they could blame us if the picture doesn't go. As it is, we both take bows if it hits, and if it doesn't they get more blame maybe than us. Anyway what do I know about production?"

The Colonel wasn't the least bit nervous about any possibility that Elvis' film popularity might one day run dry. "We've, for one, got offers for personal appearances from all over the world that start at $100,000 per night. We haven't been able to do them." Ten years later in 1974, Elvis' concert appearance offers tripled into the millions.

I didn't know whether Elvis would ever speak to me again after a lesser movie magazine piece. I had written several open letters to Elvis in my syndicated newspaper columns. Whether he'd read them or not, who could tell! Elvis' voluminous mail had to be delivered in huge zippered mail bags every week, and the army didn't allow Elvis that kind of time to read them. Elvis had said, "Don't forget me!" and I wondered now if he had forgotten me. More was the fact that I had been terribly embarrassed over a story I had written of our last meeting which appeared in the aforementioned movie magazine. The story had been a good happy light breezy honest account with plenty of quotes from Elvis. It had been quite all right, except a new editor in New York had taken it upon herself to write in and add 750 words that I hadn't, nor would I ever have, dreamed of saying. Next to a picture of Elvis with his arm around me, she had captioned me in quotes: "Standing next to Elvis I get hot and cold all over, I don't know whether I'll marry him or not—but—!" On and on it went! I could have died of embarrassment when I saw it. How dare anyone do such a thing and with my byline on the interview story with Elvis.

My lawyer advised me to sue for a million dollars and settle for $200,000. Since Martin Goodman, the publisher and his wife, were dear friends and a suit would bring headlines involving Elvis' name, I didn't sue. But the damage was done.

Grabbing a plane for New York City, I was in the publisher's office within twenty-four hours asking how he could explain this? Syndicated in 437 newspapers by King Features Syndicate and writing for national magazines, I had never in all of my experience seen any editor put quotes of what a writer hadn't said into her mouth. And this was in a movie magazine, for almost no money, but to do them a favor because they wanted Elvis so much. I didn't sue, and I don't know what happened to the editor—but I never wrote for them again. Forever after, unless a publication was a responsible one, I wouldn't risk putting myself in such jeopardy. Elvis had indirectly cost me an income of over $8,000 annually from this publisher. While my lawyers told me I was certain to win a lawsuit, my main worry was what Elvis, who trusted me, must have thought when he read it, and being in Germany, too far away for me to explain.

Now Elvis was back, and he was rushed immediately into *G.I. Blues.* His first day, I received a call to come quickly to the set to see him. First I baked an 18-egg orange chiffon cake (my specialty), and gathering two dozen American Beauty roses from my garden, I rushed over to Paramount with my "Welcome home Elvis" offering.

In uniform, slender and poised, Elvis was twice as handsome as when he'd left Hollywood, "Please, please Elvis," I was thinking holding out the cake and flowers, "don't be mad at me! Please believe the truth." There was no need for me to be trembling—with such inner silent pleas, for Elvis saw me and quickly walked over to greet me with an affectionate kiss on my cheek, and said, "I'm glad to see you." Taking the roses, he called for one of the boys to put them in water in his dressing room, thanked me for the cake, which was still warm from the oven, and took me to a quiet side of the set to sit.

"I read that story in Germany," he began. "I knew you didn't write all of that—", he said, placing a com-

121

forting hand on mine, with none of the indignation I fully expected.

"How could you not believe I wrote that silly stuff?" I asked, "since the story had my byline and all of the rest of it was correct?"

"I know," Elvis replied, "because you are a lady and you wouldn't talk that way. It wasn't your way of talking. I just knew that someone had doctored it up to make it sensational, I guess. Let's forget it."

I was so relieved I reached over and kissed Elvis without realizing it. Did he see my open letters to him in my columns? "Yes," he grinned. "They were fun. It was very nice of you to keep the fans posted for me on what I was doing, so they wouldn't forget me." The humility of the boy and now the man never ceased then, nor still, to amaze me. He was natural and unspoiled as though he weren't Elvis Presley at all!

One early (and I do mean very early) A.M., a 20th-Century Fox Studio unit man telephoned me. "How would you like to take a drive in the country about 100 miles and see Elvis? He's making *Wild in the Country* for us. As you know interviews are banned, but Elvis said he would like to see you."

Would I! Of course. Given the details for my journey which went many miles on the highway, turned off onto other less known highways, until I'd come to a certain road—a wagon road—I was to drive as far as I could until I saw a fence. When I found the gate, I could drive in. I must be sure and fasten the gate back with wire, and I was to drive across rough terrain on cow paths for several miles or so until I found another fence and gate. By repeating the process, if I followed directions, I would eventually come on the *Wild in the Country* location, away and far away from civilization!

By some remarkable coincidence I arrived. Elvis was in a scene some seventy feet away on the other side of a creek. I noticed a pretty girl, obviously a visitor, on that side of the river, too. "Who is she?" I asked the studio man. "I don't know; she came to visit Elvis. I think she's from Memphis. We never interfere or ask Elvis who his visitors are" was the reply.

Shortly here was Elvis, who'd crossed over the creek and walked the distance to greet me. "Say, is that your car?" he said, pointing to my Cadillac De Ville. "Let's go sit in it and talk," he suggested. "You know this is the same model I gave to my mother," he said. "Mind if we drive it? Handles just the same. Hers is pink. I keep it in the garage at Graceland. I intend to always keep it. Mama sure loved that pink Cadillac!"

Sitting in the car, we talked about everything I could think of. Yes, he was glad to be back making another film. He'd like to do some personal appearance, but was scheduled for another picture immediately following this one. "I want to become a good actor," he voiced.

I wanted to know his present romantic status; after all that's what everyone asked about Elvis. "There is none," he said. "What about Anita Wood, the girl in Memphis you gave a car to?" I asked if it wasn't Anita I'd glimpsed out here in the *Wild Country* visiting him? Elvis didn't allude to her presence. "She's a friend, not a romance," he countered.

"We heard about a fifteen-year-old teenager, Priscilla Beaulieu in Germany?" I began. "Oh," he laughed. "She's the daughter of one of my officers stationed there. She's a cute little kid. Romance? Oh no! She's only fifteen or sixteen." (Which was about ten years younger than Elvis.)

"Well you never know," I laughed. "I get letters from ten-year-old fans who say they hope to grow up and marry you, Elvis!" Elvis grinned.

We sat talking for some time in my car and I wondered why Elvis wasn't called for a scene. It seemed everyone at the studio was so in awe of Elvis Presley that they didn't want to disturb him, so there we sat undisturbed. That is, until Elvis said, "It's noon. Will you have lunch with me?" Of course I was delighted.

Elvis never mentioned his visitor, whom I had recognized to be Anita Wood from Memphis. Considering I was his guest, Elvis took me to lunch. We sat down at a big table with the cast and crew. Elvis ate lightly. "I want to keep the weight off. The army took it off fast," he said.

Elvis never again mentioned the fiasco of that piece which had me saying, "I felt hot and cold all over every time I stood next to him." It was forgotten. He trusted me, and he knew he well could. I also never mentioned to him that my loyalty and integrity to him over it had cost me an annual $8,000. Oh well.

Elvis surprised me by saying, "Do you want another picture?" "Oh yes," I said happily. A picture with Elvis proved that I wasn't making up my interviews with him, like all of the rest of them were. Seeing is believing!

The pictures of us taken on location that day arrived a week later and were placed on my dressing table. A burglar broke into my house taking everything of value, and the police and F.B.I., as well as I, noted that the burglars had stopped and looked all through the Elvis photos. The fingerprints were all over them. Even in a robbery, where haste should have been essential, some-one had found Elvis Presley irresistible.

For a long time, Elvis fans had been filling my mailbox with their letters. They came from all parts of the world, as many as 3,000 a month. Often I'd see the little girls standing outside my house for hours hoping by some miracle Elvis just might stop by.

CHAPTER SIXTEEN

Memphis Mafia

ELVIS' "MEMPHIS MAFIA" aroused comment and curiosity. Sinatra, Jerry Lewis, Dean Martin, and Vic Damone were never without their bands of henchmen who were their "go-fors" ("go for this for me" or "go for that"), secretaries, agents, valets, drivers, coaches, yes men—and errand boys. Elvis' boys were never explained. They were as remote to the public as Elvis was himself. No one could reach them to ask questions. They were close-mouthed. Said one, "Anyone who is a blabber mouth immediately has broken Elvis' trust, out on the outside, and never gets back in." There was no sworn oath of secrecy concerning Elvis' private life. It was that way, and everyone well knew it!

During his first film in Hollywood, Elvis discovered he had become a legend! The Colonel's obsession against overexposure, "keep them curious; they got to pay to see my boy," resulted in the Presley closed sets, and No Visitors signs strictly enforced by security guards posted by them.

Elvis became a self-imposed exile from society, whether it was to his liking or his wanting. Everywhere Elvis went, a riot started. Crowds gathered even if Elvis crossed the road to a neighbor's to shoot a little pool. Lawns and flowers were trampled, windowpanes broken, and soon Elvis himself realized that "in person" was a hazard.

"I can't go around always apologizing for being someplace and innocently causing a lot of trouble," Elvis told me. "This is the way it is. I'm getting used to it. But it's like being in prison. I can't go in a store and look around. I can't even go to a movie or places like Disneyland that I'd love to see!"

This was the big price that was being extracted from him, in return for his phenomenal fame and wealth. It was his personal freedom. Even with the strictest security guard, the world outside his door was no longer safe for people when Elvis arrived.

Pandemonium reigned the minute the word got out, "Elvis is here!" People got hurt, jammed, stepped on, and far worse. "I would never be the cause of harming anyone, so it's just no use!" Later on Elvis, after a few years of frustrated thought, devised means and ways of going about disguised with a wig, a moustache, dark glasses, or wearing working men's clothes. It became great sport at times to dress even like an old man with a gray wig, a beard, and just the right tacky costume from Western Costumes. In large cities, Elvis by devious ruses was able to make the scene and enjoy himself. He still does.

As himself, Elvis Presley, one thing was for sure, his freedom was gone perhaps forever. The fame he had and which The Colonel had worked so diligently to obtain, locked him out of the world everyone else enjoyed. As Elvis, the Super-Star, he was now actually a prisoner, doomed to be locked up in the ivory tower of his career.

Warm and outgoing, Elvis quickly grew lonely and moody. Back home in Memphis there were his cousins and his school chums, all Elvis' own age. Few of them had any more education or schooling than Elvis. One night at Graceland, when several of the boys were enjoying an evening shooting pool with Elvis, they said how lucky he was and how much they wished such luck had struck them!

Elvis replied, "You don't know how it is to be locked up all of the time, never to run down to a drugstore for a soda or go to a store to buy something. I can't stick my nose out of the door."

Red West, his cousin, a sandy-haired six-two raised in Memphis, had graduated along with Elvis from Humes High School. Red had gone along on some personal appearances with Elvis and not having any other job, Elvis had kept him with him.

Red had now become the good-natured envy of several of the other fellows. "Man, I'd like to go with you anytime you need my services, Elvis!" Elvis suggested, "Come back tomorrow and we'll play touch football here in the back yard and stay on for supper." The boys had such a good time that it occurred to Elvis, "How'd you all like to come along with me to Hollywood? You'd get a kick out of seeing a movie being made! Perhaps you can get some bit parts in the picture!"

"Yeah, man!" was the enthusiastic immediate answer. Along they went and things worked out well. Those who had no jobs to return to in Memphis made themselves so useful and handy in doing the millions of tasks that beset a star like Elvis, he simply put them on his payroll. And they stayed on!

Elvis lost the abject loneliness that had been imposed on him, now having his own friends, his own kind with him. The group became known as "Elvis Presley's Boys" until someone nicknamed them the "Memphis Mafia."

Elvis and his entourage moved about much like a president and his presidential aides. Loyalty and absolute friendship was all that was expected, along with action of any sort when it was called for. Individual duties were systematically assigned, such as dresser, secretary, makeup man, baggage man and packer, driver, errand guy, etc. Whenever Elvis felt like playing touch football or going a round in the ring boxing, or when Elvis would find himself in a tight spot in a crowd, the boys were there to rise and shine and do their best. Together they also acted as personal security and bodyguards.

Equality was the word. The young men dressed and wore good jewelry and drove fine cars the same as Elvis. They were well paid. One expressed, "This is the life—and just say you're a pal of Elvis Presley's, the girls flock to you. Wow—you get your pick."

At the same time, each one was fully aware that he was also personally responsible for anyone he introduced to Elvis or brought to his home. His own behavior must never reflect any discredit on Elvis.

Among the regulars were Alan Fortas, a muscular broad-shouldered 5′ 11″ youth who was the same age and who had also gone to school with Elvis in Memphis. The appendage of "Hog Ears" was fastened on him. Outside the in-group no one knew that "Hog Ears" was the nephew of the U.S. Supreme Court Judge Abe Fortas.

Elvis met Joe Esposito in Germany when they were buddies in the army. On their discharge he visited Elvis in Memphis, and soon he was added to the group. With his clipped Yankee talk, he was a good contrast to the Southern boys. Richard Davis, a blond and also Elvis' age, hailed from California, but he met Elvis in

Memphis. He became "runner of errands." Sonny West, Elvis' age, a cousin of Red West, proved another welcome addition. Billy Smith, one of Elvis' first cousins, blond with blue eyes, joined even though he was exactly seven years younger than the rest. He had spent much time at Graceland and begged to join Elvis' boys. Marty Locker was the only one older than Elvis. Balding, short and stout, he was the clown, always with a funny story to add to the fun. Often it would be his duty to escort Elvis in public. The other boys remained in the background unobserved, unless needed. The only Presley fan to make the group was Jerry Shilling, ten years younger than the rest. He'd hung around Elvis at Graceland, and finally struck up a friendship. Other boys were added or only left the group due to some variety of urgent circumstances. The majority, even after they all married, continued to work for Elvis from time to time.

Perhaps the only aspersion ever cast toward Elvis' impeccable and wholesome character came from a disgruntled old news hen. She declared there was something "mighty weird about a group of boys always traveling along with Elvis." This boomeranged, when I replied, "What would the old so-and-so say if Elvis traveled with a group of girls to wait on his needs instead!"

Elvis was best man at Red West's wedding in 1961. He was to become best man at many of the boys' weddings as they found wives and married. Marty was already the father of three. Alan married and made his home in both Memphis and Hollywood. He was on call when Elvis needed him. Mike married a girl named Gladys and continued to be the boy's film projector. If film broke he had to mend it and pacify his audience of the M.M. Joe Esposito became a public accountant, married, and had a daughter. Richard married and so did Billy. Billy made Elvis an uncle. Elvis was the last of the Memphis Mafia to marry.

Few of the men left the group but it was noted later that before Elvis' marriage and at the peak of Elvis' bachelorhood days, the Memphis Mafia were thirteen men including a cook. After Elvis married, only four boys remained, but all remained loyal. A glimpse of all the boys was widely seen in Elvis' early movie, *Jailhouse Rock*. From time to time they played bits in most of the Presley films.

Knowing Elvis, his habits, moods, disposition, and character better than anyone else, it was gratifying to all Presley admirers that each Memphis Mafia boy remained loyal and admired their boss as intensely as any fan. Close-mouthed, which is a ritual with all those who have the privilege of close allegiance around Elvis, there were no disclaimers amongst them. Some, who were offered fancy money to give stories to the press, or tell what Elvis was really like, or what their life with him was like, found no takers. "We are more than satisfied with how Elvis treats us. He works ten times harder than any one of us. Yet we live like kings with the King!" That was the standard reply. To receive this kind of affection and respect reveals the rare diplomacy Elvis must exercise to make no one feel a favorite, and no one to become disgruntled. Elvis is a marvelous politician, said one. Few people can handle people as well as Elvis does.

Rumors of Vernon Presley's impending marriage had from time to time been whispered in the press. In Germany that second year, Grandmammy Minnie Presley and Mrs. Davada "Dee" Stanley became friends. When the lonely Vernon became interested, Dee Stanley found herself in a precarious position. No woman could dare try to take Elvis' mother's place! The Elvis world was against it. The glamorous Mrs. Stanley, the newly divorced wife of an army man, had three small sons. She was known as Dee.

The timing was bad, with Elvis still mourning his mother. Vernon, out of respect, waited until both he and Elvis had returned from Germany and were back home in Memphis before he remarried. He had been a widower for two years. In Memphis some appraised the silver blonde, who was thirty, as bold and enterprising. Others pointed to the fact that she was religious, a lovely woman, and a fine mother to her sons. Elvis, when asked, had no comment.

In July, 1960, Vernon married Dee in a small quiet wedding ceremony in Memphis. Elvis was conspicuous by his absence. Immediately it was said that Elvis, still mourning his mother, disliked the new woman who had become his stepmother. Denying this rumor, Elvis explained that he did not resent her. He never called her mother or mom; he referred to Dee Presley as "my father's new wife." He explained that his father's happiness was the important issue. And that the reason he had not attended their wedding was because he did not want to stir a commotion that his presence might have made. "A wedding should be a sacred thing, not a circus," he said.

While Vernon's new family was welcomed at Graceland, the arrangement proved to be awkward. When Elvis was home, being a night person, he slept days. This was not conducive to three energetic little boys romping around the house. Elvis never complained. Whatever made his daddy happy was what was of paramount importance, Elvis said.

Elvis had locked the door to his mother's room. This was understandable. His grief was still too new to allow another woman taking over there. Sensing his father's discomfort as time passed by, Elvis spoke frankly to the new Mrs. Presley. "I want my daddy to be happy more than anything else in the world," Elvis told her. "It is apparent you are not happy living here at Graceland, which is my mother's home. I am willing to build you any kind of home you want, so it will be your home. You draw up the plans, and I'll have it built expressly for you."

A modern five-bedroom house was built for Dee and Vernon and the Stanley boys on the street behind Elvis' estate. Only a garden separates the two. Through Elvis' understanding and ingenuity "to right whatever is wrong," a happy family relationship developed between the two homes. At times the boys' father (Mr. Stanley) visits them. It is reported he has even seen Graceland.

"I know my daddy was very lonely without mama," Elvis said. "I gave him all the companionship I could, but in the army I was gone all day. And back home I was away in Hollywood working. I know he had to marry again to keep from being so lonely."

Dee proved to be a good wife to Vernon, and she was most anxious to cement a closer relationship with Elvis. She was happy to greet Elvis' fans, and she would invite them into her own home for coffee if they knocked at her door. She was equally praised for her hospitality and denounced as ambitious to share the spotlight of Elvis Presley.

A young man and his wife who had followed Elvis' career closely knocked on the Vernon Presleys' door one morning to find Dee and Vernon at breakfast. They invited the surprised couple, Mr. and Mrs. Jim Mills, to come in as though they were welcoming close friends, even though they were complete strangers. "Elvis is in Hollywood making a picture," Dee said. "But do sit down and have a cup of coffee. Vernon," she asked, "can't we take them to Graceland? My son John would like to see it. All of the kids at school ask him."

Vernon was completely agreeable. The group left the back door of the Vernon Presley home and walked down a garden path to a back fence. There was an opening, and stepping through, they found themselves on the back grounds of Graceland. Various animals and pets, ducks and chickens, were here and there. Elvis' famous pet monkey, Scatter, who had been one of the big attractions at Graceland, had departed. He had grown too unruly.

There were garages housing cars and in the driveways were several cars, all belonging to Elvis and the inhabitants of Graceland. Vernon Presley revealed his own office on the grounds, "where two secretaries take care of the Elvis Presley mail, and we file vast amounts of news clippings into books."

To the Mills' surprise, they turned a corner to see many people examining some of Elvis' motorcycles and his famed go-carts. People were milling about taking snapshots.

"You mean Graceland is open to the public?" they asked in astonishment.

Vernon and Dee nodded their heads and acknowledged the greetings of several people, stopping to pose for their cameras. Once inside the house, they explained that Graceland had been opened for the public since shortly after Elvis returned from the service. "People can come through the grounds until six at night," Vernon said. "However, when Elvis is at home we keep the gates locked for his privacy. Elvis and his mother always welcomed people, and we figure it is better and safer for them to come in and look around a little than to cause big traffic jams out in front. The keepers at the gate (Elvis' uncles) have their instructions to allow people in," Vernon finished. "Elvis wants it that way. When he's away, why not! When he's home, Elvis is a night person. He likes to sleep days, so at those times we keep it quiet."

"No one will believe this," said the Mills, "that anyone can walk in to Graceland!"

Dee Presley proved to be a devout member of the Church of Christ as well as an active one. Vernon and her three sons were regular attendants at the church down Highway 51 from Graceland. Since it was Sunday the Presleys invited the young couple to go along with them to church. Afterward they drove them by to see the new Memphis Coliseum where an Evangelist meeting was being held. (In spite of Elvis' popularity, there had been some holdouts who had prevented the Coliseum being named "Elvis Coliseum.") Vernon drove them all later to a restaurant for a Sunday night dinner. The Mills couldn't get over such warm, friendly hospitality. They thought perhaps Dee and Vernon were a little lonely in Memphis. There was still adjusting to be done by Gladys Presley's friends and relatives. "Vernon shouldn't have married so soon" was the general consensus.

"The only thing that troubles us," said Dee, "is that Elvis is such a religious guy and he so enjoys going to church. But he can't go anymore. His presence causes such excitement it disrupts the whole meetings. He has his Bible, though, and reads it regularly and he is planning to record some spiritual religious music."

So it was for the lucky visitors in Elvisland in 1961.

The Vernon Presleys happily announced they were expecting the stork. The news that Elvis would soon have a half brother or sister caused exclamations in all parts of the world. Excitement subsided when Dee Presley lost the baby. Little further comment was made. Elvis soon related to the three little boys, and became particularly fond of the youngest. To all three Elvis became their idol. The two elder immediately began practicing on drums and with guitars, hoping to emulate their elder step-brother. Elvis himself never referred to the boys as stepbrothers nor to himself in that term. He said, "They are very nice, well-mannered boys. I am happy playing with them when I am at home. I like them."

Families and friends were interludes who came and went, and some stayed on in the public image of Elvis. But the big spotlight always has and always seems to swing back onto Elvis as the solo figure. That is The Colonel's strategy. No one, not even a wife, is going to take the attention away from his boy. "Elvis is the star, and that's my job—seeing he stays the biggest star of them all. Anything or anyone else can be a distraction."

CHAPTER SEVENTEEN

Exclusive, Rare Interview with Colonel Parker

THE RECORDED VOICE of Elvis Presley has been heard by more people in the world than that of any other performing artist in the history of the recording industry. That statement of fact was issued by RCA Records in 1974. It was also true as early as 1956. In the early sixties, RCA released an album entitled "Elvis World Wide: 50 Gold Award Hits." By degrees into the seventies, a few rare capsule paragraphs gave the newest generation of Elvis fans a few pertinent facts of Elvis' history. There was Elvis at three years of age with his Mama and Daddy on the cover of the "Elvis Country Album." While in 1974, an album "Elvis, a Legendary Performer—The Early Years" featured an enclosed booklet "Memory Log." It jogged the memory of Elvis' own generation and enlightened the present one with news clippings of Elvis' sudden rise as "King" in 1956! Some of the controversial news headlines read, "Says the Rock 'n' Roll King"—"Elvis Music Called Good Therapy for Mentally Ill"—"Elvis the Pelvis Belongs in the Jungle"—"Critics Rate Elvis Low in Acting Ability"—Elvis records sell a million copies on release. There were candid shots of Elvis in his early Sun Record days, in 1954. There is "just enough information given to whet the appetite for more!" And that is the secret of Colonel Tom Parker's phenomenal management: "Always leave them wanting more. We don't believe in getting overexposed!" By 1957, in one year, "We do the best we can," added up to $120,000,000 in records, paid movie admissions, TV, sheet music, and a national merchandising sales program of Elvis Presley hats, clothes, jewelry, teddy bears, and other souvenirs. These alone totaled thirty million dollars in four years. Considering that two of these years Elvis spent out of entertainment circulation in the army shows, the Colonel's directing manipulative genius makes his word law with Elvis!

The Colonel himself is such a uniquely colorful one-of-a-kind showman, he is equally as fascinating as his protegé. Colonel Parker moves his offices from studio to studio along with Elvis' movie contracts. Studio personnel observe that Elvis may wince at times at some of the Colonel's flamboyant methods, but he remains perfectly disciplined and never dissents. It was also noted from the beginning that unlike many sex-symbol film idols, Elvis never went "on the make" for the

starlets or the harlots. He was gentlemanly and responded with wholesome good nature to the many
attentions being paid him. There were rarely any racy
rumors or hot gossip associated with his conduct.

Elvis did not ask for a special dressing room or any
concessions, and never displayed temperament. The
Colonel saw to it that "his boy" was given the most
luxurious dressing room bungalow on the lot—ones
that either before or later housed Frank Sinatra, Clark
Gable, or Barbra Streisand. If The Colonel had a soft
spot in his heart, it was reported to be equally divided
between Marie, his wife, and Elvis. Actually, The
Colonel is kindhearted, soft, which he tries by a brisk
manner not to show—"the better to be the manipulator
of Elvis' contracts." His formidable front is pure bluff
except when it comes to dollars and cents! Then it is
as solid as a vault in a Federal Reserve Bank!

Hollywood describes The Colonel as a "big country
boy with shoes." He is always affable, but he has
strange rules governing Elvis. All major stars have
private press agents, as well as full use of a studio, or
high-powered public relations and publicity firm. The
Colonel has never hired one for Elvis. There are so
many restrictions in The Colonel's deliberate policy of
sifting out news on Elvis, bit by bit, it is as though
when he opens another notch, urgency subsides and is
soon put aside.

20th Century Fox producers insisted that Elvis make
the picture *Wild in the Country* without any singing.
Heretofore, the consistent formula had been Elvis in a
thin story with pretty girls and a dozen songs. That
spelled sure-fire success at the box office. Now to ex-
hibit Elvis' acting ability there were to be no songs. The
Colonel signed the contract saying, "I think you people
are nuts signing Elvis without singing. But your checks
are good!" That was the only film Elvis made that was not
big at the box office. The picture was recalled, and a
song was added at the end to make it Elvis.

Richard Avedon, a highly touted nationally recognized photographer, whose fee was $5,000 called from
New York that he would like to take some pictures of

Elvis for *Esquire Magazine*. "How much will you pay us?" The Colonel replied. The astounded Avedon managed, "Don't you know who I am?" "Yes, I do," replied The Colonel, "but you gotta pay Elvis!" At the time, *Esquire* had requested Frankie Avalon, Pat Boone, and several other singers, but the wise Colonel never grouped his boy. His boy was a star who stood alone, shining brightly alone!

A lively friendship developed between The Colonel and Harry Brand, publicity director and vice-president of 20th-Century Fox. Both had a sense of humor about practical jokes. The Colonel sent Harry a portrait of himself taken in a Confederate Colonel's uniform among many others. Another picture was the back of a hippo blow-up entitled, "Lookout Below."

Like Jack Benny, The Colonel trades on being a hard bargainer and having a tight fist. This is a matter of controversy, for whenever a worthy charity bid reaches him, he is most generous and is said to often send along his check for $500 or more. News of his charitable acts is never publicized. However it is known that among others, he has helped a photographer down on his luck, he presented a group of nuns outside Tennessee with a bus to help them with their work, and a poor widow about to lose her home was saved by having the mortgage paid. It is also understandable why The Colonel never divulges his charitable deeds, since it would be humanly impossible for him to take on the financial problems of the world that might beset him.

More and more The Colonel's time was demanded in Hollywood with Elvis' various enterprises. Travel had become constant. It was hard on Mrs. Parker, to whom he has been married since they were both young, having shared the leaner days. The Colonel's affection, care, and devotion to his wife reveals that The Colonel is capable of a depth of romantic love to be envied by many a great beauty in the film business. People allude to "the lasting happy marriage of The Colonel Parkers."

In 1961, The Colonel rented an attractive small home from actor Edward Ashley who was leaving for Europe to make a picture. The Colonel paid his rent two months at a time in advance. He was such a good renter, Mr. Ashley did not ask for his house back on his return, and The Colonel and his wife remained there intact. The Colonel apologized for having a special lock put on one of the closets. "That's for where I keep my boy Elvis' $10,000 gold lamé suit outfit," he explained. "I can't take the chance of it being left in a hotel."

The neighbors noted that The Colonel's office seemed to be his patio where he spent a certain portion of each day in the sun. Three secretaries from his studio office arrived promptly for these sessions which were also business. The Colonel allowed, "I never miss taking my sun baths. It clears away worries and tensions." He is a great believer in his home spun philosophies. He did not sign contracts it was reported—his handshake was pure gold.

One of his neighbors who was invited to one of the openings of an Elvis movie in Westwood, was amazed to find The Colonel had set up a portable booth in the lobby of the theater where he was giving out Elvis pictures. "The more the better," he said. "I'm a pitchman. You've got to do it to drum up interest."

The Colonel kept adding to his and Elvis' list for Christmas cards and telegrams until the names added up to a thousand or better. Many major stars have been surprised and happily pleased to receive a telegram from "Elvis and The Colonel" on an opening night. Those closer to The Colonel receive radios, TV sets, and electrical gifts at Christmas time. I have happily received Christmas telegrams and cards. And twice also on my birthday—"Dear Miss Mann: On behalf of Mrs. Parker, Elvis, and myself, a happy birthday to you and best wishes for many more to come. Sincerely, The Colonel." A posh formal birthday dinner dance was given as a surprise for me at the Beverly Hills Hotel. Also, unbeknownst to me, 300 formal engraved invitations were sent out to those who were known to be my best friends. Knowing Elvis and The Colonel never go to parties, I was astonished to see a telegram RSVP of congratulations from Elvis and The Colonel.

Did they think I'd had the invitation sent? By the time I saw Elvis again, I forgot to ask.

The decision to make his home in Palm Springs came when The Colonel decided the heat and sun would "bake out Mrs. Parker's joints. She had been suffering with bursitis. I'd take her anywhere in the world to ease the pain," he said.

In Palm Springs, The Colonel's home became the mecca of the Parker's few select friends and, as usual, his business operations as well. RCA mentors and executives meet around the pool to decide contracts and do business for Elvis records. The Colonel loves gadgets and has a bar, an electrical barbecue, an electric ice-cream freezer, and a portable ice box among other hospitality items. Everyone relaxes and enjoys himself at The Colonel's expense while they negotiate. The Colonel still drives a hard bargain, they say. And while it is nice to enjoy hospitality, it is a long ride, a total of five hours round-trip. "We have no choice." Mrs. Parker is quiet spoken, a good hostess, and known to be very nice. "The sun rises and sets on her" as far as The Colonel is concerned. With all of the movie and show business beauties he may be exposed to, The Colonel never second-looks any of them with male intent. He is known to be a man of impeccable morals.

Hal Wallis says, "The Colonel is a fine man. Once he trusts you and gives you his word, that is it. We have never signed a contract on any of Elvis' pictures. We agree on a hand shake. The contract may be one for six weeks or six months later. The Colonel's integrity is absolute. I made several films with Elvis—all of them hits. I would like to use Elvis in another picture someday if I can find the right vehicle."

Hollywood and show business buzz with tales of The Colonel, and rather than disparaging, are sheer amazement! Only two men are said to be on The Colonel's payroll, Tom Diskin, his assistant, and Jim O'Brien, who is known as Tom Diskin's assistant. RCA Records and the William Morris office, The Colonel's agency for Elvis, furnish whatever other assistants The Colonel may need.

John Hartman, with the Morris office at the time, was on loan to The Colonel. Mr. Hartman, then a mail-room boy, drove an old, out-dated Chevy convertible that had two big holes in the top. The Colonel was delighted with the old jallopy and liked nothing better than to have Mr. Hartman chauffeur him around the M.G.M. Studio lot in it. One time when they stopped for the light signal, The Colonel saw M.G.M.'s President arriving in his chauffeured limousine. As they met to pass at the gate, The Colonel stuck his head through a hole in the torn top of the Chevy and with a bright formal smile said, "Howdy Bob!" The amazement on the other's face was all The Colonel could have asked.

One afternoon in 1957, after leaving Elvis' set, I bumped into Colonel Parker going into his inner sanctum at Paramount. "Come in," he invited. The walls of three rooms were lined with Elvis posters. Every available inch of space, outside of desks, displayed Elvis' promotion, souvenirs, and merchandising.

The Colonel's blue eyes are guileless, warm, and friendly, but they can become piercing if need be. Extending gentlemanly Southern hospitality now in expressing himself, he said after inviting me to take a seat, that he was not "talking much about Elvis these days. I'm saving that for my book." In his enthusiasm for his multimillion dollar money-making star, however, any conversation, even without conscious intent, finds The Colonel talking about Elvis.

Seated behind his desk with his Elvis hat pushed back on his head, against that background of Elvis posters and pictures in such coloful array, The Colonel talked freely. This naive writer (me) was later to learn that this was a precedent-shattering interview. Later in looking through newspaper morgue files, I finally located just one known interview with The Colonel in print. "That one," said the librarian of the Academy of Motion Picture Arts and Sciences, "was given to May Mann and appeared in a national magazine in 1957. There have been no others." Had I known of this golden exclusive opportunity that The Colonel was giving me, I'd have asked a hundred more questions!

"Elvis and me—we go three or four days sometimes without talking to each other. Sometimes even a week," The Colonel said leaning back in his chair. "Like this week it's been five days. I see Elvis, perhaps run into him, and we say Hi, and pass without another word. We have an understanding that is hard for some folks to comprehend. We say a lot to each other just with a look."

"I almost never visit the studio picture sets when Elvis is working in a film. Our contract—made out at the start is not a binding affair made out for life. If it had to have those kind of legal clauses, it wouldn't mean much in the first place. In fact I haven't looked at it for three years. We just go along working, doing the best we can."

Colonel Parker gave his Elvis Presley hat with its ensignia a twirl on his head, smiling, "I always wear this hat in the office" and continued his dissertation on Elvis.

"Everyone asks me to talk about Elvis, but I don't. Now I am writing a book about him. If I gave it all out, who would read the book? I've already sold a lot of pages of advertising in the book. So if anyone doesn't want to read about me and Elvis, they can always read the ads."

Colonel Parker, like Elvis, speaks in overlays of gentlemanly Southern politeness with "ma'am," and "Yes, ma'am," and "Sir," and "Mr." or "Miss." "I started out with the circus years back," he continued. "I'm a promoter, and I promote Elvis. I don't believe in giving away what you can sell. Elvis does his own singing and selects all his own songs for his records. Since they sell like hotcakes, he has good judgment. He has to select songs from hundreds that are submitted to him. I don't even attempt to advise him. Elvis has to feel his songs. He has to feel them to sing them the way he does."

"No, Sir," Colonel Parker reiterated, "I never interfere in Elvis' personal life, either. What goes on with

140

him away from business, I don't know. I never mix into it. When people ask me if we have a press agent to report on Elvis' personal life, I say we don't have one. I never discussed this with Elvis, so I guess he doesn't think one is necessary."

"We stay at the same hotels when we're away from home at work, but Elvis lives his life and I live mine. He has six fellows with him, working for him. And he has lots of good friends everywhere he goes that he likes to see. He mixes with young people his own age. Nick Adams (since deceased) is one of his friends and back in 1956 Nick traveled with us on tour. In fact, he worked for us."

"Would I like to see Elvis get married? Now that again is Elvis' personal life, and I don't get into that. But I'm mighty proud like everyone else that Elvis makes such a good record for himself wherever he goes. He didn't go into Special Services in the Army like most entertainers. Elvis stuck to learning to be a good soldier. I'm mighty proud of the good record he made for himself in the army."

Colonel Parker's show principle—"Always leave them wanting more of Elvis"—"is why we don't put Elvis on TV too much. Of course his appearance for Frank Sinatra for $125,000 was before we raised our price. That's because the contract was made last year. (Elvis has been paid $50,000 for three shows on Ed Sullivan before the Army. At that time $10,000 was Sullivan's rare top price.) It's like *G.I. Blues*—we didn't get as much money as Elvis is worth because it's a contract we made way back with Hal Wallis. That's only fair because he started Elvis in pictures. He's one of the few who's a genius in this business, making good films, so we're happy about it.

"Elvis finished a recording in Nashville on a Thursday after his discharge from the army," The Colonel continued. "And we left immediately for Miami Beach to tape the Frank Sinatra Show. RCA Records was in such a hurry to get this boy going again that they had the record pressed and to us by air mail two days later.

It's another gold record adding to thirty-five presently (1960) for Elvis."

"Elvis found out in Miami that his fans, even if some of them had grown two years older, were still swooning for him when he made his first appearance on that Sinatra show. Hundreds of girls screamed and fainted at the sight of him. While they had to remain in their seats during the show, some of the more imaginative crawled up on an improvised roof backstage to get to Elvis' dressing room. The roof caved in, which caused a big to-do."

According to some people in the Sinatra show, Elvis, now twenty-five, seemed a little embarrassed at all the squeals. While he went into his familiar bumps and grinds and shimmied from head to foot, he seemed a little hesitant and self-conscious to get into the mood. But the girls screamed, "Rock me baby!" "Love me Elvis!" "Go go man!" Afterward, reactionary articles appeared. "Elvis is Sex!" . . . Mothers were concerned. Their moppets "were having wet dreams—dreaming of Elvis Presley!" Bedroom walls of not only teeny-boppers, but young ladies of twenty are virtually papered wall to wall with Elvis photos, posters, and clippings.

"If we had to sign contracts for all engagements offered us, we'd be signing to the day of the millenium," Colonel Parker chuckled. "Actually, for at least five years. That's why we aren't signing any for the road. Elvis finishes this picture in time to get home to spend the Fourth of July, then he has two pictures to make at 20th-Century Fox. We don't know what they are, because we don't start something else until we get one thing finished. But Elvis will be home in Memphis about two weeks and then back to Hollywood.

"One thing," The Colonel said, "we have to play a one-nighter in Honolulu this year on an old contract. We always live up to our obligations."

As for the varying stories on Elvis, Colonel Parker said, "They make them up—most of them. If Elvis ever says two words, they come out to be hundreds.

Mr. and Mrs. Presley with Elvis at age two

Elvis in his new car, 1957

Elvis and Hal Wallis in Hawaii

Elvis with the author in 1961

The author with Elvis' ex-wife, Priscilla Beaulieu

On location, Elvis takes time out to talk to the film crew

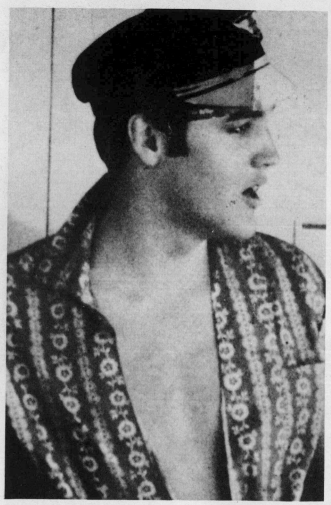

Elvis in Memphis, 1956

Elvis visiting then-President Nixon at the White House, 1972

The author with Jimmy Seagrave (left), publicity director of the Flamingo Hotel in Las Vegas, and Bill Miller, who signed Elvis to return to live audiences in Las Vegas

Elvis on location

Elvis in Hawaii, 1957

Comedian Sammy Shore, the author, Elvis and orchestra leader Bobby Morse

A rare picture of (left to right) Colonel Tom Parker, Hal Wallis, Elvis' father, Vernon Presley, and Elvis

Elvis and the author in Hollywood

Director Norman Taurog and author with Elvis in 1960

Elvis chats with movie producer Hal Wallis

Elvis and the author on location for G.I. Blues

Elvis in Hawaii, 1972

We just laugh when we read them, because most of them are pieced up from everything ever written on Elvis. We are surprised to see where we've been places we've never been. A lot of it never happened."

"Now take Elvis' records, we could keep putting them out every week. But we limit them to about four a year. The fans never get enough, and they are always in demand. Same way with TV; we keep him off by asking the unheard of price of $150,000 an appearance. Of course, if someone wants to pay us that, we can't deprive them." (That price was to jump to five times higher later on and with plenty of sponsors willing to pay.)

"And take that new album—*Elvis is Back*—that will be the greatest seller of all times. Mr. Wallis personally bought a thousand of them and sent them out. No, the way I figure," the Colonel smiled broadly, "Elvis is just getting started!"

Big time record singers cut eight discs a year. With his policy, The Colonel signed Elvis for three. Shortly after Elvis began recording for RCA Victor, it was reported that Elvis' record sales represented ten percent of the company's business.

In the beginning, The Colonel worked out of an office in his Madison, Tennessee, home. The Colonel Parker house was wedged between a gas station and a used car lot on the main highway. In early times The Colonel kept a string of ponies and donkeys that he used in circus shows, and out of season he rented them out. The Colonel and his wife kept a large garden and were often seen out working in their corn patch. In spite of his success, the Colonel always maintained "the common touch." He was proud to be known as the "Imperial Potentate of American Snowmen." "One never snows anyone other than to do good; never take advantage of anyone that you have been able to snow under."

While the usual consensus of opinion is that The Colonel will do anything to make a fast buck, that proved to be untrue in Elvis' case. He turns down many offers.

143

In Hollywood, a well-known producer tried to get The Colonel to shave a few thousand off his asking price for Elvis' services in a film. "This picture is so great, it will give Elvis the Oscar. It is worth it to him to take a small cut in salary for this once-in-a-lifetime role!"

"Okay," said The Colonel, "I'll tell you what I'll do. You pay us our price and Elvis will make the picture. And if he wins the Oscar with it, we'll refund you all of your money!" The Colonel never heard about the picture nor from the producer again.

The Colonel was approached for Elvis to sing one song on a national TV show, a talk show which features a string of celebrities weekly. The Colonel seemed agreeable. Elvis could plug his new record and new movie. When The Colonel asked how much Elvis would be paid, he was told it was free for publicity. Stars were only paid union scale, less than $200!

"Do I understand you, gentleman—that you get all the top stars for almost free?" gasped The Colonel. Assured that they did, The Colonel regained his composure, puffed hard on his cigar, and then he calmly asked, "Gentlemen, tell me—do your producers get paid?" "Yes," was again the answer. "Everyone gets paid but the stars—they do it for prestige and publicity."

"You mean," questioned Colonel Parker, "the sponsor pays for everyone on the show except my poor boy Elvis?"

The producers defended with, "Why do you think all the stars try to get on our show for nothing, Colonel?"

"That's obvious," replied Colonel Parker, "What they all need is a good manager!"

Requests from national and movie magazines and newspapers for interviews with Elvis usually number around 900 on a list that is always filed and waiting in The Colonel's office. "We'll try to get around to it" is the usual vague reply. After several years, the press stopped asking. A new writer filled with the quest of Elvis, and with the hope of making his publisher's "impossible dream" take shape in an exclusive Presley story, arrived enthusiastically at The Colonel's office. It took the young man two weeks to gain a personal audience with The Colonel. He managed this by using various contacts, one being the publisher's wife, who was vaguely related to The Colonel's brother-in-law.

The Colonel thanked the writer for his interest. He said, "That's mighty nice, young man, of you and your publisher to send you all the way to California from New York. Now tell me, do you and your publisher want the $5,000 abbreviated version of Elvis' story or the full-length $10,000 one?"

The Colonel repeats his statement annually that he himself is writing an autobiography of himself and Elvis. This explains why The Colonel and Elvis can't help out on any material, which must be kept for their own book.

One publisher called, on hearing of The Colonel's book, and offered him a $250,000 (a quarter of a million dollars) advance for it.

The Colonel replied, "Well, I guess I could let you have the back cover for that." Then The Colonel explained that he was alternating each chapter with ads. The ads cost around $2,500 a page. "They sell like hot cakes!"

As the years slip by and the book doesn't come out, it remains in the process of his own handiwork which is perhaps where he intends to keep it.

To all interview requests, The Colonel replies with his usual candor and a pixie grin, "I'm not the star. I don't talk about myself." The policy of no interviews with The Colonel and the fear of over-exposure of Elvis continues as it began back in 1955.

CHAPTER EIGHTEEN

Elvis Woos Connie Stevens; The Stars Who Woo Elvis

WHEN KENNEDY WAS president, an unusual new fresh air seemed to blow in across the country. The sixties were going to be better, freer—the liberals, at least, were optimistic at this lull in the cold war; Pope John seemed to be offering hope of an increased religious harmony in the world. And Hollywood had a buoyant rock star, Elvis, who was growing bored and tired of the routine movies he was making. Elvis yearned to get back to the action, to get before the people. As long as the public flocked to see his movies and the producers in Hollywood kept up the million-dollar offers, The Colonel wouldn't turn his back on it.

Elvis' life seemed hum drum dull locked in that ivory tower. Some critics disclaimed Elvis as walking through his films anxious to get it over with. I asked Elvis if he'd ever read *The Prophet* by Kahlil Gibran.

"No, I don't read books."

"This is such a beautiful philosophy, Elvis, I'll send it to you."

"Thank you."

Next time I saw Elvis he was reading everything he could get his hands on.

"It's such an education. I like biographies, histories, books with pictures of all the countries of the world. I'm planning a lot of travel around this old world."

Elvis was confined but his life, from the time he first twanged a guitar, was wall-to-wall girls. Gladys Presley had encouraged Elvis to invite his girl friends home. She had always made them welcome. After her death, Elvis invited girls to visit him at Graceland and Grandma Minnie Presley made them welcome. In California, there were usually several girls at Elvis' home on the weekends—those invited and those standing outside the gates hoping to be invited inside.

Since Elvis didn't give interviews, the movie producers, to publicize his pictures, arranged with the leading ladies on each one of Elvis' films to "tell how it is being with the King." As usual, halfway through each film, I would happily receive a call to interview Elvis' current leading lady. All of the twenty girls who talked to me said Elvis was just terrific, very easy to work with, was a gentleman, and never got uptight. He helped them feel at ease and often gave them the scene rather than upstage them, as stars are wont to do.

Ursula Andress and Elsa Cardenas, his co-leading ladies in *Fun in Acapulco,* told me Elvis had completely shattered their egos.

"When you're absolutely irresistible in a bikini, a play suit, a cocktail dress, and evening gown, and in the-all-together for that matter—and you spend almost two months in the arms of Elvis Presley, with his lips on yours in long wonderful kisses—and then he doesn't ask you for a date! Well—it made me furious," Elsa confided.

"It was my own fault, maybe. Elvis in the beginning sent me flowers and candy. But I had to tell him, because I am so honest, that I had an ardent man in Mexico waiting for my return. That spoiled everything! A man as fine as Elvis just wouldn't ask me for a date after that. Not even to please my ego!"

Elsa said that instead of being a challenge, Elvis treated her like a pal. One of Mexico's most sexy young actresses, with seductive green-gray eyes, like a modern Cleopatra, brunette curls piled high atop her saucy head. Elsa felt undone!

Ursula Andress, a world sex symbol, was a brown-eyed German fraulein—blonde, with such a way with her that she was well known to turn any man's head, young and old.

Elvis played it cool. That is to all outward appearances he played it cool. After investing his sentiments first in a welcome bouquet of mixed flowers, with his

147

card to greet each new leading lady love on her first day on the set, he sent each a big red heart-shaped box of chocolates decked with tiny pearls and hearts on the flowers! Then another bouquet of red and white carnations would arrive with his card. Elsa was completely puzzled. Why didn't he date her? Her engagement to another man might not have stopped another young gentleman! But Elvis, being Southern and from the old school had that old-fashioned code of honor.

With Ursula, however, Elvis was quite different. What he put in her dressing room in the way of flowers was a riot! A cabbage bouquet fancily ribboned was not exactly a symbol of romantic conquest!

This charmer said she'd spent the morning with him in the still gallery posing for poster art. Her gayety was contagious, enthusiastic, and even a little triumphant by lunch time.

"Oh Elvis, poor Elvis," Ursula laughed. "Really and he's so nice—" She giggled a little as a beauty would, when there's nothing else she can actually do about "such a handsome," she admitted, "desirable young man as Elvis Presley!

"I had a ball with Elvis this morning," she declared. "When he was posing for his single ad-posters, he'd keep saying, 'Ursula, come over here and look at me so I'll have some inspiration.' I'd laugh and make him laugh. Of course it might have been different, if I hadn't met John Derek first and married him. Elvis realized soon after we began the picture that he was stuck making love to a married woman. So he kept it all on a highly professional level. Except," she confessed with a provocative toss of her head, "I must admit that I did feel his kisses up to the top of my head and down to my toes in the love scenes—there were many. I felt them—how could I help it?"

Each of the twenty different leading ladies said Elvis had sent them flowers their first day on the set, but only Juliet Prowse and Ann Margret rated dates. Several admitted they had tried but their schemes failed.

Connie Stevens proved to be a special exception. Elvis personally called and invited her for dinner at his

Bel Air abode. Joe Esposito arrived in a Rolls Royce to drive Connie back to Elvis' house. Connie was shocked and showed it. "Why had not Elvis come in person?" Joe gallantly explained that this way was the usual procedure. But Connie Stevens was not a usual-procedure girl; she was accustomed to being pursued by all of the eligible young bachelors who did everything but handsprings to get a date with her!

On arrival at Elvis' leased mansion, Connie found several other girls and the boys of the famed "Memphis Mafia" sitting about the living room. Some were listening to records, some were watching television. Elvis was nowhere in sight.

Then suddenly the walls were parted by some electronic device, and out stepped Elvis. He took turns in welcoming everyone. Connie was accustomed to a great deal of homage, and she grew impatient at the lack of Elvis' exclusive attention. Finally she rose and informed Elvis he could take her home! This had never happened to the King. An independent girl! Hiding his astonishment, Elvis acquiesced after first trying to persuade her to stay on.

The shoe was on the other foot. Elvis had to turn pursuer instead of being pursued—if he wanted to catch up with Connie Stevens.

Elvis' open-house sometimes saw a hundred or more people milling about the big rooms. There were always friends and relatives from Tennessee, recording stars, record executives, other associates, and friends of the Memphis Mafia and the girls they invited to drop by. Motion picture studio people, nor any of his co-workers or leading ladies were invited (with perhaps the exception of Tuesday Weld). Some of the girls—girls who watched Elvis and the boys play touch football in a public park near Holmby Hills—would occasionally be invited up to Elvis' house. They reported seeing Tuesday there and that Elvis wasn't paying her much attention—at least not more than his other guests.

Elvis's parties were very informal. Everyone was free to do whatever he wanted to do—listen to records, shoot pool, watch television, talk, dance, and consume heaping platters of sandwiches supplemented with hot or cold drinks and a well-stocked bar. It was noticeable that Elvis never touched the hard stuff—not even champagne. Elvis confined his drinking to soft drinks.

Sometimes during the evening he'd disappear and return dressed in a whole new outfit. One time he changed his clothes three times in one evening—to model his new wardrobe.

The Beatles arrived in Hollywood, their first trip here. I was assigned an exclusive to be with them. The frenzy of fan worship saw us mobbed and pummeled with Ringo hanging on to me and fans pulling at me trying to get Ringo. It was pure bedlam in spite of the security guard. The Beatles had all read interviews about Elvis in the newspapers and magazines in England. "Elvis is our idol! We'd sure like to meet him," they voiced. John Lennon, however, was more anxious to meet my girl friend, Jayne Mansfield—as he did!

Our next get-together was after the Beatles' Hollywood Bowl concert. "How much did you get?" "We got $40,000 flat of the $78,000 nightly take. The Bowl had to return 20,000 checks from advance ticket reservations, because they sold out the first day."

Then—"Say, we saw Elvis! He invited us up to his house yesterday afternoon. We talked music and songs, sang a little harmony, jived and rocked! We are going to write a song for him! Pat Boone is writing a song for us. But Elvis, man, he's real groove!"

Elvis, they said, agreed with them on what they really liked, "to go about freely as people! Elvis showed us some of the disguises he uses that work!"

"John had had his date with Jayne Mansfield at the Whiskey-A-Go-Go. Elvis asked what Jayne was like in person. We said there was only one thing wrong—she brought her husband along. Elvis said there had been talk of them making a picture together. John said if it didn't work out, he'd be glad to fill in for him with Jayne!" When I told Jayne she was delighted with the prospect except, "I have to get top billing in all of my pictures and so does Elvis. I don't know how it is possible for us to get together!"

"Elvis agreed that it's like playing cops and robbers, getting shoved in and out of cars to escape being torn to pieces by the crowds of admirers. 'There must be an easier way to make a living!' Elvis told us.

"Elvis had us eat a real Southern dinner—fried chicken, black-eyed peas, and yams. That was the highlight of our U.S. tour, being with Elvis! Man, is he strong!" exclaimed Ringo. "Elvis picked up a block of wood and broke it in two pieces with his hand!!! He's way into karate—a green belt! Anybody better not tangle with Elvis, or they are a goner!"

One Christmastime Elvis sat down and answered 100 questions for me. He was due to leave for Memphis that night. We started in the late afternoon and as the hands on his watch spun away one hour and then another, I said, "Elvis let's settle for half. It's taking too long!"

"No, we said 100 questions! Keep on asking until we're finished with them all." The most remarkable thing about Elvis was his patience and the way he could remain unimpressed with himself. Still modest, manly, warm, friendly, polite, affectionate, with a great sense of humor, he was just the same as when we'd first met. He had acquired, though, a certain caution due to the millions of words written about him—out of pure imagination and fabrication.

"About all the women in your life?" Elvis grinned. "Did you know that Hayley Mills, the British star, age 19, tells me she has finally taken down the hundreds of pictures she had of you, Elvis, on her bedroom wall? Her secret desire has always been to meet you. She's working at Disney Studios, and Hayley says in spite of her many working sojourns filming here in Hollywood, she's yet to even glimpse you!!!"

"Sorry, I'm leaving for Memphis tonight."

"Fans and fan clubs and the tremendous amount of sweaters knit for you, boxes of candy, cookies, letters, love notes that exceed any number sent to any Hollywood star—what do you do with it all?"

"I enjoy all of it. The Colonel's always hoping there will be a sweater too big for me so he can have it!"

"I will never marry a girl who wears a lot of makeup. I like natural clean beauty. It will be a church wedding, too. Another thing—I like girls to wear dresses and skirts, not pants."

Among the answers that were pertinent, I learned that the Elvis fan clubs that spend considerable money and time publishing fan-club journals and sending out newsy letters to Elvis' following never receive direct word from him. "To be fair, if I wrote to one, I'd have to write to all and I don't write letters." Acknowledgment is made through members of Colonel Parker's office. "He is our King," the fan clubs say and expect no personal contact with their deity.

Elvis' long-time girl was Anita Woods of Memphis. They broke off after a six-year courtship—"over nothing really. We're still friends, but we don't see each other anymore." Other girls in and out of Elvis' life at that time were Natalie Wood, Judy Spreckles, numerous Las Vegas show beauties, and Cheryl Holdridge who later married Lance Reventlow. Elvis said most of his friends were now married. One chorus beauty from Las Vegas told of her romance, how Elvis kissed, "so gentle and tender, and his lovemaking is so marvelous." She never saw him again.

Elvis' life had been free of scandal. His character and morals were said to be of the highest. Of the Hollywood stars and starlets he dated, Elvis said of Priscilla Beaulieu: "She is the daughter of my officer when I was in the service. A nice girl. No big romance." "Of Tuesday Weld: "There was a big romance—nothing. She's a pretty kid, but that's all there was." Of Juliet Prowse: "We made a picture, and when I went to Las Vegas one holiday weekend Julie perchanced to be up there, too. So we took in some of the shows. Just friends." Of Cathy Case: "Every time I date a girl it's blown up out of all proportion as a big romance. Yes, I knew her long ago when I first came to Hollywood. I sent her red roses." Of Pat Boyd, the eighteen-year-old he called daily at Graceland: "She works for me from 9 A.M. until 6 P.M. at Graceland. She's blonde and beautiful, and she did win a beauty contest. But I didn't think about that—I needed a secretary." Of Nancy Sharpe, wardrobe girl on a picture: "She is a very nice girl, but it was just a friendship." Of Connie Stevens: "She married Jim Stacy." Of Ann Margret: "She's great fun to be with. I like her. No thoughts of marriage."

Elvis is a great showman, a born one. He never lets you see him until he is *on*. When you go up to see him in residence, it is not a casual visit under any circumstances. Even Nick Adams, who once worked for Elvis, always called first to make an appointment for a once-a-month visit.

The house Elvis lives in is always a large one sitting well back from a winding road and screened by trees and shrubs. It is easily identified because there will always be cars of girls sitting out on the roadside hoping for a glimpse of the "King."

Elvis, under no circumstances, has ever been known to answer the doorbell. If the house is leased Elvis will make many dramatic changes inside, such as deep plushy carpeting that is really lush and lots of red and orange and color in the decor. Really dramatic. A visitor may be sitting in the living room for ten or fifteen minutes alone when suddenly the walls open up —and out steps Elvis. It's uncanny because the doors are invisible; an electric contraption springs the walls apart.

Elvis is always freshly dressed. He will stand for a second with natural showman instinct and then greet a guest. After his entrance, he'll turn casual and make one feel completely relaxed and welcome with typical Southern hospitality. He offers a drink, he may talk about things—until six the next morning if he's not working. In spite of having very little education, not more than high school, he's alert and keen and brightly intelligent. He's an avid reader and he'll discuss books and poetry, and he is giving himself an education in culture and art.

In a man-to-man talk with him Nick Adams once asked

him how he "feels being self-imprisoned." Elvis looked surprised. "I don't mind it. I've always been a quiet type who likes to be at home," he replied. He runs movies, shoots pool, has tennis courts, a swimming pool, facilities for all sorts of games like darts, and a regular spot where he and his pals play at karate.

"When you know Elvis at all," Nick said, "you are approached by every writer in the world, it seems, to do a story on him. I asked Elvis once if it was okay, and he said, 'Aw come now?' He laughed like I was joking. So I can't and I wouldn't."

The Colonel always thinks in dollars and cents in spite of the fact that 90 percent of Elvis' take goes to the government in taxes. The Colonel rounds up Elvis' old footballs and helmets—anything—and with Elvis' signature he sells them from a dollar to twenty-five dollars. Each season the Colonel suggests new uni-dollars. Each season The Colonel suggests new uni-sport is touch football. The Colonel has Elvis sign the worn helmets, and he's been known to set up a table in front of a theater where one of Elvis' pictures is playing and sell the whole lot "at good money," laughs the huckster!

Nationally recognized astrologers all agreed on Elvis' personality. The experts read Elvis' horoscope (Capricorn) and simultaneously said, "Elvis was born with a splendid brain; is deliberate rather than rapid, is capable of deeply sustained emotions, and has great intellectual capacity. Elvis is a systematic dignified man with an orderly mind. He was born to lead. He will never be a follower. His is one of the most distinguished signs in the zodiac. He has deep convictions and follows them. He has many admirers but few true friends. He well knows this. The few friends he makes will be completely sincere and loyal. His one fault is thoughtlessly trying to force his ways and opinions on others. He must stop to remember that people can make their own decisions."

Elvis, according to the astrologers, "is head strong, obstinate, and at times can be unreasonable. His chart showed illness and a grave disturbance concerning his parents in his early life." He was warned to be very careful of accidents and especially cautious of air travel. He was also cautioned to guard his money, for he was prone in his early youth to give money and burden himself with unnecessary obligations on the part of relatives. He should guard his purse more closely from the undeserving. Elvis was told that among the famous people born under the sign of Capricorn were: Benjamin Franklin, Joseph Stalin, Daniel Webster, Alexander Hamilton, Presidents Andrew Johnson and Woodrow Wilson, Sir Isaac Newton, Rudyard Kipling, Jack London, and Marlene Dietrich.

Elvis prefers to pursue rather than be pursued by women. He keeps his love life shrouded in secrecy. Practical, he resents waste. He has an honest liking for intellectual things and for art and music. Things to avoid with Elvis: Don't force social graces on him; don't try to make him over; don't pry into his secrets.

CHAPTER NINETEEN

Elvis and Me in Hawaii

ELVIS PRESLEY WAS somewhere in the Hawaiian Islands, and I had been invited to fly over and see him.

Less than an hour after the jet had deposited me at the Honolulu Airport, I had registered at the Moana Hotel. I couldn't locate the Paramount Company— their telephones did not answer at the Hawaiian village —so I went walking along the beach at Waikiki. Someone suddenly reached out and turned me around! It was Elvis Presley—in person!

This was not planned, it just happened, and Elvis was the first person to speak to me!

"What are you doing over here?" he asked in surprise.

"Hoping to see you," I replied.

155

"That's nice," he laughed.

"I heard a lot about you on the jet flying in. It was the same plane and stewardess you had had," I said.

"Oh yes, I remember," Elvis replied. Suddenly I was aware that seventy-five feet away were heavy retaining ropes and police guards. Hundreds of people were on the other side. "You'll have to excuse me," Elvis said, "We're shooting. You walked into this scene!"

Without elaborating, the stewardess had said, "The Islands went wild with the anticipation of Elvis Presley's arrival. School was let out early, and kids came from all five Islands. Some held cookie sales and others did all kinds of errands and clean-up jobs to raise the boat and plane fares to Lahu and Honolulu to get a look at him!"

"The Honolulu radio flashed daily announcements, 'Elvis is coming!' The day that Elvis was on board our plane, every fifteen minutes through the three hours coming in, our pilot would receive requests from Honolulu asking approximate minutes of Elvis' arrival time. The Island loud-speakers and radios blasted minute spot announcements! 'Elvis is coming! Get down to the airport and give him an Aloha!' The last hour announcements were broadcast every five minutes.

"I told Elvis about all of the excitement," she said. He smiled, was quite calm and said, 'That is very nice!' He's shy really. He didn't have much to say all of the way. He was very polite, like a Southern boy should be," she observed, obliging the avid ears of even the adult passengers.

"He'd say in that soft low voice (it is almost like a caress) 'thank you, mam,' when I served dinner or took him a magazine. He has the bluest eyes and the way he smiles—well any girl could understand the excitement of the thousands of girls waiting for him at Honolulu Airport.

"I was a Presley fan myself when I was sixteen. I guess I still am. I guess all of his fans are. We just grew up right along with him.

156

"Honolulu, which has welcomed President Eisenhower and President Truman and royalty, never has witnessed anything like Elvis' welcome," she disclosed. "Bands were playing while thousands of teenagers and grown-ups were lined up in front of the thin fence separating them from the actual take-off and arrival grounds at the airport. Elvis had been sleeping. He woke up quick-like when the plane touched the ground and sailed in for a landing. I noticed he combed his hair and wiped his face fresh with his handkerchief. He looked like a million dollars when he stepped off. The cheers and squeals were so overpowering that no one could hear anything else, or even speak to each other with the thunderous continual rounds of cheers, screams, and squeals. 'Look over here, Elvis!', 'you're here, Elvis!' 'I love you, Elvis!', 'Aloha, Elvis!'—They must have been heard in Hong Kong."

"Elvis was quickly surrounded by a security police guard, and he would have been whisked away immediately but he stopped and smiled at the kids. He said, 'They've been waiting for hours. I want to say hello to them.' He walked over to the fence, and the crowds went wild all over again. He tried to talk to them, but there was so much squealing that I don't think anyone heard what he said. One schoolteacher near the fence told me that her whole school on the Island of Maui had come in body to greet Elvis. They'd raised money for the event by participating in a clean-up campaign for their whole town—the boys cleaning up yards, and the girls window washing, etc., to welcome Elvis and see him in the flesh.

"As Elvis came within reaching distance of the fence, everyone reached over and threw the traditional welcome leis of flowers around his neck. In a second so many leis were heaped on him that you could only see his eyes. And still youngsters were handing leis over the fence; Elvis had his arms filled. There were actually tears in his eyes at this magnificent tribute as he waved and said 'thank you' to everyone. The band played, and there was cheering long after his car had whisked him to his quarters at the Hawaiian Village Hotel. That's the way it was," she said.

Elvis was wearing dark blue swim trunks and a white yacht cap—and the movie cameras and crew were at the water's edge. The actress, Joan Blackman, in a swim suit, was stretched on the sand waiting for Elvis. "I'll be back after this take," Elvis told me. "Don't go away!" Friendly and thoughtfully he gave my arm a little squeeze.

Elvis was playing the part of the son of a wealthy family in Hawaii, just back from his Army hitch. Joan Blackman played his half-French, half-Hawaiian beach pal. Her bathing suit revealed delightful curves at the right spots, and Elvis and she sat on the sand and began their dialogue . . .

I began snapping pictures of them. This wasn't easy. The director had priority to photograph Elvis on camera, which made my shots kind of pecks between their shoulders.

As I waited I saw a familiar face—that of Tom Diskin, Colonel Parker's able assistant, emerge. "Colonel Parker has returned to the Mainland," he said genially.

Since Elvis Presley was the biggest single entertainment attraction in the world and his recording sales had passed the 77½-million mark, I asked Tom, who sees Elvis every day, "Can you explain why success hasn't changed Elvis? He is always the same—completely unassuming, remarkably pleasant at all times, polite, and considerate. He retains these wonderfully nice and endearing qualities, whereas such staggering success usually overpowers almost everyone, except perhaps Clark Gable, Gary Cooper, and Gary Grant," I remembered.

"There's only one way to explain it," Tom replied. "Elvis' talent is unique and so is he unique. That's what makes him what he is. Elvis is Elvis, and that magic combined with Colonel Parker's knowhow is a pretty great combination. Elvis is personally no different in his manners today than he was the day Colonel Parker started him on his career. It's inborn—his regard and liking of people.

"It's good to see you," he added. "It's lucky you decided to take a walk. We're leaving in the morning."

"Elvis looks great, his skin flawless and clear from healthy living. He doesn't drink, eats properly, and takes care of himself," Mr. Diskin concluded.

"I'd like a snapshot with you," I observed when Elvis rejoined me. "Sure," Elvis replied, calling a friend to take it. "Okay, let's do it right now."

We were standing there smiling into the Instamatic when a big wave (to me a tidal) surged over us. I was drenched. Everyone laughed and thought it was very funny. Was it? Elvis, being in swim trunks, didn't mind the dousing. He began brushing the water off of me. "Just stand there in the sun, honey, and you'll dry off in a few seconds with this warm Hawaiian sun."

I asked Elvis if he'd found love yet? He grinned, "Honey, we've talked that out every time, and it hasn't happened yet. I'm not looking—I'm hoping to be surprised. You know I want a church wedding, and you know how serious marriage is with me. And you know I want lots of children." Then, "We have a great wedding song in this picture, the 'Hawaiian Wedding Song.' "

"It is just ten-and-a-half hours and six thousand miles since I left New York," I told Elvis. "And why are they putting up a statue for you?" He laughed, "Well, I've read something about it, that's all I know. Look, we're filming this scene," he announced again. "I'll be back after this take," he said, giving my arm another friendly little welcome squeeze that said, "I'm glad you're here."

Elvis had come to Honolulu to play a benefit show one night before starting filming on this picture *Blue Hawaii* for Hal Wallis.

The Colonel had heard of Hawaii's need to raise $52,000. This amount would start local Congressional action to raise a monument to the USS *Arizona,* which had been bombed by the Japanese in the unforgettable attack at Pearl Harbor. Its 1,102 men still lie there entombed. A flying flag marked the spot. The island had long been anxious for a memorial monument, but they were having great difficulty in raising the money locally. Colonel Parker told Elvis, and together they devised a plan. Elvis would put on the show, sing, bring his entertainment troupe, and pay all expenses—even to buying his own $100 admission ticket for the project. With no money taken off the top for expenses, Elvis raised $62,444, which, adding to his tremendous popularity, made Elvis also a national hero in the islands.

The tickets were scaled down to $2 and Honolulu's big auditorium was filled and packed hours before the show. "No one had ever seen or heard anything like it," a reporter said. "When Elvis came on that stage, the roar of 'Elvis! Elvis! Elvis!' was overpowering. He had only to lift a finger and his audience dissolved into squeals and shouts of fantastic approval. He sang, but no one could hear what Elvis sang. We reporters just made up names of songs we knew he had recorded. I don't think anyone heard a word Elvis said or sang. He played his guitar for a couple of numbers, but you couldn't hear that either for the deafening roar of adulation from screaming, squealing, berserk kids—and adults too!"

A Paramount Studio unit man pulled me aside: "I'm sorry but you can't talk to Elvis," he said. "You have not been cleared by Colonel Parker." Without that clearance no one talks to Elvis. The fact that I had been invited to Hawaii to see Elvis by the producer of the picture made no difference. I must leave the scene.

"Won't Elvis think it's strange to walk out, when he told me to wait for him?" I asked.

"I'll take care of that," said the unit man. "If you don't come along with me, it could mean I will lose my job. It is my job to see that no one from the press talks to Elvis while we are here."

He pointed to a more pertinent reason. Seated on the patio of the Kaiser Village Hotel, facing the scene but 300 feet removed, and behind roped fences, were members of the fourth estate. The Greater Los Angeles Press Club, with all of the top L.A. Press, had chartered their own plane to fly here in the hope of getting interviews. "They had never been able to get with Elvis and you come along—the exception!" He was polite but adamant.

I had little choice but to walk back and join my friends of the Los Angeles Press and to watch from a removed distance! The minute the scene was concluded, Elvis, surrounded by six security guards as you see a prisoner going to jail (in the movies), walked by enroute to the security of his suite in the hotel. As he passed he turned back and winked at me. "Later," his lips moved the words.

I called Mr. Wallis, who had invited me in the first place, thinking surely he would arrange the interview. But Hal Wallis was very sorry—I had waited too long in arriving and since The Colonel had already left, there was nothing even he could do about it! In the morning Elvis would be gone. He was as casual as if I had driven two blocks to Paramount Studios, instead of 6000 miles straight through from New York, and I knew absolutely no one in Hawaii.

No one offered to reimburse me for my ticket, as most film companies do when they invite the press to location, nor to offer me a hotel or even a sandwich!

I often wondered if Elvis knew the politics that go on. In my precarious position, I had always played ball with the Colonel or whoever was in charge. I had never mentioned to Elvis the strict terms and disappointments experienced in being his chosen interrogator as well as friend. Many people believed I was on the Colonel's payroll to promote Elvis by the things I wrote about him. I was not; certainly not. I thought of how warm and welcome all studios and stars make you feel—and well, anyway, Elvis always did!

Not so much of the fever-heat hysteria, induced and set off by The Colonel, was reflected in the more conventional interest of spectators on Kauai. Elvis had more freedom and the six-police bodyguard escort of Waikiki was reduced to one.

Elvis was quartered in the bridal suite at the Kauai

Lodge. One night at the big festive dinner in the Lodge dining room, "The Hawaiian Wedding Song" was played with the announcement, "Any newlyweds present please stand up." Up jumped Elvis and Joan Blackman, their faces wreathed with smiles. To their surprise they were garlanded with flower leis. Elvis hurriedly explained, "No, we're just joking. She's my movie wife. And I've been put in the bridal suite. We just thought it was funny!" But they made them keep the leis.

Elvis spent some time with the newly divorced Joan, but it was not a romantic thing. Elvis always told me that when he married, "She will be like myself. The marriage of ours will be for the first and only time!"

On the next-to-the-last day of the four-weeks' shooting in the Islands (at a cost of approximately a million dollars), Elvis was singing out in the open "Ke Kale Nei Au" at the Coco Palms. If the kids in Kauai had known they would have been agog. As it was only a few at the Lodge witnessed the event. One lady reported, "Elvis just sat there singing so quietly and so beautifully." I asked him about it, and Elvis said a 100-member choir would be spliced in backing him on the sound track. This would be added on the Mainland.

As Elvis moved about some ladies began snapping his picture. Elvis turned and laughed. Then he said mischievously, "Your film's upside down." The lady gasped, and would have started pulling her camera apart if Elvis hadn't stopped her. "It's just a joke!" He was apologetic.

Every teenager in the United States and all countries where Elvis Presley pictures play soon were singing Hawaiian tunes. *Blue Hawaii,* a great hit in the past, became a big hit with Elvis. He sang 14 songs in *Blue Hawaii,* including such alluring Polynesian tunes as "Rock-a-Hula Baby" and "Aloha Oo."

Before I left Hawaii, my Elvis interview came by magic. Mr. Wallis, a little abashed at his lack of hospitality, arranged it for Elvis and me.

"I play a boy just back from my service hitch in

the army," Elvis said. "Actually I play someone pretty much like myself. Someone who wants to make it on his own and who doesn't want his life laid out for him."

"Do you play a ukulele?" "Sure," Elvis smiled. "I fiddled around with one of those a long time ago. I have always liked Hawaiian music. It's got a beat, if you listen."

One of the Hawaiian crew boys admired Elvis' wrist watch. A couple of mornings later Elvis arrived on the set with twenty-five similar new wrist watches to give to everyone as souvenirs.

In their free time, Elvis and the boys would go swimming or see some Japanese movies. Or they'd pop in for the first show at some of the Island clubs. However, with Elvis in every scene of the picture, he said, "I had to remember that early curfew for that 6 A.M. call."

"Elvis is highly proficient in the ancient art of self-defense, karate," a security guard said. "He practices every day. I've been assigned to the Elvis detail. Never saw a guy so full of energy!"

"Why did I take karate? I've always admired it as an art," Elvis told me. "I began practicing in my off-duty hours in Germany, sometimes three to six hours at a time. For practice we'd split eight two-inch boards." His right knuckle is tremendous from this activity. Anyone who would try to get the jump on Elvis would find himself a "dead duck!"

The policemen told Elvis, "We locked up Honolulu tighter for you than for any celebrity who's ever visited here. But we didn't know how to handle all of those kids at the USS *Arizona* Memorial Benefit you gave. How could you think about what you were singing with such squeals?"

Elvis smiled, "Believe it or not, I was scared. This was only the second time in three years that I've been before a live audience. I hadn't even had a rehearsal with the band. I was grateful for the kids' welcome. I love to hear those squeals which tell me they like me. But another thing I appreciated was all of that

163

yelling covering up my mistakes. And man, I made plenty."

"Three years ago," Elvis said, "I sailed on the Lurline from Honolulu to the Mainland. It was great. You should take the boat home." It wasn't seeing Elvis or members of the picture company that filled in the real story for me of what the future held for Elvis Presley, but the people on the Lurline. On the five nights sailing back to port in San Francisco, people talked constantly about Elvis and exchanged various tidbits and experiences. From several hundred passengers a new picture of Elvis in Honolulu presented itself. Elvis was the idol of the teenage world, yes, but presently he was engratiating himself with the adults. Each adult discoverer of Elvis in Honolulu had the same impression. "He's not anything like I thought he would be. Why he's polite and unassuming, even good mannered. We always had Elvis Presley pictured as some rock 'n' roll crazed kid who had a wild sex life and was pretty raw. You meet him, and you can't get over it—he has a good voice—a really good voice. He sings ballads with loads of appeal. He has a real singing voice."

This was to be the new audience of adults who were combining themselves with the teenagers to make Elvis Presley a great star of all time. The Hawaiians declared Elvis was the greatest thing that had happened to the Island since Captain Cook's initial arrival. Elvis' new picture brought a great influx of tourist business to the Islands. One native expressed it: "Our main product is the tourist who matures the minute he arrives with that green money coming out of his pockets. Now Elvis Presley brings us another boom. We just thank the Lord every sunset that it was Elvis Presley who made *Blue Hawaii.*

CHAPTER TWENTY

Elvis, 31 Years Old, Talks About Dreams of His Mother and Christmas

ELVIS, TO THE amazement of everyone, including me after knowing him for over eight years, remained the same considerate, polite, genuinely nice, unassuming young man who had accidentally found fame by his over-emotional and physical interpretation of music.

"I was just lucky. Kids were looking for a new trend and I was lucky enough to feel it and play it on records. If Mama hadn't said she hoped someday I'd be on a record, I'd likely never gone into Sun Records and made it to surprise her. Then Sun wouldn't have heard it and I'd still be driving truck. I didn't think my singing was going to last so long." Elvis was approaching his thirty-first birthday and growing more handsome with maturity. Lithe, virile, broad-shouldered, narrow-hipped with that flash of engaging magnetic charm, it was understandable why moppets of ten years of age, girls in their teens, women in their twenties, and the many who said, "Elvis is the son I never had," and wanted to mother him—all adored him. An 80-year-old lady knit Elvis sweaters "to express her joy in watching Elvis develop into a fine actor these ten years."

"It's certainly nice of everyone to be interested in me this way." There was sincere appreciation in his voice. He did not pass off such attention lightly, for he recognized and felt the merit of sincere affection. "Tell them for me I am grateful."

Elvis was only anxious about one thing—"To get back home to Graceland. I get homesick when I am away too long. There's no place like home," he added with a little sigh, for it had been a long work day, filming a new movie—up at six and it was now past six—twelve hours.

"The place I have in Bel Air is nice," he allowed, "and I have almost everything up there. But it's not home. We all know each other back home."

"There's an old saying that you can take the city out of the boy but not the country, or something like that," I said. Elvis agreed. "It's true. The way you are raised—if you had a home and parents like mine—it stays. Everyone knows how poor we were in things like a good house and a car—things like that. And how my mama even scrubbed floors in a hospital at one time to help keep things going. But we were always rich—very rich in love. Our home might have been considered a shack to a lot of people, but to me it was wonderful because there was so much love in it."

"Mama didn't spoil me either. When I ran off with the kids down to the creek and forgot to get home in time for supper, I got a whipping. She instilled in me what every kid needs, respect for his parents.

"Home means all the family and relatives getting together and all of us talking and laughing and singing and playing and enjoying ourselves.

"Like the Christmas just past, everyone was at Graceland—the boys (the Memphis Mafia)—they have wives and children and families—just everyone. We had a great time. We had turkeys and a huge Christmas tree of course, and lots of presents."

"Sure, I go Christmas shopping," he said. "My mama and I used to plan Christmas for days, even when we had no money at all. We'd work out every detail together. I enjoy it. Although the big revolving Christmas tree that mother loved so much has been stored in the attic at Graceland. It had to be replaced by a new one when the other one broke down."

"That Christmas tree has a lot of sentiment for me, for I always see my mother sitting at the kitchen doorway in her chair looking at that tree, loving the lights that twinkle as it turns round and round and the Christmas carols playing from the music box inside it. I intend to always keep it. Sometimes I go up in the

attic and just sit and look at that Christmas tree—
it is so much my mother. I surprised her with it that
last Christmas. 'I didn't know they made a Christmas
tree that could go around like this and play and
twinkle,' she marveled. Her eyes—such beautiful big
brown eyes—were as wide and childlike watching it as
any little girl."

"I'll always have to keep Graceland for my home
because there is no place else that has such a big
attic to store things. That's how we bought Graceland
in the beginning. Mama's sewing machine and so many
of the things she loved are up in the attic."

"As you well know we had lived in little places,
because we had no money. But when things got to
going for us, we moved into a better place and then I
bought a nice big home for her."

"Graceland was originally built, I believe, for a
church or something to do with one—and it was up for
sale, somebody said. My mother went out to look at it
and she fell in love with it."

"I go to the cemetery once a week to visit her
grave," he added softly. "I usually drive out there at
night when no one's around. When I am away I have
flowers placed there every week."

"There's something," he confided (and I qualify
this really beautiful and certainly touching confidence,
since Elvis knew that I, too, was an only child, and
my mother had died at about the same time Elvis lost
his wonderful mother). "I sometimes, as I have told
you, dream about my mother. I never return home
after being away a long time that I don't see her opening that front door and running out and putting her
arms around me."

"Now the dreams I have of her are always such
happy dreams. She is always happy. They have been
a great comfort to me, for the dreams when they do
come—at rare unexpected times—well, it's like seeing
and being with her again."

"On holidays—that's when I miss her the most.
At Graceland like she always did, we make the most of
Christmas. So far I've had the good luck to be sure

167

I am always home for Christmas. That has always been a rule."

Graceland to Elvis is not a place to hang your hat— or a launching pad, or a spot to place your possessions in safekeeping. Home is to Elvis, and he expressed it beautifully in the way he thinks, "the residence of the heart. It is far more than a place of physical needs, of food, a place to sleep, to dress, to eat, to go to work from. To me my home is all wound up with all the acts of kindness and gentleness and thoughtfulness that my mother and my grandmother and my daddy lovingly provided. Love was and is its foundation. All of this love still remains within its walls. It's an enduring way of life for me."

Gladys Presley, Elvis told me, believed that the most precious gift God can bestow is his children, and she loved the son God gave her. She had wished for more. With this genuine love and happiness, she filled the home she made for Elvis, and it stamped his life and remains with him. This is the real secret of the greatness of Elvis Presley—his unassuming, kind, and considerate personality. Together with his talent and his magnetism it lifted him up as a world idol.

If you said "world idol" to Elvis, he'd blush. So I didn't. He never thinks of himself that way. "Most of the time I expect to wake up and find all of this is a dream. For a long time I always thought one day it would end, and maybe I could get a job as an electrician or go back to driving a truck. But now I've changed my mind. If this does end I want to go to college and get an education. Right now I keep on reading. For a long time books didn't interest me, but now I read regularly."

"There's another thing I'd like—to get back to going to church on Sundays. Church was our way of life since I can remember. The last time I went there was so much confusion and autograph seeking that out of respect I've stayed away to make up for it. I've been working on religious songs for an album. I feel God and his goodness, and I believe I can express his love for us in music.

168

"Oh"—Elvis' face flushed. "Some say I sound like an evangelist. Maybe I am," he smiled with a self-conscious grin.

"Mama and I used to dream of, 'someday Elvis will do this or that—or that.' It was a wonderful pastime sitting there on that little porch listening to the singing of the blacks and we whites, all sitting on our little porches at sundown, singing. No one had any money. Listening to each other singing up and down the road and harmonizing maybe with the porch two houses away was real down South—our entertainment. My mama and daddy and me would sing in the church! She sang like an angel, my mother. And she'd dream such big dreams for me—like we'd go to Washington, D.C., and see everything there. And we'd go—Oh, about everything we could think of." Elvis fell silent with nostalgic recall—that the mind's eye was seeing.

The Colonel had adopted a new creed: "Don't try to explain it, just sell it!" The Colonel's sartorial ensembles, colorful shirts, unusual hats with Elvis streamers and bands, and arm bands with 'Elvis' painted or stitched on them were the talk of Hollywood—which is as the Colonel intended it should be. In spite of his hard bargaining and Garbo-technique in handling Elvis, the Colonel was well liked by regular people. "The others—the big shots—are afraid to be seen with me," he said. "Saves me a lot of time."

His picture terms for Elvis he said were still simple and without complications: a million dollars plus fifty percent of the profit plus expenses and a limited number of shooting days with Elvis. "We have to turn down many good offers since Elvis always has seven pictures ahead of him.

"I don't have to stick with a diet these days," he said. "When I first came to Hollywood, cameras, I found out, make you look twenty pounds heavier. I love Southern cooking, and besides I'd never been fat. One day in the studio commissary, I was enjoying pork chops and country cream gravy and biscuits when the producer stopped by my table. Noting the apple pie, he asked me if I could do without all of that and shed some weight. I did. For a long time I played touch football at lunch time and didn't eat at all. Then I'd slim down on either a straight yogurt or steak diet. Just protein. Now I don't have to worry any. It's strange, when I was in high school I was skinny—weighed 145 pounds, which was too light to make what I wanted in football. My mama did her best to put weight on me with her cooking."

The fact that Elvis was dining on a big bowl of mashed potatoes with country gravy, fried chicken stripped with bacon, black-eyed peas, hot bread, a quart of milk, and a slice of apple pie testified to the fact that Elvis could eat as he pleased.

He was so physically active that the minute he stepped out of a scene the Memphis Mafia and Elvis were engaging in some kind of play or pummeling. Elvis did not need a bodyguard.

"I always wanted to be somebody," Elvis said over dinner. "I figured if I ever got the chance I'd make good. If I don't do something right I work at it until I do. But I never expected to be anyone really big. I didn't see how anyone could be important unless they had a college education. Even with all of this, I always think I wish I had one. Before this I studied to become an electrician at a trade school at night. I figure I can always go back to it."

Elvis, like the late king Clark Gable, has a gentleman's view and code that excluded talking about the girls he dated. It is known he has dated most of the top movie glamor queens in his age bracket. There was Natalie Wood in the beginning who once went to Graceland to pay him a visit on his mother's invitation. Connie Stevens made him come in person to call for her instead of sending one of the boys to pick her up. "Elvis was so shy he drove to my house and sat in his car—afraid to ring my doorbell at first. I wanted to see a movie one night and Elvis said he couldn't go. We'd be mobbed. I showed him he could go to a movie. We stopped at a little movie house, went in, and enjoyed the picture. No one bothered us. But before the lights went on for the candy and snack-bar time, Elvis insisted we had to leave. He has a phobia about being close to people. Others Elvis dated included Tuesday Weld, Juliet Prowse, and Ann Margret. And his affection for Priscilla Beaulieu had continued for several years. Priscilla came with Elvis to the studio one afternoon during the filming of a picture to watch a scene. There had been continuing reports that they were secretly married. "I'm not married," Elvis told me. "If I were I'd tell everyone. I'd like to be married," he added. "I love children. I want children of my own."

Elvis at thirty-one was a far happier person than he had been in prior years. He had adjusted to the loss of his mother. He had learned to accept the responsibilities and the lack of freedom of being hemmed in as a world idol. His smile was sparkling. Elvis made you feel good just being around and talking to him. He had that rare quality.

Elvis didn't rush our conversation. "Don't go," he said. "I'll be back." He was very much at ease and more relaxed than I'd ever known him to be.

The overtures, honors, and concessions the film studios made and heaped on Elvis would spoil most stars. At MGM they had given Elvis two large dressing-room suites. This had never been done for any star. The Clark Gable suite had been given to the boys who worked for him. Elvis had only to think of something he might want—and he'd get it. Remarkably, he never asked for any favors or special considerations. He was always on time, with his lines learned; he was willing to stay overtime. No one had ever seen him temperamental—not even once.

How can you explain this? You don't try—the great secret, the great quality Elvis was born with, is one of his greatest assets.

All manner of things were predicted for Elvis' future. His directors declared Elvis had become a fine actor. "One who could undertake a difficult role if he chose to do so." Secretly, they lamented the sameness of Elvis pictures. "No story—no name cast—it leaves Elvis to carry the whole load! But Elvis' pictures, as

171

they are, are making a mint. It's a wonder he survives some of them. Any lesser personality could not!"

Elvis himself said, "My big hope is to be known as a good actor." He was far too modest to say it, in spite of all those gold records (which are a world record) that someday he'd be very proud to have an Oscar to go with them.

The fan adulation continued. A twelve-year-old girl called me to say she and some girls had managed to get over the fence at Elvis' place and get some bottles of water from his swimming pool. They were taking them to church to have them blessed. They felt since Elvis had swam in there, they would have healing powers. This is where the Memphis Mafia springs into action—to keep his fans from doing silly things, in a moment of thoughtless enthusiasm, that might embarrass Elvis.

Before I left, I left some of the Elvis fan letters I particularly liked. Elvis said, "Thank you. I read most of my fan mail—I try to read it all. They're great, all of them. I love them all."

With that he gave me a little kiss on the cheek, which was for all and everyone who loves Elvis.

CHAPTER TWENTY-ONE

World-Famed Psychic George Dareos Predicts Elvis' Future

GEORGE DAREOS, THE world's most famous psychic and counselor to the world celebrities, royalty, government leaders, and movie stars for more than sixty years first told Elvis what his future would be in ten years. It amazingly all came true.

It is interesting that twelve years ago, Mr. Dareos predicted that the new "King" of rock 'n' roll would forsake it all for Hollywood. That he would confine his talents to movies and records.

It is also interesting to recall that Mr. Dareos predicted that Marilyn Monroe would quit the screen and remain off of it for two and a half years. This was a year after Marilyn had signed her big starring contract with 20th-Century Fox and had just become a new star. Yet it all came to pass, just as Mr. Dareos predicted, even the tragic ending of Marilyn's life, against which he often warned her. He predicted that Eddie Fisher would pay a big price, almost his career, if he left Debbie Reynolds and married Elizabeth Taylor. Later he told Elizabeth in Rome not to worry, that the world which had turned against her would change, that she would win worldwide admiration again and prove herself to be one of the great stars of all time. He also told Eddie he could not hold Elizabeth.

Asked how his gift of ESP works, Mr. Dareos replied, "I look at a person, or perhaps I have only their birthdate, and sometimes a person unknown to me is just a voice on the phone. Either way, as soon as contact with me is made, I start seeing that person as though I were looking at a television screen. I see them in color, and I see what is happening, what can happen to them. Often I can help them to avoid accidents that can cost them their lives. I have done it many times. When people won't listen, often disaster has happened just as I saw it. I begged Mike Todd not to fly in private planes. He met his death in a fiery crash just as I told him he would!"

"Now, in 1969, I take a new look at Elvis Presley, to advise him of his life, some of which he presently doesn't even suspect that will take place. Foremost Elvis must stay out of planes! He must not fly. He must not fly his own plane for there would be great danger—the same as I warned Mike Todd."

"Elvis married in a year, which I told him would be the wrong year. He should have waited one more year to have insured the tranquil domestic life he hoped for."

"I see his life with Priscilla as one with many ups and downs. He and his wife will divorce after several separations that would not be made known to the public. However, I also see them returning to each other only to separate again."

"Unfortunately for Elvis, his wife is very ambitious. She also wants a career. Being 'Mrs. Elvis Presley,' many producers have and will offer her a screen career. I see her preparing for a career by taking voice, dancing, and even acting lessons, although she says it is just something to do for a hobby. But her real inner hope is to have a career. She will practice, perfect, and become good. But she will never have the color and talents and showmanship of her husband!"

"I warn Elvis that he must never let a wife team up professionally with him. The time will come. Like I warned Rudolph Valentino, the great idol years ago, I warn Elvis, great idol of today. Do not share the spotlight with a wife. It will be your undoing. Natasha Rambova was also a beautiful woman. She longed to share Rudy's career. Her influence all but ruined him! When she insisted that he not make the pictures offered to him, but that he go on a tour with her as his dancing partner, it was disastrous. People idolized Rudy Valentino, as the great sex symbol. They didn't care to see his wife in his spotlight. They resented her. And so people will resent Elvis' wife if she forces her way into his career."

"Elvis is a very fine person and a very honest man. He abides by his commitments. I don't think any woman can influence him over Colonel Parker's great management. Someday Elvis will lose Colonel Parker and he will be on his own to make his own career decisions. 'Elvis, you have a good brain and a good know-how. Always do your own thinking. Always make your own decisions.' He will always have great respect and fond memories of The Colonel."

"Elvis will always be a wealthy man, for he is a Capricorn. He is very generous and giving with his money. As he grows older, he will begin to watch his money and its handling more closely. He will start to learn to

174

economize and he will become thrifty. But he will always have money. He will never have financial troubles."

"1970 will be a good year for Elvis. There is only one danger I see in his life. He should be most careful of private planes. I warn him again: never buy a private plane of your own. And do not travel in private planes with friends who have them. You could lose your life in a small private plane, like Mike Todd!"

"I want you to pay heed to this warning, Elvis! I told the Rambo twins, Dirk and Dack, several years ago that they must watch out and never ride or own small sports cars. For five years they were most careful, and they avoided any kind of a small sports car. A friend of Dirk's asked permission to leave his car, which proved to be a small sports car, at his place while he (the friend) went East. When he didn't return he asked Dirk to keep the car. Dirk for the first time disregarded my warning. He drove the car two blocks from his home and was hit by a big car. He was pinned inside and burned to death. His brother Dack can substantiate this as being true."

"Elvis is actually a very shy man. He personally does not care too much for the limelight, but he has been lifted there by circumstances and his talents. He has gone along with other's plans for him. Alone, he is too shy to have done it. Each time he steps out to face people he girds his loins, faces the challenge, and does what is expected of him. He also, of course, has a great singing voice, good looks, and a nice character that shines through."

"People will always love Elvis Presley. But he is a loner by nature. He has to have periods of time being alone to think things out and also to recoup the tremendous energy he exerts and expends when he is performing. He is a hard worker."

"Elvis is a nice young man. If he goes to Europe, he will be a sensation! Kings, queens, and royalty will invite him. They will give great parties in his honor. There has been no universal idol like Elvis since Clark Gable and Rudolph Valentino."

"Elvis can live to be over seventy years of age if he stays away from private planes."

"He should never start drinking. Even an occasional glass of champagne socially to celebrate some immediate success could start him off. Alcohol could very easily take a hold of him, and he could turn alcoholic. I hope he avoids it at all costs. For it could be his one downfall. I said several years ago that one day Elvis Presley could become the governor of Tennessee. He laughed at the thought, and even today he thinks he has no interest in politics. Elvis, after his fortieth birthday in 1974, will stand a symbol of honesty and good character. He has given generously of his money to help the poor, needy, and children in Tennessee, as well as elsewhere. He never permits his charitable gifts to be publicized. But I know them. The people will turn to Elvis, saying he is 'the only man who can bring order and peace to our state and we want him, for we desperately need him!' "

"Elvis will find himself listening. He will realize the truth of their statements. He is loved by both the black and the white races, and with a great civil war heading for this country he will be needed as a leader. The people will turn to him, and he will not be able to say no."

"I want him to become governor of Tennessee when he is requested. I don't see Elvis turning away from what will be his duty as a citizen of this country after he reaches forty."

"I like Elvis to have a home in California. California is good for him. I also want him to keep a home in Tennessee where he will be needed. Someday Graceland will become a church once more. Elvis, who is very religious, will turn to God more and more as he goes along. He could become acclaimed for spreading God's word from the pulpit of many churches."

"I see more children for Elvis, even though there is the great danger of divorce. He makes a marvelous father. He gives a child of his more love and care than any movie-star father ever has. I don't see any of his children following his footsteps. Elvis will grow more

176

reserved and more wary of people as he goes along. But he will always be true and faithful to his real friends and to his family. Two of his best and most sincere friends to elevate him in films and in the press are both Virgos. He must always be appreciative of them for they do much for him."

"I want Priscilla to get any notions of a career that she may have had out of her head. For it is that persistence in the dream of being a star that ends her marriage to Elvis. She will always regret it. I do not see her ever becoming equal professionally with Elvis Presley. In fact, who has?"

"Elvis can become a great dramatic actor. I see him forming his own producing company. If he will give great care to the roles he plays he can one day win an Oscar. This will be a great triumph for him."

"I do not want him to ever give up his singing. I want him to take six years with his public in person. Then I want him to return to Hollywood and make great motion pictures. I want him to always make records for they will always be big money makers. He will one day head a magnificent producing company and hire other stars to appear in pictures he will produce (beside the ones he will star in). He will make a great success."

"Elvis will be an idol to the day he dies. Even if he quits his career to attend to the business side only, as he may do someday, he will still remain the great sex symbol and idol of the people of this generation."

"Elvis is a good man. He is a good influence on young people today by his honest, straightforward, sincere, fine character. I admire him and take my hat off to Elvis Presley!"

CHAPTER TWENTY-TWO

Elvis' Surprise Wedding to Priscilla

THE FIRST TIME I heard the name of Priscilla Beaulieu was in a newspaper picture showing Elvis with a pretty little apple-cheeked teenager with a mop of brown curls. Taken in Germany, the caption said she was an Elvis fan.

This was way back when Elvis was in the army stationed at Wiesbaden. Her father, Captain Beaulieu, one of Elvis' commanding officers, had two daughters —Priscilla and Michelle. Like all girls their age they were "simply dying with excitement to meet Elvis!" Their father not only made the introduction but Elvis invited them to his home where his grandma, Minnie Presley, had them stay to supper for some good old-fashioned Southern cooking. Elvis was dating a young German film star at the time, and not much attention was paid to the fifteen-year-old Priscilla who became like one of the family. "She's like a little kid sister I never had," Elvis told me on his return. Priscilla didn't consider herself Elvis' sister at all. He had given her a wrist watch with diamonds for Christmas and tears wet her cheeks when he said "goodbye," on return to the States. She asked if he'd write. Elvis said he'd call when he could. And if and when the Beaulieus returned to the States, they'd be welcome to visit him at Graceland.

Priscilla pled with her parents to permit her to accept the Presley family's invitation to visit Elvis in Memphis and for Christmas 1963 her father finally relented and Priscilla arrived, considering herself the luckiest girl in the world. Why? Because a million teenage girls and probably many others would give anything in the world to be in her shoes. There she was

178

living at Elvis' own home Graceland, seeing him morning, noon, and night, riding in his big cars, going to the night movies, the roller skating rink—well, just everything! Grandma Presley and an aunt who lived with Elvis were the chaperones. Priscilla wanted to stay on forever. Who could blame her? Telephoning her father, Priscilla asked if she could stay on until January 8th to help Elvis celebrate his birthday. Her father said no. Priscilla tearfully had to leave.

Dee Presley, Elvis' stepmother, having become well acquainted with the polite, lovely child in Weisbaden, liked Priscilla. Actually, of all of the girls after Elvis, who was a better candidate to become Mrs. Presley one day? In Memphis, Priscilla could be trained in the ways of a Southern lady and particularly how to please Elvis, become acquainted with the rigors as well as the luxuries that his career imposed. At this young age, Priscilla would be adaptable and could grow up in the tradition of a Princess Anne of England, aware of her obligations and responsibilities, disciplined to revere her allegance to the royal crown. Here in America the crown was worn by Elvis Presley, the Rock King!

Being a matchmaker at heart (well, Elvis had to marry sometime, didn't he?) Priscilla would be just perfect. She told Priscilla she could live with them and go to school in Memphis.

In no way could Priscilla's father talk her out of this invitation. Within the month she was back in Memphis to live with Dee and Vernon Presley, whose home on Dolan Street backed Graceland. It was not unorthodox or unseeming at all that Priscilla should spend as much time at Elvis' home as she did at Vernon's.

All of the time Elvis was in Hollywood dating Ann Margret and Juliet Prowse, who made headlines and columns with him, there was little Priscilla back home patiently hoping and waiting while finishing school at Immaculate Conception Catholic School. When Elvis came home she was all smiles, never letting him know the hurts she felt reading about all those famous girls in the movies he dated in Hollywood. Back home, he'd include Priscilla with his father and Dee as a family foursome. While Elvis considered her his kid sister, it was not so with her.

"What about your big secret serious romance in Memphis?" I asked Elvis. Laughingly he replied, "No, I have no one girl. No big romance. I'm still waiting for the girl to come along I can love and marry. When she comes along, believe me she'll be no secret!" He was thinking more and more of Priscilla, however, who was now twenty. One time he said, "She's the only girl I've met yet, whose only interest in me is for me." Dee's—a mature woman's—suggestions were helping Priscilla regarding Elvis. When she went to modeling school and turned out with an exaggerated high bee-hive hairdo and the all-out Cleopatra eye makeup of the day, I thought, "She's not the girl Elvis will marry, for only the day before, he had told me he liked the nice natural wholesome type without a lot of gooey makeup more, he didn't care for extreme hairdos, and he liked girls to wear skirts and be ladies. Pictures of Priscilla revealed her wearing pants and sweaters. She dressed mod!"

"Come to think of it, Elvis might be in love with Priscilla," a pal of Elvis' said. "He never talks about her, never mentions her. You know how secretive Elvis is. I think the real reason she's been in Memphis all this time, and her parents allowed her to be—is so Elvis can get to really know her. Considering Dee and his dad like Priscilla so much and Vernon treats her like she was his own daughter, that would turn Elvis on."

I talked with Elvis at length at M.G.M., where he was filming, about the kind of wife he'd like and whatever details. One thing he was strong on. "When I marry it will be a very sure thing—to be forever like my mama and my daddy. I'll have a big church wedding, do it proper, with flowers and music and the whole thing. Mama and I used to talk about a big church wedding. She wanted me to have one because she'd never had one. She and my daddy went off and got married by themselves and told their families afterward. They were all so poor, they didn't want to put anyone

180

to any expense. No one could afford wedding clothes or wedding presents. Mama realized she'd never have a daughter to dress up and she'd often talk about my wedding some day, and how she'd love me to marry and give her that daughter and some grandchildren. Mama just loved pretty things. She'd look at bridal-book pictures and say how she'd plan a church wedding. That's the way I'll be married, if and when. When I see a girl as sweet as my mama, and as beautiful, I could get married-minded right away—if the real love is there."

I suggested one of the nicest girls I knew, my friend, Annette Funicello, the Walt Disney star, who now was 20 years old—the right age for marriage. I had already asked Annette if she'd like to meet Elvis. Her big eyes lighted with a real thrill at the thought. "Annette is so beautiful, looks so much like your mother," I remarked. "Elvis, she is also not a bit actressy or movie-starish. She's a sweet, natural lovely girl with Italian blood like your mother!"

"Why," I enthused, "I gave a party for Annette at my house last Sunday. All of the leading young actors were there, just everyone, and you know something? Annette came alone. Everyone wanted to escort her home. Annette said no because she had promised to baby-sit her goddaughter that night. And it was Sunday night! What movie star girl would have done that?" Elvis was impressed. He was thoughtful, contemplating. Then he said, "Thank you but not right now."

I hadn't met nor given Priscilla a thought, since she had graduated from high school and left Memphis to join her parents at Travis Air Force Base in California, and Elvis' dates in Hollywood were concentrated on Ann Margret. Unpublicized, Priscilla, whom all of the Presleys loved as one of their own, was not infrequently a visitor in Memphis. Time and again there she was. Priscilla was also reported visiting Elvis on the set at M.G.M., but no pictures were taken nor any publicity released. It was considered a very private personal matter. Even Elvis' studio press agent on his movie, Stan Brossette, admitted to me while he had worked on three pictures with Elvis, he'd only talked to him very briefly twice. Certainly he had never asked Elvis a question, not even one. "Elvis is a very private person as you know." Not even Elvis' own studio could give out any information on their star except his films. Colonel Parker's offices were now at M.G.M. And while The Colonel and Tom Diskin and Jim O'Brien were courteous and polite, the answer to any press query was always the same. "We don't know. We never interfere with Elvis' private life!"

One night, April 30, 1967, and into May 1st the next morning, I received calls telling me to grab a plane immediately for Las Vegas and I could make the wedding reception of Priscilla and Elvis Presley. They were to be married at 10 A.M. in a ceremony in the private suite of Milton Prell at the Aladdin Hotel. A wedding breakfast was to be held in the Aladdin Room for 100 and I could make it, for any of the press who discovered it would not be turned away. This was so contrary to everything Elvis had been telling me of his kind of a wedding I didn't believe it. A hotel wedding and a press conference all in one? By the time I could reach anyone who could authenticate this, it was too late to catch a plane to Las Vegas. They were already married!

That's the way The Colonel did things. All in secrecy and with delight to see everyone scramble to make the scene. Not me. However, Stan Brossette telephoned me immediately from Las Vegas and filled me in with the details. Even he had been kept in the dark—at the start—and had only been told to take two photographers who could be trusted to keep their mouths closed and fly up to Las Vegas the night before. He was as surprised as anyone else that it was to be Elvis' wedding.

Elvis and Priscilla, her parents, her brothers, and sister arrived from Palm Springs at 3 A.M. in Elvis' Lear Jet. At 4 A.M. Elvis got the license at the courthouse. There was no need of blood tests and waiting twenty-four hours; marriages were instant on request any time in Las Vegas. Priscilla was twenty-one. Elvis was thirty-two.

Host Colonel Parker was in full charge. The wedding bower was filled with magnificent white flowers. The bride wore a traditional floor-length white chiffon and satin gown with seed-pearl trim and a six-foot train—just as though it were the church wedding of hers and Elvis' dreams. A rhinestone crown held her wedding veil, and she carried her wedding bouquet on her white Bible. On her proper finger rested the three-carat diamond engagement ring, surrounded with diamonds. Priscilla said she had designed and made her wedding dress herself. Her sister, Michelle, was Maid of Honor. Elvis' Memphis Mafia were represented by only two men, Joe Esposito and Marty Lacker. The two acted as best men!

The wedding breakfast was sumptuous: A five-foot, six-tiered wedding cake centered the wedding table, resting on white and pink roses, which also centered the beautifully appointed round tables for the wedding guests! The menu was lavish. "Love me Tender" was sung by strolling minstrels. As soon as the bridal couple had eaten, the photographers moved in for the cake cutting. "Kiss her, Elvis! Another kiss!" they cried. Then came a press conference. With all of the questions flung at them, Elvis gave the answers, saying he had waited for the right girl, and yes, his bride was the right girl. And yes, they "hoped to have a dozen babies. Give us time!"

Immediately, the newlyweds departed for Palm Springs and then to Graceland and the nearly new ranch that Elvis had stocked with horses and cattle. The joint families were reported as being upset that it wasn't a church wedding. But Priscilla being Catholic and Elvis Protestant, it had seemed the best way to settle it. The Colonel did by arranging it all in Las Vegas.

Their new mansion in the exclusive Trousdale Estates on Hillcrest Road in California was French Regency and cost Elvis over $400,000. Elvis immediately had a high fence built for added privacy. Two matters were observed in his new married life—the twelve boys who had long comprised the Memphis Mafia were reduced to two: Joe Esposito, a certified public accountant and Elvis' dresser, and Red West. All the long-time faithfuls were given jobs for Elvis back in Tennessee. And the fans: They camped in campers and cars day and night outside Elvis' house. This completely unnerved the new bride, not to mention upsetting the neighborhood, which deplored the confusion of blocked roads and the people themselves who were Elvis' devoted and often fanatical fans. Elvis would at first go to the gate and talk to them and ask them if they'd please stay away. By now it was known Priscilla was pregnant. Their constant trained vigilance and their cameras, focused with photo lens and binoculars from nearby tree tops constantly pointed at the Presley bedroom window and whatever, made her very nervous. The fans refused to leave Elvis. Soon it was all but outright war, with Elvis driving in and out of his electronic gates in extreme haste to avoid them. Elvis has a temper that can burst into flaming fire, when his toes are trod on, as many who've tried it can certify. It was all he could do to put up with the predatory types who were harassing his wife. As soon as his next picture was completed, they returned to Graceland for peace and quiet until the baby was born.

Elvis stayed close at home with Priscilla waiting. He drove her to the hospital and took the most meticulous care of her confinement. An overjoyed Elvis reacted with happy elation to the newsmen who had gathered by the hundreds, when he announced "The baby's a girl, Lisa Marie. I'm the happiest man in the whole world!"

So much was to happen to Elvis and Priscilla and Lisa Marie in the next six years.

CHAPTER TWENTY-THREE

Elvis' Fight to Hold Title of King After First 15 Years of Reign

ELVIS PRESLEY CAME out of so-called retirement in August, 1969, to make his first public singing engagement as "The King of Rock 'n' Roll" in thirteen years. The booking was for one month at the posh International Hotel, newly opened in Las Vegas. The stipend paid to Presley was one million dollars, and bets were running high that maybe Elvis had been wearing an empty crown these last few years. Maybe his draw would not be as great as some of his highly successful imitators, such as the Beatles and Tom Jones.

Even some of his most ardent admirers were saying Elvis' music, while it sold big on records, was actually dated for the now concert stage. Besides Elvis was now thirty-five years old.

All this time, Elvis had been confined to making three movies a year in Hollywood and recording. Perhaps time had passed him by. Could he still project that frenetic, arousing, electrifying, blatant sex—turning on the teenagers as he had in the mid-fifties? This was 1970—a whole new game in this crazy business. Elvis was also now a married man with a child. He was no longer the young, freewheeling romantic sex symbol he had been.

Elvis read all of this, listened to the radio commentators appraise his worth and the disc jockeys talk on the record shows. Had he slipped in these thirteen years? Was he indeed "an old man?"

Elvis was intelligent enough to justify this apprehension, and even be scared. "It's no fun to be acknowledged the "King" for fifteen years and then fall flat on your face!" he told me.

For six weeks Elvis worked out, dieted, rehearsed, worked. If he lost his crown, it wasn't going to be for lack of trying, nor lack of doing his best, giving his all to stay the "Champ!"

Colonel Parker okayed every invitation for Elvis' opening night. Barbra Streisand, who preceded him, had been blasted by the critics and had driven herself and everyone connected with her show to improve. She had won approval before her closing. I was happy to receive one of those highly coveted Elvis invitations, and I was also scared for Elvis.

This was the greatest challenge in Elvis' life to date. He was fighting for everything he stood for! What if the applause were only fair, even only polite? What if after tonight Elvis Presley was no longer "King," maybe just okay but not still great? Elvis had dieted to be skinny. His tall muscular frame had never been so slim. He looked as boyish as any teenager. His sideburns were long and black. He had an amazing new wardrobe of sharp jumpsuits, some white and some black, some beaded with silver or gold with flashing jeweled belts, and plunging V-necks to show off his virile chest. He didn't look carny or midway. No more freaky gold lamé oversize shouldered suits. He looked groomed, with class!

The band thundered the overture. When Elvis walked out on stage, I could plainly see the fear and nervousness in his eyes. But he wasn't alone. Standing in the wings was his bulwark and his strongest support, next to God himself, to who Elvis does a lot of praying —Colonel Tom Parker—who had booked him in this arena. If Elvis were to be fed to the lions at last, The Colonel figured it would be done in style!

In minutes the house was rocking with thunderous applause. The most conservative people were proclaiming Elvis again and again "The King of all pop music." Elvis relaxed and happily with it, finished in triumph.

Backstage Colonel Parker blandly lit a fresh cigar and smiled. Elvis, without a doubt, would go on like this for years to come. If Elvis had a son, the son could go on, and the son's sons. That is, as long as The Colonel was holding down the fort, and doing all the finagling to keep his boy the top attraction in show business! And, yes sir, worldwide!

I'd flown up to Las Vegas in 1970 and 1971 and 1972 to Elvis' openings at the International Hotel in Las Vegas. Elvis Presley was now winding up his third multimillion-dollar engagement. "Yes, sir," declared the posh hostelry, "Elvis Presley is the greatest box office attraction the world has ever known. That goes for this generation or any generation. Caruso and Valentino combined drew like Elvis.

"Elvis has changed the whole economy of Las Vegas. Business was way off, and when Elvis Presley is posted on the marquee, it's instant S.R.O.! People from all over the world come and fight for admittance during his engagement. Chartered planes bring his fans from as far as France, Japan, and Australia. Some little working girls, probably not earning more than thirty dollars a week, make reservations for every show and they pay in advance. Elvis is a phenomenon!"

On stage Elvis was singing "Suspicious Minds," his 52nd RCA Victor Gold Record, which had newly sold over a million discs. Teenage females were spaced way out under the proximity of his sexuality at close range. Females of all ages, sizes, and colors were weaving and swaying in a hypnotic trance—like ecstasy. Some were spiritually involved with the magnetic Presley charisma; more sexually turned on by his sheer sensual masculinity.

"This is nothing," a waiter whispered in my ear. "They're actually peeing in their panties up there in the balcony! We have to have mop-ups after every show!"

Elvis came on strong; grabbing his phallic sex symbol guitar, he swayed and rocked with "All Shook Up."

"Elvis looks kinda flat for being a super he-man sex symbol, don't you think, honey?" observed the woman across the table, who was old enough to be Elvis' mother.

Elvis laughed and grinned as the 2,000 capacity room rocked with applause. It was a shy grin, or was it, coming from this debonair handsome young man who has such great appeal for women. And who politely, still respectfully, replies with, "Yes, sir" and "Yes, ma'am"—the same as he did under his mother's supervision as a boy.

Elvis paused briefly on stage to smile, and a woman in front of me jumped up, struggled out of her husband's restraining hands, and rushed up to the stage. "Here Elvis! I did it again," she said hysterically, throwing him her panties. As he reached to pick them up, they were dripping water. Her husband swore in disgust. "Fuck him. She pees her pants every time she sees him. I don't know why I bring her here!"

A young woman, a tawny redhead, managed to crawl up onto the apron of the stage with the aid of a boost from an enthusiastic fan. Those of us at the front tables could see water trickling down her legs, as unashamedly she grabbed Elvis for a kiss. Elvis kissed the twentyish-year-old woman and grinning helplessly, he said to the audience, "Will someone please help me? What am I suppose to do?"

"Fuck her—damn you!" growled her boy friend in the audience. A man rushed from the wings and helped the woman back offstage. A waiter was already hovering around her seat for a mop-up. The man, finally grabbing the woman's arm, sat her down hard on her chair. She didn't feel anything. She was spaced out in the Elvis world as no heroin or LSD could ever take her. Elvis could and did.

When the slight commotion abated, Elvis went into "You'll Think of Me." "Damn right I will," swore an irritated husband, managing to keep his voice soft so he would not be removed from his hard-earned seat. Later, to anyone who would listen, he said, when Elvis stopped for a drink of water, "Every time I bop her, she cries 'Elvis' when she comes. What would you do if you were me?" he asked, waxing indignation which turned to resignation. "I love this broad. She's got a whole fan club of goof-offs just like her," he sighed.

What goes on nightly at Elvis-in-person concerts is unbelievable. A powder-room attendant said, "Women are streaming in here all evening bringing and dropping their soiled panties and asking for clean ones. We never stocked women's pants except for an Elvis engagement. Man, is he sexy, that man. Man oh man," she said dreamily, "I know I won't never get a piece of him, but I can dream. I dream all of the time to his records; play them all night. That 'Tiger Man' sure turns me on. I don't need no man of my own as long as I have Elvis singing me 'Tiger Man'."

From the inception of his career, Elvis Presley has been the most bombastic and controversial figure in show business. At the start, he was banned by the PTA for vulgarity, then he was revered as the best model soldier ever to serve a hitch in Uncle Sam's army. In the ensuing years, almost no one ever saw Elvis Presley in person, for he was making million-dollar movies in Hollywood. All of the films made huge profits at the box office, while his records went right on selling into the millions like no one in the record business. At the height of the Beatles, Elvis had 52 gold records to the Beatles' 31.

Yet no one really knew the real Elvis. A lot of adjectives have been used to try to explain why Elvis stays King. The few of us who learned to know Elvis as a human being quickly realized there was more to him than his unleashed fire of a tiger, his almost unbelievable emotional impact, his magnetic sex appeal, his superlative handsome good looks, his boyish youthfulness, his special unique showmanship, and way of singing a song. There is his genuine sincerity, concern, and love for people—all people. And his innate respect, gentility, good manners, and self control. He has a bundle of that.

CHAPTER TWENTY-FOUR

An Elvis Concert at the Forum

ELVIS' CROSS-COUNTRY tours, including Madison Square Garden, booked for two performances and extended to four—were sellouts. It was like it had been before Elvis made movies back in 1955. Except now Elvis was playing the biggest halls, coliseums, and auditoriums in the country!

For weeks, all Hollywood and Los Angeles were talking and speculating about Elvis' concert here in nearby Inglewood. The Forum, with its 36,500 seats, so huge it had never been packed in its history, had been chosen for one show. Four hours after the box office opened the first show was sold out. On public insistence, another show was set for afternoon. In six hours this was sold out. The clamor for a third show was loud and long. People were calling and wiring for tickets from Hawaii, Australia, Mexico, and Canada— not to mention the U.S.A. Elvis was already scheduled the next day for San Diego, in winding up his one-nighter tour. He couldn't comply with a request that six shows be added.

Teenagers, who had stood from 4 A.M. in lines of thousands to get front-row seats when the box office opened at 10, were told the front seats were already gone. Word was sent to Colonel Parker. The Colonel, whose word and integrity and belief in "fair play" is well evidenced, demanded that the box office front seats could not be withheld. They had to be sold to the kids on a first-come, first-served basis! No favorites! It was discovered that someone had held out a few front rows for friends. "Nothing doing!" said The Colonel. "Everyone pays. No passes, not even for the press!"

The press had a hard time trying to get tickets, and

if they were not at the box office those first few hours, they didn't get tickets and couldn't make the scene.

Early that Saturday morning, Elvis had flown in from his night's concert in Oakland. He was hustled as quickly as possible through the Forum's back door. Thousands of fans all ages, ten to sixty, and even older, had brought sleeping bags, attempting to stay all night on the parking lot to await his arrival for a first-hand glimpse. This had been impossible but they still hung around.

Like everyone else, for weeks I had tried to buy a ticket. An RCA Victor record executive had tried too late. "I can't get any for my children," he said. The concerts were for everyone, Colonel Parker insisted. No favorites. Miraculously due to an emergency, a lady couldn't go at the last minute and I could. That's how I got my ticket. The tickets were five dollars to ten. They could have been twenty, but Elvis wouldn't hear of it. He wanted them priced at a reasonable figure that people could afford so they could enjoy themselves.

I started to drive to the Forum forty minutes away, two hours before the concert. The roads were bumper-to-bumper traffic. No one had dreamed there would be such traffic and so many miles before you'd reach the Forum. People were singing, "We are going to see Elvis!" It was a caravan. There were not enough police to handle the traffic. It was stop, go, stop, while the minutes on my car ticked away to fifteen minutes before three, concert time, and the start of Elvis' show. There was nothing anyone could do. It was three exactly when I arrived at the parking lot of the Forum, to find it was "Sold out—no parking." Like many others, I drove for miles trying to find a parking place, without luck. Some homes nearby put up signs $2.50—park in our driveway. They had all been taken. Finally in desperation at Sears, I parked in their lot, and hiked the miles back to the Forum!

Outside were hundreds of Elvis Presley fans holding five, ten—and even twenty-dollar bills in their hands, offering to buy anyone's ticket—so they could get inside. Hawkers were selling Elvis Presley blowup pictures for $1.25. Inside I secured a beautiful color photo album of Elvis for a dollar. They could have sold for five, but again Elvis and The Colonel wanted them to be in the price range of everyone.

The first part of the show, preliminary to Elvis and which I had seen at the International in Las Vegas, was over when I climbed the stairs. In vain I kept trying to find an usher. The ushers were spellbound with the stage, anticipating Elvis; they simply could not be found. Finally on my own I wangled down to my seat, which happily was right up against the stage, to see Elvis well.

Sammy Shore, the comedian, was saying, "I knew I had a following when I joined Elvis' show. Ten thousands girls keep trying to get backstage. Elvis goes where the girls won't bother him—in my dressing room!" Then quipped Sammy, "We played nine weeks at the International in Las Vegas. I sent Elvis flowers. Was I shocked to see a funeral wreath signed from me in Elvis' dressing room. I protested to the florist. He said, 'You should see the people at the funeral on seeing your spray on the coffin with the card, 'Good luck on your opening!' "

Elvis as usual and very casual, walked onstage without announcement or fanfare. The applause and reception was deafening. More, it was with a certain complete respect. No panties or bras were thrown on stage! Not even one! Rather, the whole was awe for an idol—and respect.

It was a challenge to most of them, Elvis Presley was a legend, one they had never—or at least almost never—seen in the flesh, living, breathing, alive! What was Elvis really like? A few had gone to Vegas and had seen him at the International. Here were 36,500 people, young, old, movie stars—fans—all curious to behold Elvis actually as he was!

Sleek as a tiger—sexy, dynamic, handsome, loving all of us and clowning, he invented and improvised and did whatever he felt like doing. This he made quite clear by daringly swinging into an unmistakable impersonation of Tom Jones, with all the tight pants bit, mimicking his style! Everyone was fully aware of the hundreds who have imitated Elvis, copied him, and who have ridden to fame and millions on his shirt-tails!!!! Now Elvis was taking his turn—which clearly startled the musicians on stage. Elvis was having fun—regardless of program! Elvis' imitation was good, and he switched to Englebert Humperdinck! Next he gave us his version of Glenn Campbell. He laughed, ending with "Hot Dam!" The crowd roared. Colonel Parker came out from behind stage to see what was going on! Elvis was switching his act, as he pleased. He was joining hands with all of us as though it were a good-time party at Graceland in Memphis! It became that intimate too, before the end.

This was the Elvis everyone close to him knows—light-hearted, fun-loving, practical joker—not an awesome legend.

"Turn up the lights," Elvis said. "You can see me. I want to see you!" He went around the stage's apron for a good look, but the uniformed police would not let him off. Girls screamed, "I love you, Elvis!" One in the front row went into a fit of emotions that sent her rolling on the floor like a "Holy Roller." The girl seated next to me said, "I can't stand it—him so near!" Later she explained, "I'm a hair dresser for the movies, but I've never seen Elvis before. He's my idol. I know Hal Wallis and Dean Martin and lots of people who could maybe get me to Elvis for a hello. But I couldn't do it, not without preparing myself a long time before I could undertake such an experience!" She was an attractive young woman, age thirty.

In front of me were teenage girls with long, Jean Harlow shades of platinum hair, waist length. They sat mesmerized. The big and remarkable difference in this concert and the one many years before—this time everyone listened! No one wanted to miss a word or note of the Elvis Presley charisma.

"He's so precious!" "I love you, Elvis!" "We love you!" "We worship you, Elvis!" "You are our only love, Elvis!" exploded from all sides, the minute Elvis

193

took a breath. His entrance and exits on stage were saluted by thousands of camera flashbulbs. They made it appear psychedelic throughout the fifty minutes, except when Elvis called for the house lights turned on!

Elvis was wearing a white vinyl leather jumpsuit with gold nail-head trim, and a hand-crocheted tangy orange belt with tassels that swung around his slim hips. It was not skin tight and his body moved freely—always with the beat of the music coursing through his veins, his whole aliveness pulsating sexuality with the rhythm and the beat. It was as though he were tuned into some frenetic perpetual power of fluid sex, grace, and vitality that would not turn off. No one on stage has ever given this excitement and virility of pure male masculinity. Small wonder Elvis continues as the sex symbol of this generation and the ones before.

The woman to my right, the wife of an executive of the Forum, exclaimed, "Tom Jones and the others are vulgar sex. But Elvis Presley is sexy in an arousing, clean, healthy way."

Sex shimmers from him and envelops you, and you are caught up with its entirety grasping and even holding you. And when aroused sex is at fever pitch, Elvis laughs! He laughs at his gyrations and at himself, and his put-on; then everyone relaxes and laughs too. It is an emotional and physical tension release.

Elvis turned off and amazingly went into a spiritual. He sang about God with all of the meaning and fervor in his heart for his Maker. You believed him. You believed him more than you could ever believe a Billy Graham. This, too, is real with Elvis, for he is deeply religious. The church hymns he sang with his parents as a little boy comes through in his demeanor as well as in his voice. When you were caught up completely with the choral magnificence, with Elvis leading, he stopped. He switched to "Polk Salad Annie." Then "Hound Dog," and he gyrated to the floor and back, always with the rhythm and sexy impulse, magnetic and flowing through him and involving you with its stimulus and contagion and setting you on fire again!

Stopping for a drink of water and to wipe the perspiration from his brow, Elvis grabbed the cap from a policeman's head and had fun impersonating the officer who didn't mind a bit. When Elvis returned the cap to the officer's head, Elvis' polite "thank you" was clearly audible.

Colonel Parker decided to sit in the center of the ring of police enforcing the security of the stage, looking worried at what antics his swinging free-wheeling, multi-million-dollar star might spring next. Elvis laughingly went over, reached down, and plucked The Colonel's fedora off his head. Elvis improvised an impersonation of his famed manager. When he put it back on the astonished Colonel, Elvis again politely whispered, "thanks."

Elvis said, "I want you to meet my daddy." The house lights moved up and where was daddy? "He has to be here somewhere," said Elvis, looking all around at the thousands of people jamming the Forum to the roof tops. "My daddy has gray hair and he's wearing a blue shirt. Where is he?" Elvis pressed. Vernon Presley stuck his head through the backstage curtain and waved. Everyone applauded. They also applauded "The Colonel" wildly. "We love you, too!" they said.

Elvis really waxed personal with all of us when he bared his heart with his uttermost personal feelings, about all that has been happening to him in his private life! In a rare moment of confidence he spoke with complete frankness to deny certain unspecified, but obvious to all, allegations which had been made regarding his private life (a paternity suit) which had seemed at the time to have vanished reportedly as a hoax. "I want to thank all of you for your belief and your loyalty to me," he said. You could see his eyes glistening with emotion. Only then did you realize how deeply he had felt about the charges and of his innocence. Then he spoke of his new M.G.M. movie, the documentary—*Elvis, That's The Way It Is*—which was in current release. "It is the best film I have made in ten years," Elvis said. "I hope you like it, too!"

Elvis dropped to his knees for some numbers. At

one time he fell flat on his back. Sweat poured from his brow as he worked with all of his strength to give his fans his all, again with the famous widely imitated karate-like gestures, the sweeping turns, and the hip wiggles. There were many long-hairs and short-hairs, and Elvis, who has introduced many hair styles from his first ducktail cut, wore his hair now in a wide sweeping point on his forehead with wide, long side-burns complimenting the same point. Heretofore, his hair had dangled with perspiration on his forehead—here it seemed to have been heavily sprayed to hold its luxuriant thickness in place and control.

No one had ever seen a happier, more carefree, relaxed Elvis, as he continued his spoofing with us and asides to his entire company, with lapses also into unmistakable polite "thank you," too. Turning to his guitarist, James Burton, who was plainly bewildered with Elvis' surprise clowning, Elvis quipped, "Here you are, the world's highest-paid guitarist, standing here just goofing. What do you make, $3,000 a week? Oh, $2,500. Well, that's money," Elvis sighed. Turning, he said, "All right, let's go," and tongue in cheek, he said, "Hello, I'm Johnny Cash," and away we went with Elvis on a romp through "Funny How Time Slips Away."

Elvis tried to keep his cool while a girl behind him kept calling out such impassioned love words that he was breaking up in spite of himself. At one point Elvis actually blushed—his smile tinged with embarrassment! Then Elvis confided to us all, amid the continuous bulb flashing of brownie cameras, "That's all. Thank you. You're magnificent. Goodbye," and he walked off.

People were reluctant to leave. Many tried to hold onto their seats to await the night show. But those seats were already sold. They had to go.

Outside everyone who hadn't made it inside begged for details. What happened? What was Elvis really like? Everyone wanted to know. Through the years people keep asking.

At his unscheduled show, that night added by demand, when he finally begged off and said goodnight, near midnight, he was mindful that he was playing a concert the next afternoon and night in San Diego. And next night after in Oklahoma City, which after his all record-breaking appearances in hold-over added concerts in Oakland, San Francisco, Portland, and Seattle would wind up within the week in Denver. This was a grueling whirlwind tour for any artist, and one of such rigid timing that might not be expected of a super-star, who can afford to take his time and all on his own terms. Elvis proved he is a hard worker. "I like hard work," he said. "And when it's doing my thing before and with people, my kind of people, I make any and every effort." Priscilla had remained with the baby in the home Elvis has newly bought her in the Bel Air area. It was a luxurious mansion with more seclusion than the houses they had previously rented here. "But Graceland is and always will be home," Elvis smiled. "I feel alive again and happy," he exclaimed, working out front, instead of behind scenes, like all of those years.

Elvis next anticipated the worldwide tours. Colonel Parker anticipated those multimillions of dollars for his boy waiting for them in England, Australia, South America, Japan, Canada, and the many offers in the United States. For strange reasons, however, he kept turning them aside. So in late 1974, Elvis was still not scheduled out of the U.S.A.

Acknowledged the world's idol who could apparently do no wrong, even the most conservative newspapers were front-paging Elvis. The *Los Angeles Times* front-paged, "Elvis' enormous personal charisma, showmanship, and excellent voice shows that he is still way in front of everybody else."

The box office revealed that Elvis again was setting new box-office records grossing $313,000 a show, which surpassed the one-day record set the previous year by the Rolling Stones at $238,000!

CHAPTER TWENTY-FIVE

Married Life and Sacrifice

ELVIS' MARRIAGE TO Priscilla in 1967 made great changes in his heretofore bachelor life. Some surprised and impressed him with the fact he was now her husband. He was no longer the free swinger. Diminutive Priscilla's intelligence, a source of pride to Elvis, was now coupled with her strong-mindedness, a quality he had not fully anticipated. It brought about many differences of opinion between the two of them. In spite of their long seven years of getting to know each other in Memphis, Elvis now became aware, as a husband, his wife had the right to assert herself. Now it was their life and not just his. The twenty-one year-old new Mrs. Presley was now mistress of Elvis' four homes, the estate Graceland in Memphis, the house in Beverly Hills (which was soon to be traded for Priscilla's new house in the Trousdale Estates), the Palm Springs house, the ranch house and a house in Hawaii. Until now all these domiciles had been run with precision by Elvis' hired help. There was his cousin Patsy, who acted as his executive secretary; his cousin Billy, who was in charge of his ranch in Mississippi; his Grandmama Presley, who had charge of Graceland; and his father Vernon, who was general overseer to the help for the other homes.

Elvis had been meticulously careful not to change the the decor of Graceland which had been his mother's handiwork. Over ten years had passed and some changes were to be made. "I just replaced drapes and carpeting and furniture coverings when they were needed," Elvis told me, "But retaining the same colors and fabrics Mama had chosen." Priscilla, with a natural flair for decorating, made many changes.

The major upheaval in Elvis' newly married life was the dismissal of his Memphis Mafia. This Elvis was most reluctant to do. Priscilla wanted a full-time husband at home. She wanted to be alone with him and not always be the center of a group of Elvis' hired men. The men were more than employees—they were Elvis' long-time buddies, many from his school days. When he gave them new cars, rings, and colored television sets for Christmas he was simply sharing his success with them as they shared his career and life. They also were Elvis' security. Fans parked in campers, put up pup-tents, slept in their cars parked by Elvis' various homes, in the hope of getting a glimpse of the idol. Elvis needed his boys. But the entourage of twelve men was too much for PRISCILLA! She put her dainty little foot down, and Elvis had to agree—their marriage couldn't work unless they had their privacy in their own home. The boys were dispatched but kept on Elvis' payroll. Most of them had already married. Now instead of leaving their wives back in Memphis, apartments were taken, and they moved along with their husbands. Joe Esposito's wife Joan became Priscilla's close woman friend.

Elvis' Memphis Mafia seemed to be a thing of the past, but they were ready and on hand for Elvis' tours. Elvis, a Karate expert, well able to take care of himself now added a new form of protection. He became a deputy sheriff, with a badge and the right to carry a gun.

The Presleys began entertaining in their new home. There were dinner parties—but always for her family or his from back home. Priscilla had elected to live in California with the idea that they could be more alone and to themselves. Elvis had always maintained open house for his friends. It was impossible to turn away the many who'd ring up Elvis and drop by. This can become very tiring to a new bride when her husband's friends number half of the South, Nashville, business acquaintances, and stars.

For a long time Elvis had been studying religions. A Hollywood store specializing in occult books reported Elvis' boys had all but bought out their supply. Elvis was now interested in pursuing all forms of study. Next he was into Scientology, a religious science for self-realization. Elvis told me, "I believe in God. I always have, since I was old enough to sing a hymn in Sunday school in East Tupelo." God's favored lamb had not strayed.

On rare occasions, the Presleys entertained in Beverly Hills' exclusive restaurants. Elvis preferred out of the way places and Priscilla's dining out became more and more infrequent. It was noted that when Priscilla arrived with women friends to see a night club show— Elvis was missing.

"I can't stay home alone so much. Elvis is always gone either on tours or in Las Vegas performing or he's recording. I get too lonely." It became the custom for Priscilla and Lisa Marie to join Elvis in Las Vegas for his opening night. The ravishing beauty of Priscilla, however, was well hidden in a booth. It was only as she ran through a door, back to obscurity, that photographers might get a quick flash of her. Mrs. Gary Lewis met Priscilla at a celebration party for a very few select guests after an Elvis opening night at the Hilton. Someone suggested a photographer take pictures of the two young women. Priscilla said, "No we can't." Even with an exchange of telephone numbers, Priscilla never called. She, too, lived in that secluded ivory-tower way of life with Elvis. No outsiders, please!

Priscilla, with an unlimited checking account, full of energetic drive, decorated their new homes in California as fast as they switched residences. Her restlessness did not abate until each house was completed. With exquisite taste, the homes became luxurious palaces, although with masculine decor to suit Elvis' personality. Then what next?

Dancing lessons, drama lessons, and finally with Elvis' concern for her safety, Priscilla took up karate. From the beginning of their marriage, movie offers came to Priscilla. One of the more important was Hal Wallis' offer. Due to her fame as Mrs. Presley, perhaps, coupled with her natural photogenic looks, a leading-lady role was slated in one of his films. Reluctantly Priscilla turned down the dream of her lifetime.

Elvis wanted a full-time wife and mother for his child. No career.

How long Priscilla would be content to remain hidden in the background, when she was stunningly gowned and jeweled, when she was not permitted to share Elvis' spotlight, was a matter of open conjecture by those on the scene. The Colonel wisely said, "Only one career and that is Elvis!"

Some explained that Southern men go out and earn the living, and their women are expected to stay at home. Priscilla's restlessness found her taking long drives in her car alone at night. Police would spot her white Rolls or her Mercedes with the lone woman sometimes driving along at 3 A.M. Elvis was notified that this was highly dangerous. Confronted, Priscilla rebelled. What did he expect? She couldn't sit home forever alone.

Elvis tried more and more to spend more time with his wife. There were always distractions and demands on him beside his tight working schedules. Tom Jones, The Beatles, and other noted stars when they came to town naturally looked up Elvis!

Elvis had long considered forming his own movie company. Tom Jones anxious to make a picture had many meetings with Elvis in the hope of starring in one of the Presley productions. While Elvis acquired a new jet plane to save time—to have more time at home with his wife and baby. When you are earning top dollar and your name is Elvis, you have to live up to that name.

Priscilla never stayed long in Las Vegas, even though Elvis sometimes played four weeks. "I just go up for the opening and closing nights," she explained. "I don't want to be around to bug him."

Elvis was long accustomed to rumors and manufactured phoney news concerning him. He never confirmed nor denied, for that was The Colonel's idea. "Always keep them guessing!" Priscilla, however, couldn't understand it all when she read such as: "Elvis Presley

201

Has Split From The Church of His Mother and Father: The Assembly of God Church in Memphis!" "Elvis Joins an Occult Cult in Hollywood!" . . . "Why Elvis And Priscilla's Child Is Not Baptized!" . . . "Elvis on Dope" . . . "Priscilla Falls Down Steps and Loses Elvis' Baby" . . . "Priscilla Waits Elvis' Second Baby" . . . "Priscilla Has Miscarriage" . . . "Elvis Gives New Cars and $500 TV Sets to People To Stay With Him." So went the news reports daily on Elvis.

"Why do they make up all of these horrible rumors about us?" Priscilla worried. They began to close in on Priscilla with alarming upset. Elvis began to worry. When they touched his child—they got to him. Elvis for the first time couldn't understand why the press would make up absolute lies. He also had to re-evaluate his position! He could sue and stop them. Or he'd have to reconcile himself that rumors always beset public idols. Actually he laughed at one, replying, "What's new in the rumor factory today?"

Priscilla, on a plane enroute to Las Vegas for an Elvis opening night, remarked sadly and apprehensively, "Why do they persist in making up all of these stories about Elvis? About us? Why?" She still couldn't understand why.

When the demand is so great to know more about a super-style star, public idol, she was told—that's why, Priscilla! That's why! The super, long-time stars have a saying, as Wallace Beery used to say, "As long as they spell my name right, let them print what they want!"

Some of it on Elvis is too far out to be ignored, like the one he had split from his church to join an occult faith! That was going too far!

How did this one start? How can such a rumor grow, in fact, in print, so the world, or whoever reads it, believes it?

"Actually that was years ago, when I was working in a picture at Paramount Studios for Hal Wallis," Elvis told me. "A lady had an occult bookstore across the street. Some of the boys bought some of the books. I began reading and it was interesting. That was all."

202

"I became very interested reading about religions. I was interested in self-realization—in finding one's true self. Who isn't? I have never left my own church." On that he stands firm.

Life styles predicated on babyhood, boyhood, and growing up with a mother and father in church don't leave you overnight. Not when you are a sensitive, intelligent man who has the deepest respect for his upbringing, as they do in the South. An inquiring, maturing mind wants to learn. Elvis has given himself a self-education by reading books on every subject.

"I'd like to go to college to learn more. But again I know that wouldn't work," Elvis dismissed, shyly envisioning how classes at U.C.L.A. or elsewhere would be disrupted by the presence of Elvis as a student! Elvis tuned in to higher knowledge by continuing to read books.

"Priscilla and I often talk about taking some joint courses at U.C.L.A. when we are out here in California, but it wouldn't be fair to the other students," he concluded. "When you go to school, you go to learn."

The question of why Elvis completely shared his good fortune with his family and the boys who work for him was answered by his cousin Red West. "When it all first began, Elvis gave all of us suits and rings and cars as gifts. That's because Elvis has real humility and he never lorded his riches or his fame over us. We were always all for one—and one for all. He's more than generous. Elvis never makes us feel obligated. It's like we earn it all along with him, being with him as co-workers."

Concerning more of the way-out rumors besetting Elvis and Priscilla, I was told: "Elvis has not left his church. The reason his baby, Lisa, has not been baptized is the fact that Priscilla is Catholic and Elvis is Assembly of God. The baby will be baptized when she reaches the age to make her own decision." Priscilla laughed when everyone exclaimed, "For a pregnant woman, you certainly have a slim figure." "I was not pregnant and I did not fall down any stairs. I did not suffer a miscarriage." Elvis said, "We are hopeful of having more children and that possibility is in the hands of the good Lord. It could be any time."

Elvis was certainly not on dope. He never has been, nor will he be. His mother so ingrained in him the logic of a clean mind, clean body, good health, honesty, and integrity.

At this time Elvis had never been happier than in his marriage. Equally radiant was Priscilla, with a huge diamond pin, Elvis' Christmas gift, which she wore proudly. Priscilla, always beautifully dressed, made Elvis, who is very clothes conscious, very proud.

Priscilla at last accepted the fact that her husband was not unlike all the great idols of the past who were victimized by female adulation coupled with imagination. Clark Gable and Rudolph Valentino were beset with rumors and gossip and fans. Women actually dreamed dreams and took them to court on paternity suits—only to have it proven to them that they were just dreams after all.

New stars coming up instruct their press agents and managers to study the Elvis charisma in the hope of learning the secret of his continuing long-time popularity. One who tells it as it is, is Dixie Jones of Tampa, Florida.

It is so nice to read something real about Elvis. It is always, he runs alone without his wife, the newness of his daughter has worn off, he is not as interested in her as when she was born, he drinks, etc. From his songs and his actions alone (I saw him last year here in Tampa) he was still great. I kept telling my husband how great he was, so this year I asked my husband if he would take me to Alabama to see him. Now my husband is just as enthusiastic an Elvis fan as I am. Last year I took snapshots and about eight months later, I sent Elvis one to see if he would sign it for me. I never thought he would. Two weeks later, I got my picture back, signed "Best Wishes, Elvis Presley." He also sent me an 8 x 10 picture signed. After all these years of making people happy, he deserves the best and the loyalty of his fans. Thank you for always being honest with Elvis. I am twenty-three. (signed) Dixie Jones.

CHAPTER TWENTY-SIX

I Prevent a Scandal

IT'S HARD TO believe, but Elvis Presley turns down the largest dollar offers made a single performer. "According to Australia's *Daily Telegraph* April, 1974, Elvis snubbed a million dollars up front to perform only two concerts in Sydney," reported Hank Grant in the *Hollywood Reporter*. Wire service reports of various other multimillion offers overseas appeared in the newspapers. Since the press through the years never had access to Elvis, little was seen or read about him in print. "If The Colonel won't play ball, we won't build Elvis' career," was the press decision from the start. Publicity apparently made no difference in the Elvis charisma, his records and his concerts were sellouts. "It's performance that counts," was The Colonel's belief and with Elvis it was just that.

What was so superior about Elvis' in-person singing that had hundreds of fans turned away an hour after the box office opened, when the "Sold Out" sign went up?

On Elvis' opening night in Las Vegas, his first in fifteen years, he looked plain scared when he first walked on the stage. He was putting his reign as King "on the line." Amid the clamor and applause, Elvis knew after his first numbers he was home safe. He was still King.

Alex Shoofey, manager of the International Hotel, tried to sign Elvis for the next ten years and at the stupendous one million Elvis was getting for that first time. "No," said The Colonel. "We don't sign longer than a year ahead, because next year we might want to do something different." Turning to Elvis, The Colonel asked, "Right, son?" "Yes," Elvis replied. As it turned out Elvis played the International twice a year and was paid the double figure.

Elvis meticulously rehearsed. The Beatles said, "We never rehearse—because the fans yell and scream and can't hear anything anyway." With Elvis, some of his shows were recorded live on stage. Others were filmed live for Elvis' Television Specials. Yes, The Colonel got triple money all the way.

Elvis Presley's opening night, his third in a year at Alex Shoofey's posh International Hotel, found me there again for the third time, too. It also found thousands of Elvis Presley fans—all ages. Some had to wait many days and nights to get a reservation in the big 2,000-seat room to see him during his four week engagement.

It was indeed the most exciting and the most elegant opening night in Las Vegas history. Elvis had been rehearsing right up to show time to the point of exhaustion. He literally knocked himself out for everyone there out front—the most blasé critics and the most affluent people rewarded him with a standing ovation and nothing but raves.

Elvis said after the show, "I wasn't as good as I can be. I'll be with it all the way by tomorrow night. I've had to learn sixty-one new songs, memorize the lyrics and the arrangements, and in a period of time where I usually rehearse six or ten. This was because of the movie they were filming live. Every night we'll do a different set of songs so the M.G.M. people can take their choice of the best for the film."

"Will there be any of your personal life, Priscilla, the baby, Graceland, or your father in this picture?"

"No, nothing personal," Elvis replied, "It will be entitled the *Summer Festival* for the people all over the world who want to see me perform but can't get here or I to them. I wish I could go out on tour about the country, like I did fifteen years ago. I love the feel of the audience, of people, being with people again. Man, I've loved every minute of it here in Las Vegas. You don't know how it has been, making movies, reacting to a box (camera) instead of getting with it, swinging with real people. I really need them to turn on."

The Colonel found time at last, since Elvis' movies had become not much more than "quickies without much thought or direction." As long as they were money-makers and Elvis was paid his million-and-a-half plus 50 percent of the profits and full recording rights, it was okay. Finally even the most ardent Elvis fans stopped seeing them, while Elvis himself declared he couldn't make another one until he had a decent script. The time was right to return to his people in person! Elvis appeared first in August, 1969, at the International at a million dollars for four weeks. He was promptly signed for another engagement for February, 1970, at another million, and entertainment director Bill Millar signed him again for August, 1970, as the biggest attraction in show-business history—exceeding the revered greats: Al Jolson, Frank Sinatra, Caruso, *ad infinitum*.

"I'd sure like to go on the road and play all of the towns I once played," Elvis told me with nostalgia. Sure, there were offers at millions of dollars to play a Canadian tour, an Australian tour, and another—a million pounds sterling—to play London. Colonel Parker refused them all. "Not going to overwork my boy. We don't want too much exposure."

Since Elvis Presley motion pictures have never been known to make less than a six-million-dollar profit, M.G.M. signed Elvis for the *Elvis Festival* film.

Elvis' opening in Las Vegas found the big room fused with giant panavision cameras and lights. Elvis admitted, "The cameras made me a little nervous at first but once I settled down, it wasn't too bad."

For a week the M.G.M. crews had been at the International filming the phenomenon of two generations —Elvis Presley.

Colonel Parker had Elvis banners, kerchiefs, flags,

ribbons, and straw hats on the dealers and waiters, building the excitement of the *Elvis Festival*. This gave the elegance of the hostelry quite an air. No one, not even Elvis himself, second guessed that after his show, in the early wee hours of the dawning, his greatest wish was about to come true.

If you were not one of those who flew from all parts of the world—Paris, London, Japan, Australia, Canada, or from much more available places like New York, Chicago, Miami, Los Angeles, and all of the towns and cities in between to attend Elvis' Summer Festival—"You need not put out your dollars for plane fare and hotels and all like I did," I reported. "It would also have been quite worthless for that magnificent Elvis Presley opening, if you were not on Colonel Parker's approved guest list. So come right along for free and I'll share it with you."

Fans, teenagers, teeny boppers, twenty-twists, thirty-merst, and those of all ages of the Elvis Presley world were there. Hundreds couldn't get in. Many milled about outside waiting for reports and waiting, too, until they could get a reservation with the maitre de, Emilio Muscelli, who was sold out (but who was always smilingly confident that there might be a chance later on).

So you walk into the big room into the blinding lights of movie cameras and you survey the scene. Sammy Davis, Jr., is there with a table of eight beautiful black people. Sammy received tremendous applause and told me, "That was because they could recognize *me!*"

Necks swiveled for George Hamilton back to double takes for his Alana Collins, wearing one of the first complete see-throughs, chiffon pajamas with the barest bikini pants and bra underneath. A gorgeous girl with waist-long brunette hair was discussed as possibly being Tina Sinatra. Oh no, she was Priscilla Presley, standing up at the hidden Presley booth to look around. With Priscilla was her girl friend Joan, who was Mrs. Joe Esposito, whose husband was a member of the Memphis Mafia. The next booth seated Vernon Pres-

208

ley and his wife Dee. And there were The Colonel's brother-in-law, Tom Diskin, and Mrs. Parker and The Colonel.

Repeatedly over the loud speaker, a voice announced "Tonight we are filming an MGM picture, *Elvis Festival.* Your presence here is your consent to be a part of the film." If anyone wanted to not be in the film, they could go. No one departed. And that included Cary Grant, Nancy Sinatra Jr., Jim Aubrey, now head of M.G.M., Greg Bautzer, attorney for Howard Hughes, Kirk Kerkorian, Juliet Prowse (who once dated Elvis), Sergio Franchi, Dale Robertson, Herb Alpert, Jack Benny, and many more. All were evidently quite willing to be *gratis* in Elvis Presley's newest motion picture.

"The lights dimned, and the Elvis Presley Show was on. People stopped eating dinner or dessert or whatever and riveted their eyes on the big stage. Opening the show were the Sweet Inspirations and the Imperials, then comedy star Sammy Shore, all who had been with Elvis on his three preceding shows. And just when everyone had settled down to wait for Elvis on the second half of the show, in he walked. Gasp! He looked sensational in a white kid leather jump suit with fringed shoulders, slit down his chest with a beaded streamer belt fringed around his hips. Elvis smiled and went right into singing, which hushed the screams and gasps. The excitement and potency of his presence was electric and it held you. Movie lights on poles flashed off and on as the cameras dollied in for closeups, but Elvis ignored them. The greatest drawing power in show business was in full control, and his every move was deliberate and assured, pacing his timing playfully as a master showman. Even so, his eyes were laughing and even a little embarrassed at his own daring after his sexy pulsating gyrations! Most astounding was to see that naive natural sweetness that is Elvis clearly shining in his eyes. It remains uncorrupted by his adulation, staggering fame, and multi-millions of dollars pouring into his bank accounts all of these years! That's the wonder of Elvis, and his strength and his charm!

His "Polk Salad Annie" turned on women until they were screaming. A girl seated next to my escort began nudging him, moving closer and closer, and finally she whispered in his ear, "I'm not married to the boy with me—maybe???" The mercurial sex radiating, zinging, bedazzling, caused a frenzy of squeals from the balcony, uninhibited to burst into full crescendo! Elvis looked up and waved, "Hang on you girls up there, I'll try to make it up." Then with his chief characteristic, which is honesty, he was laughing at himself and his antics—even going so far as to exclaim, "I feel like an old stripper!" This from the world's No. 1 Sex Symbol!!!

Elvis stopped from time-to-time under the hot lights to borrow proffered napkins to wipe the sweat pouring liberally off his brow, while women and girls reached up for them to press his dampness to their breasts!

No one works harder knocking himself out than Elvis does on stage. On this particular night he was sheer exuberance and we, his audience, as always were right there figuratively in the palm of his hand.

It was not all rock 'n' roll, the dynamics of song and music, as it had been the two previous engagements. It was surprise! Elvis took all of us into his confidence, explaining, "We don't know what we are doing up here! We've been rehearsing—whee—I had to learn so many new songs I've never done before, for this movie! But by tomorrow night we'll be all with it." Elvis was as informal as though it were a rehearsal—until pow!— he swept us off into a new set of dynamics—fluid motion—sex—the karate power holds—and then he was nostalgia with romantic "I've Lost You" and "The Next Stop is Love"—two of his newest recordings.

An M.G.M. executive intoned in the mike, "Elvis is being photographed tonight with no script, no artificiality. There are no constructed sets, no makeup, no direction for the star. Elvis is on his own. And that is good enough for anyone!"

When he sang, "I Can't Help Believing," a hush descended over the big room as people were swept into a new emotional take with his mood, and then he went into "Sweet Caroline" and "Bridge Over Troubled Water." But was Elvis himself at his best with "Tiger Man," "Love Me Tender" and "Mystery Train," with all of the impact and emotion moving through his body, self-induced.

Elvis said, "I have so many songs, like fifty arrangements, and lyrics, spinning around in my head!" He laughed, but he didn't miss a word. He was free, relaxed, and occasionally he leaned down to kiss a lady or a girl who'd dashed up to the stage and begged him for a kiss. The kisses were full on the lips. None of this cheek business with Elvis—when he gives, he gives!

A tiny little girl was held up for a kiss. Elvis took her tenderly in his arms and even at age four, she reacted as all femmes do under the mysticism, charisma, and the gracious sweetness that is Elvis Presley, the idol of two generations.

Elvis, twelve glasses of water later, closed with "Can't Help Falling in Love" and he was saying good night. He had been singing scarcely stopping for breath, for almost two hours. And you didn't have the heart to applaud him back, although everyone did try. No one had had enough Elvis. They wanted more of the old Elvis favorites, such as "I'm All Shook Up," "Hound Dog," "Heartbreak Hotel," and "In The Ghetto." "I'll be singing them all with different songs every night," Elvis consoled and bowed off."

Elvis went to his dressing room, and a pretty girl came to my table. "We all love you," she said, "We Elvis Presley fans. Because you tell the truth as it is about Elvis." She said, "We hate those who try to break up Elvis and Priscilla. She is such a doll—and that beautiful baby, Lisa Marie. All Elvis wants is to have more children, lots of babies. And how he'd like to go on the road and see everyone. He wants that so much. He loves people and wants more than anything to go back singing for them, even one nighters as he did in the beginning. But he's such a big super-star today. It doesn't seem likely."

When I asked her if she wanted to give me a full story on her friendship with Elvis and Priscilla, she shied away. "I wouldn't capitalize on my friendship with Elvis and Priscilla, it's too sacred."

While everyone was departing the big room, Elvis was now upstairs in his dressing room showering. However, Colonel Parker was seen herding the key men of RCA Victor and MGM into a sales meeting. An hour later the word filtered out that Elvis was about to get his biggest wish realized! It was decided that to fully capture the world of Elvis Presley, he should go out again across the country on a concert tour. He had been hoping for this year after year. And here it was! And why?

It was felt the movie of Elvis would be more spectacular, showing the exposure of Elvis with the crowds of people in the different cities where he would play.

The tour would be brief. It was scheduled to start in two days, following his closing at the International. He would play Phoenix, St. Louis, Detroit, Miami, Tampa, and wind up in Mobile!

You should have seen the excitement in Elvis' eyes when he heard the good news! "Just what I have been wanting to do all these years," he exclaimed in delight. "And to play the South again!"

The big surprise of Elvis' first opening was never to be repeated, although it was always a hopeful subject of conjecture by the press who came from far and near —and at M.G.M.'s bidding—to exploit the filming of the Elvis Special. A mysterious message was whispered in several ears on that initial opening that Elvis would hold a press conference as soon as he had showered and dressed.

The metropolitan press, had they known, would have flown in immediately for this unexpected bonanza after all of these years of Elvis' unavailability. But no way could they fly in from Los Angeles, New York, or Chicago and reach Las Vegas on thirty minutes notice. As usual The Colonel had timed it to "always leave them wanting more."

The heavily security-guarded conference room found The Colonel smiling and welcoming the very few and some extraordinary press. Some represented the underground papers and some rock sheets of devious circulation. However they were press and The Colonel always said, "We treat everyone alike!"

Whispers and intents filled the room in full realization of this rare history-making occasion in which we were about to participate, asking Elvis any questions. It boggled the minds. Seated in front of me were some nondescript characters of uncertain age, who were plotting. "How'll we get a headline out of Elvis for that hundred bucks? I long distanced pronto, and the editor said, 'Ask Elvis anything that will make a scandal for a headline.' " "Ask him if he's a fag. Either way it will make a headline," agreed the other one.

To do such a thing to Elvis—who had just covered himself with glory!!! And 2000 people had given him such ovations! How could these two characters seeking sensationalism mar this big night for Elvis! As for such a question—Elvis with wall-to-wall girls all these years —and a wife and baby. How dare they? How could they be stopped? I was at my wits end to stop them! But how? Righteous indignation all but overcame me —that by Elvis' and The Colonel's generosity these two ingrates were about to make a spectacle! Then there was Elvis walking in with his father. He apologized for keeping us waiting. Whew, he had had to shower and change. There Elvis stood unprotected by any clever press agent or anyone to jump in and deal with the horrible situation that was about to take place!

One or two pleasantries were asked and then it turned hard-core. "Elvis, do you dye your hair black?" A little startled, Elvis replied, "For a movie sometimes when they want it for the lighting effects!"

Just as one of the plotters began to rise to his feet, I jumped up and began talking—which forced them to remain in their seats.

"Elvis," I said, "we are all so happy for you here tonight—your return in person after fifteen years—to see you and hear you in person! Everyone in this room is filled with pride and a deep respect and affection for you, and the fact The Colonel has given us this rare opportunity to participate in your first press

213

conference in as many years! Long may you reign as King of Rock 'n' Roll and we all want you to know we love you."

That set the trend. Who would dare to ask any inflammatory questions after that. The two in front of me slunk down in their seats, realizing well that I had overheard their nefarious scheme for headline making.

With one look at both The Colonel's and Elvis' astonished faces at such an accolade and eulogy, I turned on my heel and fairly ran out of the conference room! I couldn't take time to explain that if I didn't make that 2:30 A.M. plane back home to Los Angeles, I'd be in trouble. There was a plane strike and Jim Scagrave of one of the hotels had used all sorts of pull to get me on that last plane. I had only twenty minutes or I'd be grounded in Las Vegas. Princess, my pussycat was at home without a sitter, and I had been gone two days. Also I hadn't had time to get a check cashed and I had spent all of my money. It was a dire necessity I make that plane.

Also running for the plane at the airport was George Hamilton. After we were air-borne, George came to say hello to me, and for the first time in my life I asked for loan for taxi fare so I could get home. Readily he offered me a hundred dollar bill—I settled for a twenty and gave him my check. It had been quite a night! I doubt that Elvis ever knew nor did The Colonel, who both stood open-mouthed with amazement at my grandstand speech for Elvis, why I had done it. I heard later that closed the press conference—but good!

214

CHAPTER TWENTY-SEVEN

Elvis Presley for United States President

ELVIS' LIFE IN 1971 had settled down to become prosaic humdrum as far as any news of him was concerned. It was always the same old thing, his record sales, the mobs of girl fans, his tremendous success in Las Vegas and his P.A. tours. One night at Hugh Hefner's mansion at a party some show people were discussing Elvis. "But his image has become so dull—boring!" they were saying. "He needs some revitalization, some color. Elvis needs a clever press agent like in the days of Russell Birdwell when stars were stars!" They went on dissecting Elvis—my friend!!!

Well, I could stir up some color and excitement for Elvis I decided. I called Memphis to learn that Elvis was turning a hand-crank ice cream freezer of fresh peach ice cream. And the family were sitting around waiting to have ice cream and cake! Wow!

Then it came to me, since Elvis had nobody else pushing him in print, that it was up to me! This wouldn't be the first time I had positively brilliant ideas (I thought) to inject some glamour in Elvis' image. Why it was perfect. I'd announce and propose Elvis Presley as the no. 1 candidate for President of the United States! How about that! *Fabulous Las Vegas Magazine* cover-lined it: "Elvis for U.S. President" and since *Fabulous* was circulated in every state in the union, my Elvis presidential column brought about all sorts of reaction. When Elvis recovered from the initial shock, he laughed. But then it also started him thinking. First people raised eyebrows. Ridiculous! Elvis for President, . . . ? How could a rock 'n' roll singer from Tennessee aspire to high political office as a world power and leader of nations? Crazy—insane! "Easy,"

I affirmed. I had my stroke of genius all thought out. Even the most irate scoffers had to agree when my logic set in. And the facts; "the voting age majority in this country is under 30; Elvis is an all-time world idol; he is loved by both black and white; he is probably the only man today who can unite the North and the South; Elvis has an excellent and admirable service record; he is highly knowledgeable and interested in world affairs; Elvis has honesty, sincerity, integrity, a well-known fine character, a love for his country and fellowman; he has guts, courage, and assurance; and he is a born leader! Who else?

"Youth today rebels for the state of affairs that our presidents haven't been able to do very much about, have they?

"Why not give such a winner, a highly respected young man a chance, a try? Let youth try it! That is, if Elvis and The Colonel will consider it! At least Miss M.M. proposes it in good faith. And you can all take it from there!"

"I am also proposing it in my columns (nationally and internationally and world-wide). Let's see what happens."

The Liberals, the Conservatives, the Far-Outs and the Republicans and Democrats saw my point. They were eager to get Elvis!

With the new eighteen-year-old voters, Elvis could have his own party. In fact my brilliant idea saw Elvis being drafted and petitioned by thousands of young Americans to head "causes." "Aspire to office, man, and get voted in by the people! Help run our government!" One black said loud and clear: "Straighten things out, man, before we overthrow the system completely!"

Elvis' sudden and first visit to the White House to see President Nixon was passed over lightly; a star saying hello. Probably he was making arrangements to sing at one of President and Mrs. Nixon's socials. Or could it have been a Nixon campaign request?

It was far more, as far as Elvis was concerned. Offers to entertain at the White House had not been accepted by Colonel Parker.

I heard Colonel Parker was far less enthused with my idea. "Why Elvis would only be getting $200,000 a year to be President. Shucks, that was chicken feed Elvis could pick up in a night!"

Elvis' visit with President Nixon had far more significance than idle conjecture. Elvis had told me when I first began interviewing him back in 1957 and we became good friends, "I'd like more than anything else to visit the White House some day and meet the President of the United States." Modest and actually shy in person, Elvis never made such a request. "That would be a great honor," he'd said wistfully—not quite believing it would happen. Now Elvis was not only invited—he was sent for to discuss urgent needs of tremendous national importance—and to ask Elvis' ideas of promoting "the blending and knowledge in today's living and political views of today's young!"

Since then Elvis has taken quite an interest in the affairs of our country. Hadn't Elvis left his career for his service hitch in Germany and acquitted himself with distinction and honor! He had refused to take the easy way as an entertainer. He dug in as a buck private, shed his duck-tail hair style for a regular army butch and asked no favors. The people had recognized the patriotic, serious vein of Elvis Presley's character. He was far more than "Sir Swivel Hips" who took chorus girls home to Graceland. Gubernatorial election ballots and presidential ballots often found Elvis' name written in.

Ever since Elvis had moved into Graceland almost twenty years ago, young people have been gathering at the big iron gates in the hope of seeing the King of Rock 'n' Roll. When Elvis is in residence, they do. Elvis began spending longer hours at the gates, answering questions for his views about today's problems— our government and our American way of life.

The complexion of gate talk in the early sixties had changed by the early seventies to the mood of anger and frustration which was behind much of the activism

217

and violence of students on college campuses. They expressed it openly to Elvis. The blacks, the welfare poor, and the minorities, moved by a feeling of terrible frustration, declaring the "system" being what stands in the way and must be destroyed, is what they talked about with Elvis—instead of getting his autograph!

"There's got to be a way to make this country better," they'd say. "How can we get anywhere with the corrupt systems we have?" To the blacks, Elvis Presley is an idol—a poor white who sings black-blues—their music—one of them who has made it big. Elvis can be heard—will he be their voice?

Elvis found himself in the role of moderator and pacifier. But above all, Elvis honestly levels as he sees it with the truth! Standing talking to Elvis Presley became a sounding board of the real thinking of people in saner moments, when they were not caught up in the hysteria of mob marching, revolution, and violence.

"Justice and safety are the basic goals of any society," Elvis told a Black Panther group. "Hang on for justice man! Violence gets you no place."

Elvis' ability to speak out won him rounds of applause and brought the attention of Tennessee politicians to his real worth. No one else in a decade has influenced youth as has Elvis Presley, the entertainer. Today, as the thinking, deeply patriotic man—his worth in world affairs, they realized with a jolt, can be powerful.

"You've got to sit down and evaluate yourself as a person. Up to the marijuana thing, most of us have gone along as is. I've never taken the drug scene. I don't need it. Look around man and see what happens to those strung out on dope. It's a mighty bad scene.

"A lot of our lives have the ups and downs—one way or another. But don't go against the law. It's our only hope. Work to make better laws. This is a free country man—your country. You can!"

Elvis is conservative establishment. "I believe in law and order man. Any way I can help my country, I'm right here to do so."

"My mama," Elvis had told me, a little embarrassed,

when she was still living, "thinks maybe someday I can become president!" Elvis laughed with self-conscious shyness at the remote possibility of such a thought. "You know how mothers are," he'd qualified, "How they can believe in a son. I tell her, 'Mama, that is one thing I can't give you.' I try to make it up to her and give her everything else."

Fifteen years later however, the possibility of Elvis becoming President of our country became a real possibility. Who else can talk to the young who are besieged with anger and emotional violence, who have tried to destroy the system with campus outbreaks, burning, murder, and destruction? Who else would they listen to?

"Politicians in both parties are seeking leaders," I wrote. "A new leader who has the confidence of the young, new, eighteen-year-old voters! And those who are so against the establishment expressing themselves in draft card burning, war moratorium rallies, and actual revolution. Many who are determined to overthrow the United States democracy."

"These are the people who will listen to Elvis Presley! Elvis has already been quietly approached by various delegations at Graceland, seeking his consent to name him on the 1972 presidential ballot. Some Republicans would like Elvis as running mate for Nixon. Some Democrats would like him to run with Los Angeles Mayor Samuel Yorty!" So I persisted.

Elvis began evaluating, while Priscilla became frightened at the idea of Elvis facing the hazards and dangers that beset all public political world leaders today. "I don't want Elvis to be a martyr," Priscilla said, with tears of worry and even fright.

"Our government is worth saving," Elvis said. "This is the greatest country in the world today."

The idea of Elvis for President I had first propounded, publicly, declaring Elvis was the natural leader for today's young in the U.S. brought cries of "What, Elvis for President? Ridiculous!" Second thoughting, now everyone agreed!

Priscilla reading it, was at first very proud! Then a realistic reaction set in and she wept. "I don't want to lose you Elvis. You'd be exposing yourself to such danger!" Elvis comforted her. "Don't worry. There is nothing to worry about." Elvis was appearing again at the International Hotel in Las Vegas. Priscilla was with him. She'd left Lisa Marie at their Bel Air home tightly security-guarded.

Priscilla was mindful of the murders of President Kennedy and then his brother Robert Kennedy. She became almost hysterically fearful for Elvis.

"Elvis, please don't go into politics. Please for our sake, for the sake of our Lisa Marie and your family. I couldn't stand it if anything happened to you. It's such a risk campaigning in mobs of people. I'd be so afraid for you!"

Elvis reassured Priscilla—but the realization, the need, and how, and what he could do to help his country stayed and silently grew in his mind.

Elvis had long ago reached the point where money doesn't mean much. It has already bought and furnished him and his loved ones with everything they need and their hearts could desire. And still, in spite of the big homes and arrays of custom cars, the Presleys have remained simple folk.

When you have been and are staying securely at the top, breaking all records of your nearest would-be competitors as Elvis has done, and you have his drive and strength plus his innate goodness and concern to reach out and do something for humanity—and you want to pay back your own blessings—maybe this is the way.

"I've been reading the biographies of the Presidents and the governors and the history of our country," Elvis told me. "I find them very interesting. My one regret is that I didn't go to college during the time I was in Hollywood making so many pictures—and get a good solid education. It seemed improbable then, because I didn't want to disturb or disrupt classes. But I've been getting an education on my own, by reading."

Elvis realized the full seriousness of affairs in our

country when it hit home, not as newspaper headlines, but when there were open kidnapping threats to the safety of his child and family. He visited the local sheriffs in Memphis and Los Angeles and the police departments. He was given means of protection and made a deputy sheriff. (He has collected deputy sheriff badges, and he is a card carrying member of several district attorney's offices.) He takes his citizenship seriously. Elvis was named and awarded the honor of being one of the "Ten Most Outstanding Men in the Country" by the U.S. Chamber of Commerce. Elvis, who rarely shows up for awards, showed for this one. Among the ten were young statesmen, including a senator of the United States and the President's appointment secretary.

Elvis' character is impeccable. He would win the votes of the older people as well as the young, agreed the politicians. Elvis at this time was 37 years of age— a man in his prime. He is still the idol of the teenagers who have newly acquired the right to vote. According to the census, two-thirds of the people in this country are between the ages of eighteen and thirty-five years of age.

Will Elvis one day consent for his name to be placed on the ballot?

Elvis made it clear. He will not be dictated to by any political machine. He is aware of graft in politics, and he refuses to be a part of it—"robbing the poor. My daddy was on welfare; we were dirt poor when I was a kid. I'd like to help this wonderful country restore the peace and to live and let live. If it were any sacrifice on my part but I knew I could really help— man, I'm for it."

This may come as a surprise to some of Elvis' rock fans—especially the revolutionaries. One of the "gatees" at Graceland asked Elvis: "Do you really think our society is worth saving?" Elvis replied, "You can believe it is man." Elvis has a convincing discourse which is as highly patriotic as Abraham Lincoln's. In fact, he quotes Lincoln often from some of the great martyred President's speeches which Elvis has read.

221

In a less violent world, any young woman with Priscilla's beauty and refinement would be excited at the thought of being First Lady of Tennessee and living in the Governor's Mansion. Or being the wife of the President of the United States. But today, where people's homes are virtually iron-barred arsenals for protection, where the streets are not safe from muggers—the young are pessimistic, brooding on a dire and deeply pessimistic future. Priscilla begged Elvis to stay out of politics.

Elvis' current swing around the country for the past few years in concert, seeing it as it is—is the reason he gave that he and Priscilla hadn't had another baby. "It could happen any time, but I don't think it would be fair to her with me being gone away so much now."

Elvis' final decision not to make a motion picture that has been scheduled for him six months before in Hollywood, instead to continue P.A.—was to get the real flavor and feelings and moods of the people. Many people carried placards, "Elvis for President 1972." His tour kick-off was Buffalo and included Knoxville, Tenn., University of Tennessee, Neland Stadium, Little Rock, Ark.; Hampton Roads, Va.; Richmond, Va.; Roanoke, Va.; Indianapolis, Ind.; Charlotte, N.C.; Greensboro, N.C.; Macon, Ga.; Jacksonville, Fla.; and San Antonio, Texas. Hundreds of thousands of cheering people of all ages turned out to see him.

Elvis' appeal to all ages registered in Texas, where an eight-year-old child with terminal cancer begged to see her idol in person. Elvis sang a special song to her. His infinite caring and his deeply emotionally loving and instant involvement impressed officials even more.

One night in Charlotte, North Carolina, Elvis spoke to a large group of young blacks who'd waited for him. "Man help us," they begged. "Help us change this lousy world!" To their surprise, Elvis responded with a largeness of view rather than any provincial narrowness—to include them all. "We must remember we Americans are not a chosen people, even though we have been raised to believe we are. Our history books tell us we are. But we are all human, just like anyone else. And we will not be spared any terrible retributions for wrongs we commit on others. I don't believe, in spite of some wrongs in some specific cases, that on the whole Americans are guilty people. We are naive, honest, genial, innovative, and sometimes we blunder, but we so believe in our heritage in this country and human rights that when someone blunders—we can't believe it.

"We have such high ideals. We've all been raised on idealism and when the system goes wrong at times, we feel bruised and hurt, and some of us march and protest. Violence is no answer. That's been well proven. It gets you nowhere."

"Here we have men on the moon and they were almost ignored for some bedlam on earth. It takes great men of courage to go to the moon. It takes adventuresome people to reach outer space. That's where it is—our future today."

Jane Fonda and Kathleen Kennedy, the twenty-year-old daughter of the late Senator Robert Kennedy, avidly in politics, each said they would like Elvis to join them. Many causes sought Elvis.

Elvis fans—the very young and the middle young and those who've grown up with Elvis—are the millions who turned out 35,000 to 100,000 strong a night to see and hear him. They can, no one can deny, make him the great new power, the voice and the leader of our country.

Elvis may long consider what he will do; and if he will accept such an awesome national burden on his capable, strong shoulders. My plea "Elvis for President" was only the beginning.

CHAPTER TWENTY-EIGHT

Elvis Sued on Paternity Charge by Waitress

THE TURN-ON FOR "Elvis for President" was not only considerably dampened, but turned off, when a waitress by the name of Patricia Parker (no relation to The Colonel) filed a paternity suit against Elvis Presley! She claimed him to be the father of her unborn child.

The suit was filed August 21, 1970, by a highly credible and noted attorney, Paul Caruso, in Los Angeles Superior Court. The twenty-one-year-old waitress alleged that on an opening night on a specified date in Las Vegas, Elvis had made her pregnant. The specified opening night found fourteen members of Elvis' family and his wife, Priscilla along with noted stars from Hollywood at ringside. After the show Elvis had entertained them all in his special suite at the hotel. Where could Elvis possibly have had a dalliance with the Parker girl on such a night?

Elvis was so shook up when he first heard the news of the law suit and was shown a picture of himself with the girl, he gasped, "How could she do this to me? Sure I pose with a fan like this when one catches up with me. My fans have always been wonderful, but this one I've never seen. I don't remember her!" Indignantly he added, "I am innocent and will fight this to the last ditch!"

Filled with indignation, Elvis grabbed a plane to Memphis to confront Priscilla and his father with the news before they read it in the papers. He called them and told them he'd be there in a matter of a few hours and to get together and wait for him.

Rushing into the house, he told Priscilla and Vernon what had happened. He declared his indignation and his innocence. Elvis has always been truthful. They knew he was telling them the truth. The Presleys stood strongly behind Elvis' decision to fight the charges. It could have been so easy for The Colonel to have paid the girl and kept it hushed. But no—Elvis said he was innocent and it would be blackmail. He'd fight for the truth!

Elvis had been warned many times by The Colonel not to pose or talk to the girl fans at the gate and not to permit them to take pictures with him. But Elvis believed in his fans. He loved his fans. Not one would ever think of harming him. But there it was, the official papers stating the plaintiff Miss Parker expected her child to be born during the latter part of September, 1970. She didn't have sufficient funds to support nor maintain the child, and she asked for support and all bills for the child and for the defendant to be declared the father. It further asked that the defendant be restrained from annoying or beating or harming her.

This was curious, for Elvis, when he first came to Hollywood, read a script where he was to slap a girl. "I can't do that sir," he told the director. "I would never strike a woman." He was surprised how Hollywood used tricks to make it appear like a slap when it was not. Either way, Elvis would not be any part to slapping a woman. But here he was being charged.

The highly credible attorney, Mr. Caruso, believed the girl's story while almost everyone else believed it was either blackmail or imagined fantasy. Hollywood was surprised it had not happened to Elvis before. Being a screen idol, it was the name of the game. Clark Gable, Cary Grant, almost all idols were sued on such a charge at one time or another. Most of the time after the court action, it would be discovered the accuser had mistaken the identity of the man, that it wasn't the screen idol at all. But there was Miss Parker with a snapshot with Elvis.

Elvis was indignant and dismayed in turn. How could a fan betray him with such a false accusation, and who was the girl?

It was finally learned that Miss Parker was a Presley fan who had managed to get her picture snapped with

Elvis when a group of fans had been waiting for him. They'd all stood around outside the hotel and when he came out their cameras went into action. It was said the rest of the group had been cut off, so it looked like Elvis and Miss Parker alone. There are always people around celebrities who are trying to figure ways to persuade them to give up money. Now it was even more understandable why the Memphis Mafia was brought back to be with Elvis wherever he went—for protection!

Lotta Von Strahl, a handwriting expert, who works with the department of parapsychology at U.C.L.A., examined the Parker woman's handwriting. "My oh, what an imagination this woman has. And what a great ego. Her "P" is written to show she thinks high in the clouds. She has psychological problems. She was very nervous writing her name as it shows on the complaint."

Examining Elvis' handwriting the noted lady said, "Elvis has a very good sense of humor. He can be aggressive but not in a personal way. He is completely objective. His handwriting shows that if it is a matter of business or career he can be aggressive, but not for himself as a person. He is outgoing. He observes, and he holds back much. He is extremely sensitive and he does not place his affection easily. While he is shy, he is full of ideas and he is very creative. His "P" goes up which shows his ambition is not enormous but healthy. His letters show that he loves people, but can completely pull himself back from them. His moods vary from high spirits to low depressions. He can be very critical, but he is not calculating. He has no big ego. If he gets upset he crawls back into his shell. When he gets angry he gets furious. He can let off plenty of steam. Watch out! But it's soon over. He has intuitive feelings and there are few people he knows he can trust. When he is hurt he says "to hell with it," and hibernates. He is a child of his surroundings and he has learned to adapt marvelously. I wish he would build a bigger ego with which to fight what is going on in the world about him. Elvis is one hundred percent male. She has to be someone very special to attract him physically. That person is very rare. He has a high sense of humor and he always wants to do the right thing."

Elvis reiterated, "How can anyone do this to me? I am completely innocent. I will fight it to the last ditch."

The worry and the cloud of this suit hanging over him caused Elvis concern. The questions of it went round and round in his mind.

Elvis' shows continued as a smash success in Las Vegas—breaking his previous records which had already broken all records in show business. Little public importance was evidenced in the suit. Even the news media surprisingly forgot it or ignored it or buried the item—as a fantasy of a fan. Such was the Elvis charisma—The knight in shining armor!

There were four people in this world Elvis knew he could count on forever: Priscilla, Lisa Marie, his father, Vernon, and his grandmother, Minnie Presley! Yet even one of those he trusted and loved the most— was to turn from him.

CHAPTER TWENTY-NINE

My Forbidden Words and Picture with Elvis

ELVIS LOOKED EVERY inch the royal King in his black fur suit with the 18-karat gold buttons, his white silk shirt ruffled at the cuffs and neck and his diamond rings flashing. More was his stance, head high, body lithe with a careless grace, and there was a ready smile on his lips. Elvis had come a long way in these twenty-one years since he had been acclaimed King of the pop world at the start. He still stood head and shoulders above his nearest contender, England's Tom Jones.

The English singer said it louder than all the rock stars, that he was Elvis' biggest fan and never expected to even come close to Elvis' enviable record. Several times the two had spent considerable time discussing a movie that Tom was anxious to make. Elvis was still playing around with the idea of going into motion picture production. Tom was eager to be his first star. Elvis' annual income was now reportedly a soaring five or six million a year, and it had been for many years. He could well afford to make movies or do anything else he chose. But movie-making was business and business remained as always, in control and by decision of The Colonel.

Elvis by now had lost track of his gold records. They were reported to be over a 100 or just under. Others said the correct number was sixty-one gold records and then there were his gold albums. With the release, in 1974, of some of his early unreleased Sun Records on R.C.A. label, they jumped to the top of the charts. Elvis' youthful singing still had the volume pull, while today's have unequaled special musical arrangements, agree the music critics.

There had been good times and there had been the year previous, when Elvis had been panned by the critics for giving an indifferent performance. The trades and some critics "murdered" Elvis' annual Summer Festival Show in Las Vegas. "He's forty pounds overweight; unenthusiastically he belts out his songs in a bored fashion. He's coasting on his past mystique of sexuality which has paled. Elvis has become a parody of what he was." Elvis had never experienced such vicious harsh reviews in his twenty years! One report said "The King is Dead!" A few nights later, Elvis had visibly trimmed down—by not eating at all. He had pulled himself together. He was with it, proving the King was far from dead! Injecting some gutsy vigor into his show, Elvis, heart-sick and staving off pneumonia, was fighting to hold on to his crown.

His divorce from Priscilla earlier that year had shook him up and depressed him. Illness had put him in the hospital. There had been that paternity suit still pending. Elvis hibernated at Graceland, under doctors' orders, after two days stay in the hospital. He didn't look well. His career—was it over? "No, not at all," said The Colonel. "Why son, you're just getting started. We've got great plans!"

Linda Thompson, the shapely 1972 Miss Tennessee, and Elvis wore identical his and her custom tailored suits—which set off marriage rumors. She was a visitor at Graceland and in Las Vegas as well as Elvis' bachelor home in Holmby Hills. Then other girls were seen with Elvis in Las Vegas and the gossips became confused. Elvis himself said he had no marriage plans. His heart was getting over his first, slowly.

The sun was shining down brightly again on Memphis' favorite son when Elvis opened his early fall engagement in Las Vegas at the International. Bouncy with zest and high spirits, Elvis was again in the pink. The critics reacted accordingly and sang his praises. "His voice was never better. Elvis is still the King!" As usual, no matter the critics, The Colonel was turning down million dollar offers from all parts of the world. "When we feel we can use a million, we'll let you know," was The Colonel's reply to Australia, England, Germany, France, Japan, and Canada. The wire services duly reported these turn-downs in the news media. Capital cities continued offers, "Elvis can't possibly refuse." And refuse The Colonel did!

It was said Elvis might have played England, but his musicians would not be allowed to back him, because of unions and English law. The thought was abandoned in the making.

The logistics of the phenomenal outdoor rock concert held at the racetrack in Ontario, California, with a 200,000 turnout in April, 1974, inspired rock promoters to try anew for an Elvis concert. "Man, if 200,000 people would turn out for lesser rock stars, how many would come out to hear Elvis! A million at least!" The Colonel was not of a mind, he replied, at the present time. Elvis was booked a year in advance to play the larger forums across the country. But Ontario's was no Woodstock. It was orderly, carefully planned, and well managed, came the plea of the promoters. The Colonel just smiled. "We'll let it pass for the time being. What would Elvis do with more millions?"

Having attended four of Elvis' big opening nights in Las Vegas by invitation, I was a bit amiss in my schedule and didn't make the present one at the Hilton International until I found myself unexpectedly in Las Vegas for a weekend. It was opportune to catch Elvis' midnight show. No one knew I'd be there. It would be great fun to be a paid admission and observe, I thought.

A lady at the next table, as we waited those first few minutes for the lights to dim and the orchestra to boom forth with a stirring Elvis medley, on recognizing me said she was from Hawaii. She'd seen Elvis' show for the last three successive nights! "He's glorious! I became an Elvis fan when I was twelve. I save my money as a waitress to come to hear Elvis here every fall."

Elvis fans usually stop to talk about Elvis. "Look around," observed another. "There are those white-haired mothers, the teeny-boppers as well as we fans who have grown up with Elvis. We are all still loyal, not to mention all of the new Elvis fans! Some are married and have children and are in their late thirties or their forties who dig Elvis. Elvis is loved by all ages."

A fan letter in my purse summed up "Elvisitis" well. It read:

I was sixteen when Elvis began to blaze his trail over night to the very top. I was crazy over Elvis, like all the kids of our generation. We had Elvis Presley block fan clubs in every neighborhood in town. Our time was filled with Elvis' record sessions, with earning money to buy Elvis shirts, hats, jewelry, and blouses, with calling radio stations and badgering them if they didn't play an Elvis record at least 100 times a day. Some stations did as much as 179 times in one day. We were all writing to our Elvis—from whom we never expected a reply, nor did we receive any.

Somehow we managed those long treks when he appeared on the Sullivan show, Sinatra special, or wherever he was appearing, that we had no time to become delinquent and get into trouble.

Our boy friends, too, soon caught on, and they sported duck-tail haircuts, blue suede shoes, and tight pants with bell bottoms. We carried on in a world of Elvis Presley. Knowing that Elvis was religious, well-mannered, loved his parents, and never smoked nor drank, had a tremendous impact on our generation. We didn't cop out—we wanted to be true to the Elvis tradition!

When Elvis fans were lucky enough to catch his show, we didn't need applause cards or anything. The sheer excitement of breathing the same air as Elvis was a sustaining force that kept us all on our toes at high speed with wild applause and screams of elation! It was all so fantastic and so spontaneous.

Today, here we are, a generation later. I am thirty-five with two children, and my husband and I went to Las Vegas last week and caught Elvis Presley's show. Our boy was great, and even greater than ever. Elvis in all of these twenty years had not lost that magic that makes him so unique! Equally important is the wonderment of it all—that he has retained that sweetness of character and demeanor—which so endears him to everyone. Do you agree, Miss Mann? Every Elvis Presley fan, and there are legions all over the world, read every word you write on this super-star of stars. We read you saying that Elvis remains just as you first knew him, in demeanor, kindness, politeness, warmth, and affection, as when you first met him. This is a blessing of pure gold and a treasured asset few if any other stars possess.

If Elvis has changed in any way it is to have even greater control of his audience. Every move he makes, because it springs right from his heart, is deliberate, and a lesser personality might have distorted the power he holds over us and not know how to handle it. Elvis, right from the very beginning, was a polished showman. I can get excited just thinking of those days, and today, when we saw Elvis in person again.

Mrs. E.J.L.
Tacoma, Washington

Elvis also keeps a firm grip on the public's tastes, which keeps him still on top of the coveted box-office polls for a third decade. At forty, Elvis is gradually turning more and more to gospel singing in the rock style, with a depth of pulsating emotion that is holding audiences in the palm of his hand. He also has a whole new motion-picture audience wordwide awaiting him, which sum totals, by every indication, that the King's crown will shine in glory a third decade and a fourth as well, and probably a fifth and sixth or as long as Elvis so desires to reign.

Finally it was show time. The orchestra began the medley of Elvis' latest gold-record hits. And without further ado, Elvis was on—in great form, top voice, rich, and with wide range, filled with emotional intonations and fascinating—at times spellbinding with quick changes of pace and moods. Elvis sang, danced, executed sexy karate moves with his legs, teased, and laughed, epitomizing the sheer joy of life and that he at last was fully living it all again! His happy mood, highly contagious, embraced all of us. It was sheer delight.

After Elvis' final bow-out and the lights turned on, I received a message from Sammy Shore, the very fine comedian appearing on the first half of Elvis' show. "Come back to my dressing room and say hello," it read.

As I parted the curtains at a side exit to proceed backstage, I was stopped by two armed security guards. I showed them Sammy Shore's note and happily they waved me to proceed. At the elevator two more security guards asked for my magic pass. As I stepped out of the elevator on the second floor, two more security guards, also fully armed, stopped me. One of them, still disbelieving, led me to Mr. Shore's dressing room. At the opposite door stood an armed guard. That is Elvis Presley's personal security I was told.

Then I was with Sammy and his friends on the show, laughing and chatting, for everyone was happy and exhilarated with the wonderful night it had been. Bobby Morse, the orchestra leader, remarked, "Elvis never comes off stage after a show that he doesn't stop and shake my hand and thank me. He's the kindest and the most considerate star I've ever worked for. We've been working for a long time together." Sammy was equally enthusiastic in admiring Elvis. "Everyone on the show idolizes him," he said.

I had my little Instamatic camera in my purse, and I brought it out and took their picture. Sammy remarked that when he first worked with Elvis he'd brought his camera to a rehearsal and asked Elvis, "If I could have a picture with him for a souvenir?" The Colonel said, "No pictures!" Later on, The Colonel brought a special photographer for some stills of Elvis, and he pulled me aside and said, "You can get a picture with Elvis right now!" I did. I learned that no one gets photographed with Elvis, not anyone unless it's a piece of the action of business. Why every star appearing in Las Vegas has had their press agent call over to see if they could come backstage and get a picture taken with Elvis.

Bobby said, "Does Elvis know you're here, May?"

"No, I don't think so."

"Well, he'd certainly want to say hello to you if he knew. Everyone reads your columns on Elvis. You are his only biographer, the way it looks. I'll go next door to his dressing room and tell him you're here so he can say hello!"

Sammy returned in seconds a bit crestfallen. "The Colonel was in there with Elvis. That's strange, he never stays on after the show, but there he was. I told The Colonel you were here and he said, 'I saw her out front.' Then he turned away and I didn't get to ask Elvis."

Bobby, fortified with an extra glass of champagne, declared, "Well, Elvis has the right to know May's here. He's right through that wall, and I'll go tell him!"

The next thing I knew there was Elvis walking through the door all smiles—and with a kiss and a hug he said, "Am I glad to see you! I heard you were out front, but I didn't know you'd come backstage." Seeing my little Instamatic still in my hand, he said, "Been taking pictures?" "Yes, I just did!" Then, "Would you like to get a picture with Sammy and Bobby and me?" "Of course," Elvis smiled. Zoom, there were the four of us grinning into the camera, and the flash bulb popped and that was it. Suddenly my feminine intuition reminded me I was talking to Elvis Presley without The Colonel's clearance. Carefully, I did not ask Elvis one single question but made a sudden excuse that I had to leave. My honor system was shining very bright, so bright it was becoming overpowering and blinding me. I didn't want The Colonel to get any wrong ideas—that I had on purpose come backstage to see Elvis, which I had not.

Elvis said, "You leaving already?" "I have to," I said. "Goodnight. It was so good to see you." Elvis kissed me on the cheek with affection. Sammy and Bobby and Elvis and I were all so happy. Elvis had made it such an exciting night on stage and off. What a good friend he is, I thought, as I fairly danced back to the elevator and passed the guards who were beaming with happy smiles at my radiant mood—and so out into the night.

I was lunching at the Flamingo the following day with Bill Miller, the famed impressario who booked both the Flamingo and the International. He was responsible for signing Elvis to make his debut in Las Vegas at the International, which was no little triumph. While his contract gave Elvis a million dollars an engagement, there were always a half million more for the hotel, as well as triple business.

We were interrupted by the grim and harassed face of a hotel executive who joined us at the table. "What's wrong?" I asked cheerfully, still in my happy Elvis mood from the night before. "You look like you have lost your best friend."

The man was hesitant to tell me, but finally he did. "The Colonel called a staff meeting early at nine o'clock this morning at the International. He said that the Hotel had abrogated Elvis' contract, which has a special clause stating at no time is Elvis to see or speak to a member of the press! The Colonel blamed the publicity department of the hotel for your speaking to Elvis last night! Three men in the publicity department face losing their jobs. The Colonel said to haul Elvis' name off the marquee because he won't play tonight. His engagement is automatically canceled, since the hotel didn't live up to its contract!"

In shock, I looked at Bill Miller! What should I do! He was stunned. "That's so unfair," I exclaimed, as reaction set in. "The publicity men at the hotel didn't even know I was there! They are not to blame. If anyone is, it would have to be Elvis and me! And we are innocent, too, all we did was say hello."

"Bring me a telephone, I'm going to call Colonel Parker right now!" As I waited for my call to come through, I observed to Bill Miller, "As you can see, The Colonel runs a tight ship. I can understand if he let one person of the press get away with seeing Elvis, then he would soon lose control of his no-interview policy. Obviously, he thought I had planned this to see Elvis, when I had no idea I was going to see Elvis at all."

The Colonel was as hard to reach. I wondered if Elvis were being reprimanded about his part in just saying hello to a friend, when that friend is also a member of the press!

Tom Diskin returned my call for The Colonel. When I explained everything to Tom, he said, "Well, don't worry, now that we understand, I am sure everything will be worked out."

"I want to be assured those innocent publicity men at the hotel will not lose their jobs," I countered. I was assured that the matter would be looked into and hopefully remedied.

235

To be certain, I sent The Colonel a letter immediately. It was a long one, three pages, single-spaced. The essentials were:

Dear Colonel Parker:

Since you and Elvis are and have been dear friends for all of these years, I want to clarify my saying 'hello' to Elvis after seeing his show. I did not plan it, and honestly had no idea that it would be wrong to congratulate him on his show. He was tremendous. How I enjoyed it. How everyone did. And that warmth and winning smile is the same magic that Clark Gable had. I don't know of any other. You may or may not have heard that Clark Gable gave me all of his interviews exclusively and no one else, (this meant *Life, Look,* or any publications) for years. Which Howard Strickling can substantiate. It was never a romance, but just a wonderful friendship. Clark Gable was a great gentleman as you are and as Elvis is.

I was invited backstage to see Sammy Shore as I told Tom (Diskin). There was no thought of an interview, nor was there one with Elvis. Sammy, naturally filled with enthusiasm, said it would be nice to congratulate Elvis as all of his friends do. I am a friend always. Sammy came back and said you had said no. Truthfully this really embarrassed and hurt me. At the same time, I said perhaps you had a press policy, I didn't know about at this time, for I always go backstage to congratulate friends.

In seconds Elvis came in and just as we were taking a snapshot with my unprofessional ten-dollar Instamatic of Sonny and Bobby and me, I told Elvis how I enjoyed the show and how glad I was to see him so happy enjoying the show, too, which shows. Without thinking anything wrong about it, I said, "Elvis, you want to be in this snapshot with us?" He said yes and that was all there was to it. I never asked him any

236

questions. I have always stuck to the rules with you, as you know.

Over the years I have written much on Elvis and objectively the truth. Since I have never written you a letter like this, Colonel Parker, and probably never will again, I will add that when Elvis was in Germany an irresponsible editor at Martin Goodman's took an Elvis story of mine and added 750 words of her own to my story and put them in my quotes. I not only made a trip to New York and had a big talk with the publisher but quit working for him entirely which meant a loss of $8,000 a year of my income, which was a matter of my personal integrity. I was embarrassed, for she had me saying that when I stood "next to Elvis, I went hot and cold all over and I thought of love, etc." It was so ridiculous and so embarrassing. When I saw Elvis next, I explained, and he said he realized that something had been added because he knew I wouldn't say things like that. Elvis trusts me.

I was pleased that you had invited me for the initial opening of Elvis at the International. That was nice. During the surprise press conference, someone seated in front of me was plotting a big embarrassing question to ask Elvis in order to make a headline for themselves just by the asking. I didn't know how to circumvent this, except to pop up and say something which sounded very corny, but which would set a trend and would prevent them from asking any such questions. So I said, "We all love and respect you, Elvis, and we are so proud and happy for you tonight." You may recall that. With that I walked out, as I had to catch a plane. I didn't stay for a picture, which I would have loved for my column which is so avidly followed by Elvis' fans. In fact, their mail has been a big headache in trying to handle it when it goes up as high sometimes as 5,000 a month. Then it simmers down and bounces up new again. These fans know by pictures I have had with Elvis that I know him. Thus they write constantly to ask me to write about Elvis. I have been accused of "Elvis is your pet." So I reply, since he is everyone else's pet on all polls, so he is.

I hope in the future I can ask to talk to Elvis briefly for publication. This time I did not, since I had not asked you first.

As you know, I have a deep respect and affection for you and Elvis.

With love,
May

P.S. I was pleased that you remembered I'd made you and Elvis cookies. I'll send you some first minute I get time to make some. You and Elvis are the only ones I've made cookies for. I just wanted to return your kindness in some way.

Elvis' twenty-first year in show business finds him at the pinnacle. Magazines are still covering "a new career"—"a new love for Elvis?" Girls he might marry are still being named. Million-dollar contracts are still being offered. New fan clubs are still being formed by the new generation of teeny-boppers, who are as enthusiastic as the past generation of bobby-soxers. The charisma of Elvis goes on with the assurance of long waiting and anxious new worlds to be conquered—personal appearance concert tours in Europe, Asia, South America—motion pictures with an enviable Oscar in the offing to win—

George Dareos, the noted psychic sees Elvis becoming a holy man, a religious leader. It will come about through Elvis' gospel singing. Elvis can become governor of Tennessee and bring order and brotherly love to the whites and blacks. One day the South will nominate Elvis Presley to become President of the United States.

Happy Birthdays, Elvis and The Colonel, in the years ahead—with so many ways to go!

CHAPTER THIRTY

Priscilla Leaves Elvis for Another Man

IN 1971-1972 everything seemed to go wrong for Elvis Presley—even though a lot of confidence had returned to him on being still acclaimed "King" at the box office. This was again acknowledged by Tom Jones, who admitted he had copied Elvis but never would expect to equal him. Elvis, however, was a distraught, visibly unhappy man. He had become unpredictable, even professionally, at times, cutting his shows short. He had just finished "Suspicious Minds" when some braggarts, slightly stoned, climbed up on stage and attacked him. Elvis gave one a karate kick which sent him back on a table amongst the glasses. A second who tried to drag at Elvis was head locked. Elvis was furious and offered to fight the rest who slunk off. The audience screamed, "No, Elvis!" Elvis calmed down and picked up the mike and said, "Ladies and gentlemen, I'm sorry." The audience applauded! With a grin, Elvis added, "I'm sorry I didn't break their goddamn necks!" Elvis said he was always glad to shake hands, but any who started a rough house he could quickly stop it, as he had demonstrated he well could with karate.

Everywhere Elvis played to sell outs and enthusiastic crowds. The critics used superlatives as though adjectives were all they knew. Then it happened, and Elvis suddenly began reading about himself in harsh terms, that were not quite true and which dumfounded not only him, but all Elvis-ites.

A news poll in England that Elvis had topped for years in 1967 had headlined: "New Poll Shows Elvis and Beatles both Fading." "The popularity of Elvis showed a big drop from last year. Andy Williams has

239

replaced Elvis as No. 1." That had perhaps motivated The Colonel to drop movies and return Elvis in the flesh to live audiences. The result—Elvis quickly regained his top position. Now, however, the critics were pointing to the fact that while Elvis' records were still selling in the million, he hadn't had a new hit in five years. They were all the good oldies. While the same critics who had lauded Elvis' openings in Las Vegas after so many years away making movies, suddenly turned. Wrote one, "It is obvious that Elvis Presley can't be a leader forever. Elvis set the trend and revolutionized music of the 70's which he had started with his earth shattering new rock n' roll in the 50's. That's two decades of being on top. Where is the challenge today? He has no competition. It became boring, and 'The King' shows it, to compete only with himself. Still no one else has even come close to his all-time record of gold hits. While he is still the greatest rock performer the world will ever see in this lifetime, it is sad that he can't energize the electric magnetism that he showered on his audience when he returned to show business in 1969." The worst was a simple headline: "Elvis Washed Up?"

Elvis would forget some of the words to a song. He would stop the orchestra and admit that he had in fact forgot the lyrics. Then he'd start again. Elvis was known for his remarkable memory and recall. "When he first reported to film my picture," David Weisbart the producer had said, "Elvis had memorized the entire script; his part and everyone else's. He can real a page once and it is memorized."

Later Elvis confided regarding the critics' scoldings, "I was nervous and went blank in the middle of some of my songs. I was really shaking out there on that stage. Everything was going wrong. It was awful. Our amp system was turned down by someone who had no business touching it in the first place. I just wasn't myself nor at ease at all."

"A couple of times Lisa called. That's the hardest part—her crying and asking when her daddy would be home. And me having to turn her off to rush on stage. Man, it grabbed me!"

One critic reported: "It's true, Elvis is not sparking with electric sexuality on stage!" Elvis was having behind-scene problems that no one knew about. Elvis was doing well to even appear at all. No one knew then the real reason—Priscilla had left him for another man!

Other critics reviewed Elvis. "Only 60% with it." More said, "Elvis is a big disappointment!" One said, "Elvis came on stage with his mind so far removed from his audience, that after twenty minutes, he excused himself and left. He did not return." After all the golden years, Elvis was compounding one disappointment on top of another. He was unable to hide it. It plainly showed. "Perhaps Elvis is having off nights," one critic reviewed. Then he also pointed to Elvis' newly released albums. "They also suffer from a lack of care and direction in both material and Elvis' handling of them. In spite of Elvis Presley being the most influential singer of his time, he who alone revolutionized the entire music industry, he is now alarmingly slipping! There were many audience complaints about 'Elvis' lackadasical appearance on stage.' He has to get off!" A record critic announced, "Elvis was the leader, never the follower. Today he is selecting other singers' hits, rather than his own, for his night-club audiences. While Elvis is still flashy when he gets with it, and he is still breaking all box office records, his heart is no longer in his singing. There is no longer the intensity nor the dynamics, nor the sensational accentuation beat with all sorts of sensual moves and sexuality. He is now merely going through the motions. Of course Elvis can't go on being a leader forever. He's obviously tired of his audiences." Another reported: "The real trouble, it seems, is Elvis' own interest level. He's still great, but he needs to apply himself if he wants to stay King." During all of these mishaps and press barrage, behind scenes Elvis had a fever of 104. He was going on rather than to disappoint audiences. Next only to his mother's death was the tragedy of losing his wife. Elvis, highly sensitive, was emotionally shattered. On the persistence of The Colonel who had "to save my boy—see him through this terrible ordeal—Priscilla finally flew up to Las Vegas to be with him. She cut her visit short, however, by immediately taking a plane back to Los Angeles. This was minutes before Elvis was to go on stage. Priscilla's power as Elvis' wife had never been fully recognized until now. She had never been allowed to participate in the spotlight with Elvis. She was always brought in and seated in a booth, well hidden after the lights went out. She was also escorted backstage before the finale and the lights came on. That can be very disappointing to such a beauty, rarely permitted to be shown proudly on her husband's arm but who was always shunted into the background. Colonel Parker concentrated on Elvis exclusively. That's what kept the King the world's greatest, wasn't it! His wife and family and baby were his private life and not a part of his career.

More and more kidnap threats were also frightening Elvis. With extreme worry over all of the pressures, Elvis was frantically calling home constantly for even greater security. At the same time he had to go on and do his shows. To top that, he developed a severe eye infection. While the critics, unaware of his problems, blasted him roundly.

Immediately following this engagement, Elvis, always radiant with good health, went into a hospital for eye treatment and actually also from complete collapse. He recovered after a long rest at Graceland.

Elvis was filled with remorse and was upset that he hadn't given a better show recently in Las Vegas. He was sorry that he had cut some of his shows short. He was depressed over the reviews and the rumor that he would not appear at the Las Vegas Hilton International for a long time, that his future engagements had been canceled. The rumors were incorrect, for Elvis returned as scheduled.

Priscilla was now openly seen dating her karate instructor, Hawaiian Mike Stone. The gossip shook

Elvis to his very toes. His wife was his for all time and eternity, and now the world was clued in—Priscilla had left him, not for a competing idol but for someone of far lesser stature. In his abject humiliation, "the King," "the reigning sex symbol of three decades," it took superhuman courage for Elvis to face audiences again. He didn't need the money. He plain didn't care. A man meets his responsibilities and Elvis' image was "super-man." He had no choice but to ignore the whispers and the gossip and go on with the show!

A TV Elvis special *Aloha from Hawaii* in Hawaii was sent live by satellite to the Far East countries and to Australia and New Zealand. Within twenty-four hours it was sent to twenty countries in Europe by satellite. Americans saw it later on as an NBC special.

Elvis' jumpsuits in white or pale blue and studded with jewels or metallic studs, with long sweeps of fringe or shoulder capes, were copied by all of the rock stars—who were completely unabashed to be as much like Elvis Presley as possible.

Mike Stone was reported already married, but in the process of getting a divorce. All that Elvis had dreamed and visioned of togetherness, of himself growing old with Priscilla and having more children, and someday grandchildren, had blown up in his face. Elvis was heart broken. Way down deep he clung to the hope that it was all a bad dream. Priscilla would return.

The supercharged excitement and magnetic drawing power, sustaining Elvis Presley as the super-star of stars, finally returned along with Elvis' confidence. Again the critics raved, "Elvis is incredible!" "We have seen all of his imitators and no one comes close enough to rival the real genuine diamond of rock n' roll that is Elvis Presley!" The *Hollywood Reporter,* a powerful trade paper, headlined, "Elvis Dazzles Hilton Crowds." The review reported "an irresistible lure and the Hilton's sole reason for dusting off its rarely used balcony is Elvis here for his *Summer Festival.* The star's colorful karate romp is back full force. The Presley repertoire, always a subject-to-change program, included his hits. But we missed his electric 'Suspicious Minds' and 'Polk Salad Annie.' Whatever Elvis does, or for that matter, doesn't do, has little effect on his attendance (he is by far the box office champion), his generations-spanning appeal, or the fierce loyalty of his public. Audiences will forgive Elvis anything short of not showing up."

Variety opinioned, "We do not begrudge the Beatles nor Tom Jones nor the numerous and various who have made it big, nor the lesser imitations of Elvis Presley who originated, created, pioneered, sparked and fathered rock 'n' roll—the whole new sound and concept of popular music for this generation. Today the real Elvis is back with us. He carries on with slight variations to top all music sounds!"

"The Beatles who took me along with them on a horrendous night at Hollywood Bowl," I wrote in my show-business column, "when they first appeared in America, and by their fans pulling on me, and Ringo not letting go of my hand and trying to get me inside the door—I was all but pulled to pieces. So their popularity at its height is well cemented in my mind. Then those crowds greeting Tom Jones, and the Stones— had it been Elvis, they'd have had to call out the police department and the fire department and drop Mr. Presley on stage by helicopter. How about that, Colonel Parker? Ambitious managers have studied and aped the colossal management of The Colonel to make millions, I'll agree, but the records show clearly that Elvis remains the King of them all—and right at the top!"

RCA's release of a four-record album in 1970, containing all fifty of Elvis Presley's million-dollar sellers, entitled "Elvis Worldwide, Fifty Gold Award Hits, Vol. 1" spoke for itself. (Who else could lay claim to fifty gold records in world history?) In researching who had even come close to Elvis' popularity, it was still the Beatles with thirty-two gold records to Elvis' fifty. Runners-up were way down the line. Name any of your greats in the music world and one discovers some have perhaps one or maybe two gold records.

Elvis had certified in the U.S. alone fifty each which sold a million copies. Couple that with fourteen gold albums. With each new release adding up more gold hits. Elvis crown as "King" seemed secure.

I congratulated Elvis, who had just concluded a twelve-city tour—all sell-outs—naming Elvis as the biggest draw in show business. Elvis smiled. He was once again more of his old self. Fans who had flown in all the way from Bad Nauheim, Germany, recalled when Elvis was stationed in the army there in 1959-60. "Elvis hasn't changed. He's still just like one of the rest of us. No swelled-big head. At first in Germany Elvis seemed afraid to come out of his house. He thought he'd be mobbed. Soon that strain passed. He was accepted by our town and he accepted us. He'd play football on a field behind his house, and he'd buy food at the local grocery. We taught him new German words every day. He still remembers them."

"One day, however, three cars with a dozen girls drove into town blowing horns and shouting, 'Where's Elvis?' As if by a prearranged signal—we all kept still until the intruders left. Yes, Elvis is still one of us. That's why we chartered a plane and came to see him."

"Burning Love" hit the top of the charts all over the world. His new single "Separate Ways" was sad, like Elvis parting with Priscilla. In the Hawaiian Islands, when asked to what he attributed his many years of success, Elvis replied, "A lot of praying." Asked about his marriage breakup, he replied, "It's pretty hard to work the two together—marriage and a career." *Elvis on Tour,* a documentary, was released in 1973 and was duly reported, "Fantastic in contributing the excitement and electricity of Elvis concerts and tours. It showed him rehearsing, on stage, traveling, and in his dressing room, his ad-libs denoting his humor." Elvis spoke directly of Lisa Marie, who was seated out front at his Long Beach, California, concert. "It's the first time she's ever seen her daddy make a complete fool of himself in front of 14,000 people," he quipped in the middle of some clowning on stage.

245

Then for Lisa he sang, "Lord You Gave Me a Mountain!" As girls screamed, "I love you Elvis," he replied, "Aw, honey, I love you, too, but there's nothing I can do about it right now." The audience loved his repartee. Once more Elvis had risen above tragedy. It was fun time in Elvisland!

CHAPTER THIRTY-ONE

Elvis Confides His Innermost Thoughts

RUMORS AND SPECULATION now had a field day with Elvis' private life after he had filed for divorce. Little Lisa Marie's love of cuddling with her daddy and mamma together as a threesome, it was reported, brought about a reconciliation with Priscilla and Elvis at Christmastime. It was a joyous homecoming at Graceland. The Presleys in Memphis, very fond of Elvis' wife, rejoiced! Alas, the rumor was just that. Elvis took Lisa back to Graceland but not Priscilla.

"There's been a lot of second-thoughting on Elvis' part over the divorce," it was said in Memphis. "In Las Vegas Elvis no doubt thought it was the only proper thing to do! But now he's back home amongst his own kind of people in Memphis, and especially at Graceland, Elvis is overnight a changed man. Close to his father, Vernon, and his step mama, Dee, who all love Priscilla, Elvis plain wished he hadn't been so hasty."

"Family and religion are a big part of the Presley's life style—for all of them. Divorce is just something that never happens in their families. Certainly Elvis didn't want it. Then how did it all come about?" That's what all of the Presleys kept asking among themselves. "Course Elvis is close-mouthed. He won't discuss it, no matter."

"Elvis has spent his whole life being bossed about in

his career," said a Presley. "Naturally when a boy grows up to become a man, he likes to do his own thinking. And when he can't do much about decisions on his career or his own life—it rankles him way down deep inside. The Colonel owns fifty percent of Elvis—but not his soul. And Elvis has a real beautiful soul—a generous one, 'that places the benefits he confers beneath his feet, as the old Southern saying goes. And the benefits he receives—which to him are not the material ones—nearest his heart."

"Elvis, being the soul of honor and decency will always keep his bargain and his word with The Colonel. No wife is going to change that. But I've seen him secretly rebel inwardly at some of the Colonel's decisions. Elvis never lets on at all about that."

"Then here is his wife Priscilla now, suddenly stepping up and taking her turn, trying to boss his private life—even giving him ultimatums. A Southern-born gentleman can't bear that, no way."

"You've got to be in the South to know how Southern men consider their women. A Southern man is head of his household. His woman is his to love, care for, and to adore. More important, she's to stay home and look out for their personal life, welfare, and well-being. This especially applies to their family."

"Priscilla these past two years began stepping out of line. Maybe she got the idea of Woman's Lib or something! She plain began disregarding what Elvis was asking her to do. She rebelled, of all times, on his birthday. Priscilla made it clear she'd lead her own life if Elvis wouldn't concede to her ways."

"We Memphis Presleys fairly consider both sides of the trouble of Elvis and Priscilla. There was Priscilla just dying to be accepted in the limelight as 'Mrs. Elvis Presley.' And there was The Colonel's astute business head, which said there was only one star in the family and that was Elvis Presley!"

"At Elvis' last opening night in Las Vegas, Priscilla flew up. She got so miffed, she stayed backstage. She wouldn't go out and take her rightful place in her usual booth. That's because it was always after the lights went out. The way she always had to sneak out there, she resented. You can't blame a pretty woman like Priscilla for wanting to go out and let folks take a good long admiring look at those pretty new dresses and the jewelry Elvis showered on her!"

"The big trouble was—Priscilla was plain lonely for attention, mainly her man's. She had been hidden away too long! Her movie offers, Elvis believed, are mostly to exploit the Elvis Presley name. Priscilla angrily refused to be sold short. In her own right, she has worked hard, studying dancing, singing, and acting—so she can become a full-fledged star. Her original idea was for her and Elvis to make a picture together. The fans would love seeing his real-life leading lady play in a movie!" The Colonel thought otherwise. Priscilla said Elvis could insist on his rights!

"This independent flare of spirit in Priscilla is what angered Elvis. He could foresee it could break up their marriage, which he didn't want to happen."

"When a wife openly opposes her husband, and he's Southern, watch out! Elvis is always accustomed to a lot of beautiful women flinging themselves at him. They don't mean much. This has happened to him for years. One of the girls had a broken-down car, so he made her a present of a new one as a means of transportation. Elvis gives a car as a gift, like I'd give an ice cream cone. With his kind of money he can. And he does. It hit the columns. Priscilla was furious."

"Now you can't go on telling Elvis what he can and cannot do. He's had that all of his life. And he's not going to take it from his young wife. That's where Priscilla made her fatal mistake with Elvis.

"Adding fuel to the fire, Priscilla went directly back to Los Angeles from Elvis' Las Vegas opening night. What did she do but stand at the door and act as ticket-taker for her karate instructor Mike Stone's exhibition match!!!"

"Of course what upset Elvis were those pictures of Priscilla with Mike Stone at karate exhibitions. Elvis had told her not to go out with him like that."

"The photographers could see if they'd wanted to

look," Priscilla had told Elvis, "that my mother and my sister were along too. Except they didn't take pictures of them. It was all just plain nothing!"

"Well you know how stubborn Elvis can be. And now here was Priscilla, equally as stubborn, declaring her rights to do as she pleased! 'I am tired of staying home as a doormat always waiting for Elvis.' "

"If Elvis would just make movies, go to Hollywood, and make do his acting chores in front of a camera, come home to her at quitting time, say six o'clock every night, and take her out even twice a week, Priscilla said she would be content. With it the way it was, No!!!!"

Elvis was booked for weeks and weeks all of the past year on concert tours. Priscilla, who wanted to accompany him, was told she could not! She had to stay home with Lisa Marie. Or was a mere wife excess baggage and in the way of a rushed schedule of one-night stands?

"If Elvis really loved me and Lisa Marie, I would be more important than any concert tours," she declared. "We don't need the money. We do need each other! I'm not asking for any more than any other wife of a husband!"

There was more than that, too. Priscilla resented the showgirls and friends who always come to pay their respects to Elvis. His hotel suites are always hospitable to all of his friends. Priscilla was always left safe back home in Holmby Hills. Elvis would call two or three times, day and night, to know that she was safe.

Except suddenly when he called, Mrs. Presley wasn't at home. Where was she? Why, she was out to see karate matches with Mr. Mike Stone, her karate instructor. "It isn't proper for her to go out with him!" Elvis was angry. His wife completely ignored his wishes.

Elvis had asked Priscilla to learn karate for self-protection. God knows the kidnaping threats that pour in on them and the threat for not only his safety, but also Priscilla's and especially their child.

Priscilla going out with Mike Stone looked like dates! Looked like an unfaithful wife.

Elvis issued an ultimatum to Priscilla! She ignored it. Elvis' manly pride demanded—there was nothing left to do, he warned her, but get a divorce! If she continued her ways, then he would get one.

She did and he did. Except Priscilla told Elvis she was now in love with another man. No matter how Elvis tried to keep this deep hurt private, it was to come out for all the world to see.

CHAPTER THIRTY-TWO

Divorce and Tears

CONTINUOUS THREATS ON his life, his wife's, and his child's made Elvis so uneasy he was now carrying a loaded .45 in his hip pocket, while closed-circuit TV guarded every door in his various homes to enable anyone to check out a visitor before pushing a button for admittance. When you are a hundred-thousand-dollar-a-night super-star you are a natural target as well of crackpots. Elvis wasn't taking any chances and the security tightened around Priscilla to become almost unbearable.

Like any loving parents, Elvis and Priscilla took movies and snapshots of Lisa Marie. On her birthday, they'd both pose lovingly with her. To insure Lisa Marie's safety Elvis never allowed photographs of her for publication. When she was present at some of his shows, he would sing a song especially to her. He would talk about her calling him on the telephone and tell how she could mimic his records. "She has her own record machine and plays it and sings my songs better than I do. She'll be up here one day, and I'll be down there listening."

Home snapshots were taken to a private printer with the guarantee than no one else would see them. Then one day it happened! A print of Elvis Presley and Priscilla and Lisa Marie appeared on a movie magazine cover. Someone reportedly couldn't resist making an extra print. It sold for three thousand dollars. Elvis then set up his own printing and developing dark room to insure the privacy he required for Lisa Marie, to protect her.

"Lisa Marie has nothing to do with my career," he said. "It's her safety that I have to think of. A picture of her isn't going to help my career or show business. My career is for everyone, by my home life and Lisa are the only things I have private for me."

Priscilla's plane trips, alone with Lisa Marie and without Elvis, brought about divorce rumors at first, then headlines: "Elvis Presleys Headed For Divorce Over Career Demands." Elvis was shaken up considerably at any thought of a rift, and took time off to take his wife for a Hawaiian vacation. Priscilla's absence however, was noted on their return and at his Houston's Astrodome Show. Seating 72,000 people, it was sold out for four shows. Priscilla was no longer at their house, and the Memphis Mafia was back in full force.

Elvis took time off again to be with Priscilla and Lisa Marie. It seemed all was well.

"Lisa means more to me than my life. She is my life," Elvis said. "I'll do everything to make her happy and to protect her." He was deeply moved, and the sincerity in his voice sprang from his heart—you could tell. He was holding his beautiful little daughter on his lap as she hugged and kissed him. Lisa is tiny—smaller than her age. At three years, she was the size of two, "Petite like her mama," Elvis smiled, "But oh so smart." Indeed Lisa was.

"I'll never exploit her or allow that. Never!" he added.

In a change of mood, Elvis, who'd just been barbered, grinned. "I'm glad they didn't want my hair this trip. I have plenty but not that much to go around."

This was the day that station wagons—two and three —were being loaded with Elvis' clothes and costumes in front of the new Holmby Hills mansion he had acquired. Priscilla was helping. The neighborhood was mystified. There were two reasons for conjecture. How could any one man have so many clothes? And, where were all of Elvis' clothes going?

Colonel Parker had gathered all of Elvis' wardrobe ("except my shoes, socks, pants, and shirt I'm sitting in," laughed Elvis) for a good cause. The cause was coming out that September. It was Elvis' new RCA Album with the title "The Touch of Gold." It would cost $25 and, according to any Elvis fan, "worth double." For it would contain an actual piece of Elvis' personal clothing, including shirts, pants, ties, scarves, even his underdrawers. This piece of Elvis in a tiny plastic bag, plus a large full color, pullout reproduction of Elvis today, was to be the album's special bonus.

Elvis is always with the new in men's fashions. His duds, most of them scarcely worn more than once or twice, were taken directly in the station wagons from Elvis' house to the cleaners. Next, they were carefully cut up for the bonus album. Some fans lamented— they would prefer to have had them not dry cleaned!

"I need new outfits. People get tired looking at me in the same old things. It's part of show business—keep moving with the new."

At Elvis' recent opening night at Lake Tahoe, he'd blazed out in a white suit, very different from the long fringe swinging gear he'd worn last season. "I guess the tailors sat up nights thinking up something new. They really got with it this time. I like these modified fringe numbers. The long sphagetti noodles kept tangling into my guitar."

Elvis' new, smart white suit, with the jacket spangled from the navel into red sunburst and the sash a part of the jacket, was glorious to see, everyone said. He came on stage with a red scarf tied around his neck— and that was soon gone with a girl grabbing it off when he reached down to kiss her at ringside. More important—Elvis looked exuberant. He was a smash hit.

His "Bridge Over Troubled Waters" and his new RCA single, "I'm Leavin'," were met with standing ovations. Priscilla and the wives of some of the boys came out to take front seats a second after dimout. You could see the flash of Priscilla's diamonds when the spotlight swung across the room.

The Tahoe Hotel said Elvis had broken all records again. They had jammed in 3,400 people a night. They could have had more, except for the Nevada fire laws which prohibited it. Elvis had a week's rest and then he opened at the Las Vegas Hilton (formerly the International) where Elvis again broke all records.

Elvis always changes his act around with each show, as the mood moves him. Sometimes "Sweet Caroline" is in the middle, sometimes at the beginning, or at the end. This creates all of the happy by-play and informality between Elvis and his Boys in the Band which fans love. No one is certain what song is next! Not even Elvis.

Elvis himself looked sharp, lean, and happy—happier than he had looked for a long time. "All's well with my family and at home."

At this time Elvis was faced with the demand for Lisa Marie!

Thousands of requests from all parts of the world asked Elvis to record an album of lullabies—interspersed with some daddy and little girl talk with his little three-year-old. Wow, and with Elvis holding Lisa Marie on the cover! What an album that would make!

"Lisa is my life—my very own," Elvis repeated. "She's all I have left that is personal and private for me. Everything else about me, and including me, is for everyone—for the fans and people who enjoy my work. But my baby—that's a different matter!"

Elvis agreed that little Lisa sings his songs right along with him. "She's learned the words from my records. She has a sweet, little baby voice—very appealing. It goes right to your heart. She'd outsell me any day." But until Lisa grows up and decides herself that she wants to sing for the public, I'll protect her as a father should. There isn't anything I wouldn't do for her. I love her completely." Elvis' eyes moistened with the sincerity and deep love he has for his little daughter with the golden hair, and the expression in her eyes, of Elvis himself.

Parading little Lisa on an album cover was out. Nor would RCA even suggest it. It was the demand of the public. No matter the wall of love and security that Elvis surrounded his child and his wife, he had not been able to shield them entirely.

Elvis is so proud of Lisa that he would love more than anything to walk her right down Beverly Boulevard in Beverly Hills for the world to see. "She's so cute in her little dresses." Lisa has a little gold ring with a tiny diamond. Her little gold lavalier on a gold chain is around her neck and a gold bracelet on her arm. Elvis would like to buy her everything he sees. He restrains himself, knowing that a little girl should enjoy babyhood with baby things, not be entered into adult life with adult tastes too soon. Now his delight was a pony and a pony cart for Lisa. The pony cart, with its lacy, fringed top and silken ropes and pink cushioning, together with the little golden-headed beauty, is a beautiful sight to see.

On rare occasions Elvis has ventured forth with Lisa sitting beside him in one of his long sleek cars. When he takes her for a ride, he doesn't stop. Any danger that could possibly threaten a child of a famous personality is always on his mind. His own enjoyment and pride of Lisa comes secondary in the thought of her well-being and security.

In Memphis, back at Graceland, Elvis couldn't resist. Lisa had just awakened from her nap. She was rosy and white and pink, pretty, pretty—her skin smelled so baby-clean, and her eyes sparkled as she walked into Elvis' study, took a tiny bow, and modeled her new pink organdy dress. Elvis swung her up in his arms and kissed her. And Lisa, truly feminine, rebuked him, "Daddy, don't mess my hair. Mama just combed it. She wants it to look nice, Daddy! Don't run your hands through it or it will get mussed!"

Elvis put her down and standing back, he took a new look at his baby. Why, already she's growing up— too fast—into a young lady. But at three years? He marvelled! "Yes," Lisa said, "Mama put a wet comb through it and she said not to muss it, Daddy." Lisa was completely serious.

Elvis and Lisa walked to the front windows and looked out at the big iron gates fronting Graceland. Hundreds of tourists were standing there hopefully, as they had done for the past sixteen years, with cameras and autograph books, hoping that Elvis would come out and say hello.

On this day, Elvis and Lisa stood looking out the window when the little girl suddenly became aware of the people standing at the gate. "Who are they, Daddy?" she asked. "Why don't they come in? Don't they want to?"

Responding to a sudden whim, Elvis lifted Lisa up into his arms and out they went to say hello at the gate. A security officer rushed forward. "No, Mr. Presley, it isn't a good idea," he warned.

Elvis smiled and proceeded down to the gate with Lisa Marie. He was so proud, he couldn't resist showing her off. Some of the people began taking snapshots and Elvis didn't object!

"What a risk, Mr. Presley!" the security guard warned him as the happy two returned to the house. "Those people, Mr. Presley, can sell those pictures and you'll be seeing Baby Lisa in newspapers and magazines all over the world."

"No," Elvis said. "Those people are my friends. They wouldn't do anything to endanger her."

"How do you know?"

"I know," Elvis said. "I know inside here in my heart!"

A call at Elvis' home found him relaxing and playing with Lisa Marie. "She's just learned 'Sweet Caroline.' I've recorded her," he said, "on tape. I tell you Lisa could run me out of business. She loves to sing," he said proudly. "She learns the words by playing my records over and over and over and then she's so proud. She says, 'Daddy, sid down. I want to sing you our latest song.' There she is singing 'Sweet Caroline.' "

The Presley family was all gathered, as they usually do on a Sunday. "We're making a freezer full of home-

255

made fresh strawberry ice cream. Excuse me. It's my turn to get the dipper to share it with Lisa."

At this time Jerry Hopkins had written a book entitled *Elvis*. "I've never met Elvis," said Jerry. "I had to talk to lots of people who worked with him. He sure is a nice guy, according to everyone. I didn't meet anyone who had anything bad or even wrong to say about Elvis. In fact everyone close to Elvis clams up. It was hard to write, but there had never been a book on Elvis. I had to do the best I could with no help. I sure would have liked to have met Elvis or The Colonel—or just seen them—or even caught a glimpse of either one. I never did!" "Always leave them guessing" had applied as usual.

Just when the world and all Elvisland was happy that Elvis' marriage had weathered a good four years, it was now discovered it wasn't working at all. In fact Priscilla told Elvis she was leaving him. She moved back to the Trousdale Estates home, leaving Elvis in nearby Holmby Hills.

Then suddenly there it was in cold print in the newspapers dated August 19, 1972. "Elvis Presley sued his wife of five years for divorce in Santa Monica Superior Court citing irreconcilable differences. Presley, thirty-seven, and his wife Priscilla, twenty-four, agreed she will have custody of the couple's four-year-old daughter Lisa. Presley said a major reason for the divorce was the pressure of his traveling six months of every year."

CHAPTER THIRTY-THREE

Elvis' Settlement Makes Priscilla
a Millionairess

ELVIS HAD BECOME a very private person who had successfully managed, as the Colonel had planned it, to let people guess but never really know what went on in his personal life. Now here it was, what he dreaded most, the intimate details of his life with Priscilla fully exposed for the whole world to read.

The property settlement, to avoid all of this, had been signed. It was only a matter of Elvis picking up a default divorce in California. Since he did not pick up the divorce, it now appeared a reconciliation was possible. Then Priscilla filed, accusing Elvis and his attorney of getting her to sign an unfair property settlement, one that gave her $100,000 and a thousand dollars monthly for herself with $500 for Lisa. Filed in Los Angeles Superior Court, she requested the court to vacate the default entered so she might "obtain a fair division of our community property together with spousal support and child support."

Priscilla said she felt she "had been led around by the nose and legally hoodwinked." In part, her petition read: "Since I was 16 years old, I've been living with my husband, his father, and other persons associated with them. During our marriage I was never involved in my husband's business or financial matters. I was never informed of my husband's income, nor the nature and amount of property which we had accumulated. My expenses were paid through an unlimited checking account upon which I wrote checks. Deposits into that account were made by my husband's business managers. Although I signed Federal Income Tax returns,

I never examined the returns and do not know what income was disclosed by them.

"My husband and I separated in February, 1972. In August 1972, my husband told me that we should agree on a division of our property."

"My husband felt the sum of $100,000 would be a proper amount for me to get. My husband also agreed to pay for furniture for my new apartment and to pay the rent for that apartment. He did not tell me how much money or other property we had. He asked me to make my decision then, and I told him that I would accept the $100,000 because I assumed it was fair. On that same day, from what our family attorney E. Gregory Hookstratten said at that time, I got the impression that he believed it was a fair and proper amount for me to receive as my share of the community property."

A few days after signing, Priscilla revealed, "I received a check for $50,000. I was told by Mr. Hookstratten that I should put the money in the bank and leave it there so that I could have it for my future needs. After that, I began receiving $750 twice a month. This money is not good enough for me to live on, and on several occasions, I called Mr. Hookstratten, asking him for money which I needed for my apartment. I called Mr. Vernon Presley, my husband's father and business manager. He would send me checks for furnishing my apartment, but such checks did not provide funds for other living expenses. My daughter and I cannot live on $1,500 a month in the style in which we lived during our marriage.

"I am attempting to arrange my affairs so that I can be gainfully occupied and yet have time to take care of our daughter. I believe I can be successful in designing and selling women's apparel, and I have gone into that business. It is essential not only that I have some money in order to get this business started but that I have enough money to dress in a manner consistent with one who is designing women's clothes.

"Had I known that I was entitled to one-half of the community property and adequate spousal support based upon my husband's income and our previous

258

style of living, I would not have signed the Property Settlement Agreement or the Marital Settlement Agreement, nor would I have permitted the default to be entered against me."

Elvis' counter petition was filed, which declared in part: "To my knowledge, the reason she permitted the default to be entered was her announced intention to me, as early as Christmas, 1971, that she wanted her freedom. She left our home at that time. At Christmas, 1971, I had already heard about her relationship with one Mike Stone, and I asked her about Mike Stone later in February, 1972. She expressed surprise that I had known about her relationship with Mike Stone and her desire to have a separation and her freedom. In mid-July, 1972, when it appeared that my wife was determined to get an immediate divorce and her freedom, I decided to discuss with her the prospects of seeking a final settlement.

"I asked my wife what she wanted. She told me that she wanted nothing; that she simply wanted her freedom; that she knew the type of person I was and fully trusted me to provide for the reasonable needs of herself and our daughter at all times. She stated to me that she wanted 'nothing,' that she did not want any part of the property, and said further, 'I know what I can do and can't do.' She said she just wanted 'to live comfortably without worrying about it.'"

"I told her that she should get a cash settlement and suggested without consultation with anyone, a cash sum of $100,000. I asked Priscilla to make a list of her needed monthly expenses for herself and Lisa. I readily agreed to her requests for $1,000 a month child support. At the same time, my lawyer, Mr. Hookstratten, explained to both Mrs. Presley and myself the procedures regarding dissolution in California, including that we could obtain a quiet no-fault divorce based on irreconcilable differences. She was advised that, in order to assure the privacy and safety of our daughter, she would assume the use of her maiden name, Beaulieu, and that if I filed for dissolution of our marriage,

259

her new name and address would not be disclosed in public. She agreed."

After the dissolution agreements had been signed, on August 15, 1972, Priscilla went to stay with karate instructor Mike Stone in Hawaii. Near the end of that year, Elvis received a phone call. "She called me to advise me that she had a quarrel with Mike. She then told me that she might want to come back to me. I told her and I cautioned her that she should not take that for granted.

"Since then, it is clear that neither Mrs. Presley nor I anticipate or desire a reconciliation. Both of us concede that irreconcilable differences have resulted in an irremediable breakdown in our marriage."

Elvis' petition denied that Priscilla "did not know the nature or value of the assets owned by me, nor that she was entitled to half of them."

Elvis declared Priscilla knew of his assets, earnings, and properties; that she signed joint income taxes with him, that they jointly purchased their California home by her wishes. He also said he was surprised at her court action, because she knew he would always take care of her needs, and she replied, "I do not want to take you. I only want to know I can live comfortably."

Presiding Judge L. J. Rittenband indicated he could find no fraud, that she said she wanted her freedom for another man and willingly agreed to the property settlement.

The Romeo and Juliet marriage of the century, the King and his Queen of Hearts, was at last dissolved with Priscilla winning a multimillion dollar settlement. This made the ex-Mrs. Presley, in her own right, a millionairess.

Elvis' ego had suffered a shattering blow, losing his wife to another man. There were always beautiful girls aplenty after him to give tea and sympathy. One whom Elvis took more seriously was Linda Thompson, Miss Tennessee of 1972. A home-town girl from Memphis, she and Elvis seemed to become inseparable after the divorce was first filed. The fact that she was often seen with Lisa Marie cemented the solidarity of their relationship. Also important, with Lisa Marie spending so much time with Elvis, Priscilla and Linda became friendly.

Other girls' names popped into print with Elvis from time to time. Then frequent marriage rumors said Linda saved Elvis from going into abject despondency over his divorce. She'd be the second Mrs. Elvis Presley.

Elvis said he loved Linda, but he did not mention engagement or marriage plans. He was impatient when Linda tired of waiting around, went out with her girl friends, for Elvis was accustomed to having "his woman" all to himself.

Linda was different from Priscilla. More sophisticated, she liked to mingle with people and be free. Declaring she loved Elvis very much, she said it meant giving up a certain amount of freedom to live his life.

To off set marriage rumors as much as possible at his San Diego (1973) concert, three limousines pulled up outside the stage door. A lone girl quietly entered one and was driven away. Bystanders and fans were not aware she was Linda Thompson, whom they expected to come out with Elvis. Later Elvis and his own henchmen walked out to the second and third limos and departed.

Elvis continued once more to be fiercely protective of his private life. While Linda confided after the first year that while she loved Elvis deeply, she now had no hopes of marriage. "I don't think Elvis will every marry again. He desperately wants more children, but his pride was badly hurt when he lost Priscilla to another man. He won't get over that hurt for a long, long time."

Elvis was more than generous with all sorts of presents. And beautiful clothes. Many look-a-like pants suits were made for Elvis and Linda by his own tailors in white, orchid, beige, black. Linda's fingers glistened with jeweled rings from Elvis—but not one was more than a friendship ring.

Scheduled to open in New York for three nights that summer, Elvis flew home from Nevada to rest in Memphis. His doctors declared his strep throat was chronic and he should take a long vacation. "How can I?" he asked. "I'm booked on tour months ahead!"

When the newness and shock that his wife had fallen in love with another man had lessened, Elvis demurred, "Perhaps I took Priscilla too much for granted. But I was working to give her and Lisa Marie everything I could. And well, I lost her. I thought it was like Mama and Daddy who were married forever to stick through thick and thin. I thought she understood.

"If I could have settled down and made a picture," Elvis pondered. But management, even though Elvis was now past thirty-eight years of age, had not agreed: it was the quick and ready money Elvis draws by personal tours. Some in Elvis' confidence said, "The day is coming when Elvis will rebel, and for the first time in his entire life, will make his own decisions, be his own free man. Elvis for too long now has inwardly felt he was a puppet on a string, who when told to dance or sing, turned on and did as he is and was told."

"Elvis has the greatest respect for Colonel Parker and follows his judgment," said another. "Anything personal Elvis wants to do or change, he does. Otherwise he goes along with The Colonel's plans which have made Elvis not only a legend in his time, but one who is constantly in demand and many times a millionaire."

"I want to breathe free air. I've been a slave too long," Elvis exploded in one of his rare mercurial moments. But those moments are rare.

With the constant crowds of fans and curious, standing at all hours in front of his house in Holmby Hills and at Graceland, with Elvis cooped up as a prisoner somewhere inside, there are always events of humor, of threat, of praise, of condemnation. Pickets have paraded in front of his Holmby Hills estate hours on end, carrying signs "Elvis Come Out!" "Don't be Afraid!" "Talk to us Elvis!" The high iron gates remain securely locked. Sonny West has a police dog trained for attack, loose inside. There's also a ferocious Great Dane for protection.

One night Elvis drove in and stepped out of his car,

to have the Great Dane, then new, mistake Elvis for an intruder. The dog leaped at Elvis' throat. If Elvis hadn't been well trained as a wrestler, to twist himself out of the dog's grasp, and deliver a well-aimed karate chop, Elvis might have been killed.

A tourist bus lolled outside the gates to scrutinize the house and grounds "where Elvis Presley lives." Someone inside the house by mistake, or perhaps even Lisa Marie or one of her playmates, pressed the gate's open button.

The gate swung wide open. A fan ran to the gate telephone. "Can we come inside and see Elvis?" Secure in the knowledge the gate was closed, a voice jokingly replied over the intercom, "Sure, sure, come right on up!"

At that, the bus pulled forward and up the drive, while an assortment of people began running up the road to the house.

Half way up, Sonny West and Lamarr Fike came running, screaming, "Get back! Go back! The dogs are loose. Run!" Everyone began running back to the gate, except the bus which had to go full circle in order to turn around.

There was much explaining at the gate by all sides. "Sorry," said Joe Esposito, "it was all a mistake."

"We're going back to Memphis," Elvis said, "to be home as much as possible. Linda gets homesick for her family there. I do for mine."

Elvis and Priscilla remained friends. Her car was often seen at Elvis' Holmby Hills house. Lisa Marie lived with Elvis five days a week to go to school. On weekends, she joined her mother.

Priscilla busied herself with her new boutique store. In partnership with a girl friend, the two opened an atelier of young swinging rags and costume jewelry.

CHAPTER THIRTY-FOUR

My Sudden Friendship with Priscilla

ELVIS GENEROUSLY CONTINUES to share his good fortune. Periodically he cleans out his wardrobe closets and drawers. Spreading out his give aways on the kitchen table, they will be costumes, suits, and assorted items he no longer uses. Elvis invites his friends to take their pick. One who'd previously worked for him happened to stop at his Holmby house one day when Elvis was "cleaning house." "I'll be in Memphis tomorrow," Elvis told him, "but you come back and I'll have a lot of things here for you." He did, and found he had acquired a full-length white velvet cape with a luxurious white fur collar, several jeweled jumpsuits, some kerchiefs with "Elvis" stamped on the corners—which Elvis gives away in his shows—plus shoes and socks. This veritable gold mine of Elvis memorabilia was scattered around among the deserving and faithful of Elvisland.

In 1973-74, Elvis went on a royal cycle in his dress, which was considered way out. He wore velvet suits of all colors, copied from pictures of royal kings of history and replete with long fur capes, boots, and even special fur hats. When Elvis made an entrance in these lavish costumes, which were not his show duds, everyone looked! On Elvis they looked great. On anyone else, it would have been as though they'd just come from out of a period costume movie.

During a show in Las Vegas, a young woman, who had painstakingly herself made Elvis a silver and turquoise ring, managed to make her way to the apron of the stage while Elvis was performing. Handing up the ring to him, Elvis stopped his song and accepted it. "I made it for you," she said. "Thank you. And you must take a ring of mine in return." Taking a sapphire from his finger, he gave it to her, and then continued his song. When she had it appraised for insurance, the Elvis ring's value was $600.

Ms. Pris Presley swung into Saks Beverly Hills parking lot, let the attendant take her Mercedes, and smiling radiantly, paused for a moment for a photographer who'd jumped out from the shrubbery popping flash bulbs.

"Let's just say I'm tired of running," she said to the photographer, who voiced his pleasure and his surprise at her cooperation. "I hope you got a good picture." Ms. Pris Presley smiled a beautiful smile. You can anticipate seeing her as a cover girl on the fashion magazines, for she's free at last to be herself, rather than living in the shadows of the man she really loved.

"No more living in an ivory tower," she told her parents, who had tried to talk her out of leaving Elvis. Imagine any girl in her right mind marrying Elvis and then not wanting to go on with it!

Elvis was conditioned to being fenced in, to stay in; always afraid to go out, with his long inbred conceptions that mobs of people would be after him! "In the beginning I accepted all of this. Then one night I wanted to window shop on Wilshire. It was springtime and a lovely night. 'Let's go to Will Wright's and have a soda?' Elvis was apprehensive. He called Joe (Esposito) and Joan (Mrs. E.) to go with us. They were out. Why couldn't we two go alone?" Priscilla persisted. Elvis discovered to his surprise and perhaps dismay that they could go out for an ice cream soda—just young marrieds and no one bothered them. No one at that late hour seemed to recognize Elvis behind the dark glasses. However, Elvis wouldn't let it become a habit. Next time Priscilla wanted ice cream out—it was the usual format—the boys went right along to protect them.

In the spring of 1974, I received a hand written invitation from Priscilla Presley. She had opened a boutique shop "Bis and Beaus" in Beverly Hills, and she was celebrating with a champagne party. Priscilla's handwriting was beautiful. While I had never met Priscilla in person, I had glimpsed her in Las Vegas and at times in Beverly Hills. I sincerely thought she was certainly one of the most beautiful girls I had ever seen. I soon observed she was also very intelligent, a perfectionist with many talents, and the drive to accomplish whatever she wants to do.

I telephoned my R.S.V.P. of acceptance. On the day of the party, having the flu, I decided it was better for me not to go. A few weeks later I called Priscilla and made a date.

Priscilla in person is even more beautiful than her photographs. She has a Dresden doll quality with a flawless complexion, a completely natural look with her fresh-scrubbed face, her large amazing blue eyes, her slight figure, and her long pale red-brown hair. If ever a girl was "the perfect dream" in appearance for a wife, Priscilla was, I thought.

"I'm a very private person," she smiled as we secluded ourselves in a back room of her shop to talk.

"I'm a good friend of Elvis, as you know," I offered. "Although I have always been completely objective about him."

"Yes I know," she replied. "Elvis and I, too, will always be good and close friends because we admire each other and we love each other."

Then why the divorce?

"I just couldn't go on the way it was any longer," she said in her lady-like voice, soft and feminine, now dropping almost to a whisper. "I had to get out and be free and do things. (In mid-1972) I finally realized that things would never change in our way of life. I had been alone too long. It was too lonely. I kept hoping our lives would be different, and then I realized it would always be this way. I had to live, too, to express myself, to have some identity as a person, as a human being. I felt caged."

Priscilla had known during those six years before their marriage Elvis' way of life. She had lived in

266

Memphis. She knew his busy life was surrounded by everyone else, with the constant demands and pressures. There was no assurance that it would change at all. "One day he showed me the ring and simply asked me to marry him. Even though we were content as we were at that time, it wasn't nice for people to live together. So we found ourselves suddenly married.

"It is not true that I wanted a career. I turned down the movie offers. I saw the demands on Elvis and I wouldn't ever want to live my life like he does. I want to do what I want to do, have freedom, and it is not possible for Elvis. That is a shame."

"I used to make all sorts of plans for birthdays and anniversaries, and sometimes Elvis could make it home, sometimes he couldn't. I grew to accept heartbreaks and disappointments, but I kept thinking, we'll make it. We're young, it will work. I adjusted in every way I could. And I'm sure Elvis did, too, but it was impossible to adjust the career which consumed him to the kind of marriage we really both wanted.

"I knew if I went on being so confined, so lonely, I'd go crazy."

"For a while I did my own cooking and housework, perhaps that would be the answer. It wasn't. I had so much inside of me—wanting to be and to do and to live. Now I can scarcely wait, after I get Lisa to school in the morning, to get out and start living. I used to go shopping, buying things endlessly, just to have some interests—something to do. All of the clothes, I'd have no place to go to wear them."

"Now I'm active, and we are making this, my business, a big success. Elvis now understands why I had to be free, to start living. I had been cloistered, pampered, protected, and confined too long."

"Elvis is happy that my business is successful. He sent flowers for our opening. He has driven by at night to see it. We respect and care for each other and we always will."

Priscilla said she was not getting married to Mike Stone or anyone else at the time. She was busy moving into the new mansion in Beverly Hills that would be her permanent home. "Elvis will naturally be coming to our home often," she smiled. "With Lisa, naturally we will always be family."

CHAPTER THIRTY-FIVE

Universal Elvis Fan Club—Money and Lives Dedicated to Elvis

ELVIS PARKED HIS white Stutz Blackhawk, lifted Lisa Marie from the front seat, and taking her tiny hand, rapidly strode into a Sunset Strip shop in Hollywood. His white shirt with ruffled sleeves, white tight pants, wide belt with expensive silver and turquoise buckle, his hair modishly cut, his sideburns wider to the face, his body slim, set off his high spirits as Elvis approached his fortieth birthday. Happy, too, was bearing in mind that all Elvisland of thousands of fans for years had been making great plans for this international event. Coupled with his twenty-first year in show business as super-star, the double celebration would again proclaim him "King, Long Live The King!"

Elvis' voice had matured glorious, strong, mellow with wide range in any key he chose. At both his 1974 engagements in Las Vegas and Lake Tahoe, the critics and reviews were pure praise. His clowning and wit on stage and on his tours bespoke his good humor, his love of life. His past two years, beset with troubles, those few bad reviews during his divorce, upsets with Priscilla, and the kidnap threats against his little Lisa Marie on her birthday, which had caused him to walk off stage after twenty minutes, had smoothed out with such problems long since solved, resolved, and abated.

Elvis walked like a free man, ready to meet the

world on its terms or his own, whichever. He had the virile strength for it either way.

Lisa Marie, now six years old, petite and a real beauty, had been staying with him for the past ten days in his California home in Holmby Hills. He was taking her to Hawaii for a vacation.

The only possible flaw no longer concerned him— the Patricia Parker paternity charge had not been finalized. There was still a third blood test pending and his deposition. Elvis, who has never been known to tell a lie, again declared: "There is no truth in it. If he was my child, I would accept full responsibility readily and gladly!" Elvis remarked, indignant on that sole matter.

Elvis fans in 1973-1974, outlined great promotional plans for The Dual Celebration, "Elvis' 40th birthday and 21st Year as King." They had spent countless hours, dollars, stationery, and postage, writing every magazine, newspaper, radio, and TV station in the world—alerting all news media to join the celebration. Even The Colonel couldn't have thought up nor masterminded a more magnanimous nor brilliant plan. Even the new ten-year-old fans wrote, "I wasn't even born when Elvis first became King! We want to know all about him from his beginning, please."

Elvis Presley fan clubs sprang up in Hong Kong, London, Sydney, Rio, Montreal, Moscow, Paris, Honolulu—beside every city in the United States from the very inception of Elvis' career. Organized, they put out fan-club journals detailing minutely Elvis' latest activities, if not his every breath. The larger ones sustain themselves with annual dues of two dollars or so, and selling copies of snapshots any fan is lucky enough to acquire of Elvis in person. A lively trading, selling, and barter, beside the dedication to the cause of always promoting Elvis is their lifeblood. The smaller Elvis fan clubs often find salary-earning jobs in offices, themselves paying the costs of printing, mail, and postage for their Elvis journals—which may be less than a hundred dollars a respective issue. The clubs celebrate Elvis' birthday with gatherings from far and near for a birthday party. A big Elvis cake with candles, the exchange of any news of Elvis, and running an Elvis movie is the theme and objective. And again Elvisland renews its allegiance to the King!

Pledges are renewed to boost Elvis record sales and write to Elvis himself without any anticipation of a reply from the king. Their letters to Elvis, which are never answered, give the dates where Elvis will next appear in concerts, urging members to attend and to voice demonstrations of their absolute loyalty. They are to save their money to insure at least once a year making the pilgrimage to Vegas, or wherever Elvis is scheduled in concert to appear in some part of the world, no matter where nor how far and remote they are—to be present to worship and renew their allegiance at Elvis' feet! Chartered plane loads of fans arrive from all parts of the world, with advance reservations for specified dates to insure their presence at an Elvis concert. Those who can afford it will have reservations for as many as six or seven continuous nights of Elvis' show. A few pay in advance for every night. The majority of Elvis' fans are in the small-salary earning groups. Some of Elvis' generation are married and their husbands pay. Today's generation of moppets beguile their parents for Elvis money.

What do they get in return? Does Elvis make personal appearances at the clubs? No, never! Does Elvis answer their letters? No, never! Is there an Elvis press agent to give them news of Elvis? No, never! Elvis has no press agent. What cooperation do they get? None. Then what inspires this continuous, rabid, loyal devotion to a star who is so inaccessible to them. It is only by sheer luck of waiting for hours, days, and even nights outside Graceland or one of his many homes in California or Hawaii that they may get a glimpse of their idol coming in or out. And if he stops to sign an autograph, they have reached the pot of gold at the end of the Elvis rainbow!

From the prexy of the long-established Blue Hawaiian fan club, who asked that her name not be given, "because I wouldn't want to capitalize on Elvis," came the explanation that motivates an Elvis fan. "It's because no one in the world is nicer to you when and if you do get to see him—even if it is only for a second." In 1974, at twenty-eight years of age, she is intelligent and pretty, employed as a secretary. She faithfully compiles and puts out an Elvis Fan Club journal four times a year. She became an Elvisite when she was addicted to his records at twelve years of age. To 1975 and continuing, she has exerted her energies and her life to promoting Elvis with his fans. "I doubt I'll ever get married. But I have no day dreams of marrying Elvis. He'd be too possessive. I like being his friend, even though I may just glimpse him at a distance, and even though I only get to say hello once in two years. The outstanding loyalty we all give Elvis is sustained for what Elvis gives back to us. Just playing his records makes you feel glad to be alive. And then on those rare occasions if you stand outside his house here or in Memphis, and for one lucky minute, he finally does come out or in through the gate, no one can be nicer and more wonderful. If he smiles, and that light in those blue, blue eyes turns on and he says 'hello,' that warmth and real sincere friendliness stays with you forever. It's his sincerity, so rare in this phoney world, that sets him so apart, beside his voice.

"Now that he's a super-star, it's hard to be friends with Elvis. He has to be guarded with ever tighter security. If people were turned loose to go to him in a crowd, they'd lose control and mob him! They'd actually kill him with love."

Some say if The Colonel didn't keep Elvis so hidden away from his fans, the fans wouldn't be so apt to go wild—crazy and try to tear him apart—when they do get a chance to see him. It's because they never get to realize that he is a person, that they go crazy over "the image." Not one fan would by intent harm a single hair on his head, but in the excitement of touching a "sudden vision," they have been known to grab his hair and pull it out by the roots as a sacred memory. That is another reason why, from the very start of

Elvis' phenomenal career he has to be covered with bodyguards constantly, and no less than six strong able-bodied men at that.

At the Las Vegas Hilton during Elvis' 1974 show, he reached down to kiss a woman leaning on the apron of the stage begging for his kiss! As he kissed her, she took a stranglehold on the expensive jeweled necklace Elvis was wearing and wouldn't let go. She pulled so hard she broke it and then ran with it. Elvis muttered, "Son-of-a-bitch," under his breath. It was his favorite birthday gift from Lisa Marie and probably cost a couple of thousand dollars. Security guards caught up with her as she tried to run out. The next night, another girl grabbed his chain and pendant, which cut deep into the back of his neck causing bleeding all over his white costume. In the hysteria, women are so carried away, they forget decent dignity and the rights of another person—going hog-wild to get a piece of Elvis to keep.

"Elvis is about the only star of the 1950's still around today at the top. That's why his twenty-one years as the King is well-worth celebrating, and all we Elvis fans are doing just that in every media we can think of around the world," the fan-club president said. "A Chinese girl from Hong Kong asked me to take over the Hawaiian Club, and I've been after it ever since. My mother sends $35 for flowers for Elvis' mother's grave each year on Elvis' birthday."

"I had been an Elvis fan for ten happy years," she wrote in "Elvis' Golden Decade 1956-1966," a small booklet with pictures. "I followed his career from the Ed Sullivan Show through the Army, and I twice visited Memphis and permanently left my home in Hawaii to be closer to Elvis. Elvis was not in Memphis, but his Uncle Travis, a younger brother of Elvis' mother, is one of the guards at the gate at Graceland. He was very kind."

When Elvis is in residence, the gate is kept closed, and at times Elvis comes down the winding road from the house and visits with the fans. When Elvis is away, the gates open and fans are admitted from

6 A.M. to 6 P.M. and they can snap pictures of the grounds. Graceland is a white Georgian colonial manor house set in the midst of fourteen acres of lawns and trees. The garages are at the left and a music and record room and pool are at the right. Elvis' den is wall to ceiling filled with trophies, awards, and his gold records. They are so many even his own record people have lost count on the certified number world wide, which by 1974 was reported to be over a hundred. Elvis' suite is upstairs and his mother's and father's suite, since her death, is occupied by his grandmother who is in charge of the house. The big kitchen with the back door steps is the favorite gathering room for everyone. The fragrance always emanating from the stove is honey as it was when Elvis' mother was alive. Uncle Travis laughs and jokes with the fans. He also tells some funnies. Many ask, "Does Elvis drink?" Uncle Travis replies, "He sure does man!" He waits for the initial shock to wear off, before adding impishly, "Elvis drinks loads of water, milk, and soda pop." Elvis had a myna bird taught to yell "help." The bird yelled "help" when Elvis was with some visitors. Perturbed, they turned to Elvis, who with a straight face replied, "Oh, I got a couple of girls tied to a tree out back, and they're yelling for help!"

Elvis was on his tractor mowing his front lawn when a tourist bus stopped. Seeing Elvis, they climbed out and right over the fence! They made a rush to reach Elvis, who just made it inside the door. Elvis who is meticulous and a hard worker, unexpectedly came home once to find the guards gone and the gates locked. He backed up and ran his car right through the gate. The gate guards never went moon lighting after that incident.

Another tourist attraction nearby is East Tupelo, where Elvis was born. The Elvis Presley Youth Center is a recreational park, a gift for the children from Elvis. Well-equipped, the building features a big dance floor, kitchen, rest rooms, lesson rooms, and outside is a children's wading pool, a swimming pool, a basketball court, and a baseball diamond. There are swings and slides and picnic tables. Elvis' old swimming hole is now stocked with fish.

The little two-room white-framed house, the Presley's first home, when they were sharecroppers and where Elvis was born, stands on a small hill as a memorial. It is locked since souvenir hunters stripped it. Today, looking through the four windows into the small two rooms, there is the front room where Elvis was born, and the back room with its kitchen table, four chairs, and an open hearth for cooking. The outhouse has been removed, and the old hand pump has been disconnected from its spring. In the little adjacent Southern towns are many relatives from both sides of Elvis' family. They consider Elvis another Presley, except he goes to Hollywood, make movies, records, and goes on tours. At home again, they insist he is still "the same unspoiled fun-loving boy, generous and kind, with a temper that can flare on occasion if justified." Most of them have their walls plastered with Elvis photos, posters and other souvenirs, which enable the family in sharing Elvisland vicariously.

Meeting Elvis, fans say he is everything they had believed him to be, except his Southern talk. "Ahm sure glad to met yoau," he says. He is unaffected, natural. Since the few fortunate who encounter Elvis face-to-face are usually struck dumb at the proximity, Elvis is known to counter with, "Hi, how are yoau?" Fans explain it, "I looked into those beautiful blue eyes, and everything I wanted to say flew out of my mind!"

Since news is not handed out on Elvis by any source, the fan-club journals work harder than any of the professional news media to pick up any tidbits of news they can get. Justifiably, they pride themselves that whatever their news is, even if it's a "yes, suh," reply, it is authentic.

Elvis at the beginning didn't "have a future" according to the critics. "Elvis the Pelvis" is a flash overnight sensation to be forgotten. Here it is twenty-one years later, and Elvis and The Colonel haven't even begun to explore Elvislands and the hundreds of personal appearance and concert offers that can keep Elvis busy for the next three decades, or for the next sixty years, when no doubt he'll celebrate his 100th birthday and his seventy-nine years in show business. Likely he will still be reigning as the King.

Will he reign alone? The outside pressures and constant demands of his fabulous career isolate him from the everyday normal millstream of meeting and getting to know people, especially the one woman he'll want to be his wife.

The question that will always bother Elvis' subconscious is: Will a woman he loves love him for himself alone, or his public image—"Elvis Presley The King." Can he find lasting happiness as "Elvis Presley the man?"

CHAPTER THIRTY-SIX

Elvis, Father of Rock 'n' Roll, Recognized Inventor-Creator-Genius of the Century

HISTORIANS OF SHOW business one day will record the just acclaim long overdue the "Presley-Parker Team," what critical writers of the fifties through surprise and dismay failed to do. Through lack of understanding of Elvis Presley's new undisciplined, sensual, wild, vibrating sounds, the critics refused to recognize the whole new era of music Presley created. Only Elvis had ushered in this distinctive new sound which catapulted world wide.

Knowing only the traditional standards set by Tin Pan Alley, and singing stars such as Sinatra, Dinah Shore, and Bing Crosby, the critics, mostly middle-aged, had not the foresight to go with it. Being from a different generation they didn't "turn on." Instead they disclaimed Elvis as either freaky or vulgar. Some were downright outraged that his sound could be called music at all. They dismissed the dynamics of the young new supercharged singer, who sparked sex shooting in all directions. The new exciting quality of his singing they saw through older eyes as a sideshow!

Elvis' alert young body's wild and showy vibrations, reacting with every word, every move, springing from his heart, readily transmitted to teenage youth. His own generation, responded with hypnotic approval. The kids swayed, stomped, and clapped! They called it "rocking and rolling with Elvis!" It caught on like an epidemic of cyclones. Even so, the staid music critics refused to take it seriously. They insisted it was all a disgusting passing fad! While overnight, rock 'n' roll flared into an international trend, hundreds of imitators bought guitars and twanged and gyrated. To be a copy of Elvis Presley became hundreds—even thousands—of new singers' goals. Some caught on to enjoy great success, but no one had ever been able to supplant or duplicate the unique style and sound of Elvis Presley himself.

From his smashing success at the International Hotel in Las Vegas, however, the critics, now twenty-one years later, declared one and all, "It looks like 'Elvis the King' will go on as uncontested champion." He had broken every attendance and box-office record of a performer in world history. In four weeks, he drew a staggering 101,500 persons at $15 per person minimum. The receipts added up to one and a half million dollars for the engagement. The million was for Elvis and The Colonel. They continue repeating this fantastic record wherever they play.

Alex Shoofey, President of the International back in 1969, asked Colonel Parker for a signed ten-year contract at one million a year for Elvis' services. The Colonel replied, "No. We don't want to be tied up that long. But I'll tell you what I'll do," he said characteristically. "Double or nothing!" Turning to Elvis, he asked, "Right, boy? You play for ten years for 20 million. If I lose, you play for ten years for free?" "Right," Elvis readily agreed. Mr. Shoofey refused to take the gamble, while Elvis garners a million for his four weeks each year as long as The Colonel will sign Elvis to appear.

Elvis as the star and The Colonel as the manager don't need to point to the more than 350-million Elvis records sold worldwide. No singing sensation, including those inspired by Elvis, who took up his sound to become rock 'n' roll kings—the Beatles, Rolling Stones, Tom Jones, and a hundred or more lesser names on the charts, have even come close.

Elvis, the father of rock 'n' Roll with its subsidiary antics, the twist, watusi, frug, and the whole range of today sounds and movements that have emerged as ever improvising versions of Elvis' first concepts, is still the idol. He is the most popular with the teens, pre-teens, and those in Elvis' own age bracket, stemming from three generations and three decades. His music is now acclaimed as a healthy emotional outlet and release for preadolescents.

Now, twenty years later, when Elvis and I discussed the initial persecution he had experienced in introducing his music, he smiled. "They did make quite a fuss when I started. Now everyone understands it, all ages. I guess new things are always controversial until people understand them. I always said I played the way I felt inside. That's how all of the kids react. And now the grown-ups do."

Simply bursting with pride and excitement for Elvis' phenomenal success, it suddenly hit me: the amazing truth!

"Without a doubt, your creation and contribution to your generation of rock 'n' roll music, which has engaged the whole world, will establish Elvis Presley with the same acclaim as the world's acknowledged pioneer geniuses and contributors of this generation. As the Father of Rock 'n' Roll,' you have to be acclaimed and go down in history right along with Edward Teller, father of the H-Bomb; Enrico Fermi, father of the A-bomb; John Steinbeck, Nobel Prize winner for literature; Pope John III, winner of the Balzan Peace Prize; Samuel Eliot Morison, American historian; John Glenn, astronaut; Neil Armstrong, who first set foot on the moon; Dr. Jonas Salk, scientist—all outstanding pioneers who have contributed 'their thing' to benefit the human race and mankind!"

By his eyes, Elvis was disbelieving, and his brows arched with a slight frown. "You aren't serious," he said.

"Oh don't be so modest Elvis," I countered. "The honor is long overdue. When an entire world embraced rock 'n' roll, your own original invention, how can you ask? It is there. It has to be recognized in world history for the impact it made—is still making! You know I'm right!"

Elvis silently digested this new phase of being Elvis, then with a smile he said, "Thank you for thinking so." He really didn't believe me or it.

"Facts are facts," I said. "And when historical encyclopedias of your decades are written, they have to include Elvis Presley "The Father of Rock 'n Roll" —the music which captured the whole world!!!"

Since early in the sixties, Elvis' name has been written on ballots for President of the United States. By 1975, it's been generally conceded that "Elvis Presley for President" was not offbeat at all. Elvis is a national idol with an impeccable character of honesty, integrity, guts, and leadership. Born in the heart of the cotton country, Tupelo, Mississippi, not far from Memphis, Tennessee, he is loved by both the black and the whites. They understand his blending of gospel, blues, and country music which is the sound of rock 'n' roll. The majority voting age in this country is under 30. Those who have again and again urged Elvis to run for President, say he could do no worse and hopefully much better than many recent presidents for his country.

I introduced the facts in my column first in Las Vegas and again in 1974, in a national magazine. Both times it was cover featured, "Elvis for President." At first glance it was greeted with astonishment and dismissed with a laugh. However, I pinpointed fact by fact why Elvis could be elected President and without a political machine. Facing such facts, people agreed. My columns were reprinted in the nation's press with varied comments. No one thanked me for my enterprising enthusiasm, except Elvis.

Elvis and The Colonel disclaimed any political ambitions. Elvis said, "I'm an entertainer. That's all I want to be." While The Colonel, with his built-in adding-machine-mind, calculated how many million it would cost Elvis if he laid aside his career to enter the White House. "Politics are not for us," said The Colonel.

What The Colonel says goes with Elvis. However, by 1972, Elvis was giving more heed to the call of U.S. youth to make him governor of Tennessee. A paternity suit and a divorce that hit Elvis at this most inopportune time dismissed any further political talk. The time was not right. It was still in the future.

Colonel Tom Parker is the commander-in-chief of the Presley mint. The coin is still split down the line—25 percent for The Colonel and 75 percent for Elvis. Ten percent off the top goes for an agent. The Colonel takes his and insists he still puts at least half of his take back into the business side for advertising and exploitation.

Strangely, with publicity considered a necessary fifty percent of any phase of show business, The Colonel has no budget for it nor any press agent for Elvis. Instead he still continues rigid control with his "Garbo Technique"—no interviews, no press to interview Elvis.

"I don't believe in over-exposure," repeats The Colonel. Almost no interviews have ever been given by Elvis. His motion picture sets were always closed. When he appears in nightclub engagements, the press can sit out front like any other ticket buyer and see Elvis perform. No one is allowed backstage to talk to Elvis. This peculiar form of non-exploitation evidently pays off. The Colonel's attitude continues, "Always leave them wanting more."

In recent years, The Colonel himself has also adopted the policy of no interviews, no information. When I managed to catch up with The Colonel, who is as difficult to reach as Elvis himself, I again asked if he would recall his days bally-hooing Hadacol? "Never heard of it," replied The Colonel blandly. "But I've heard from good sources that you were the big medicine man who went on tour in a caravan with a host of country singers to attract the people's attention," I insisted. "All I want to ask, is it true that drugstores which stocked Hadacol had to obtain a liquor license to sell it?"

"I'll tell you something," responded the cagey Colonel. "The first thing to learn about advertising and publicity is to never tell the truth. Always keep people guessing. I never heard of Hadacol," he winked and walked away.

Since 1957, The Colonel has been writing that often referred to book on Elvis Presley. The book is staggeringly unique according to any literary standards, for The Colonel sells pages of advertising in it. Hal Wallis, the producer of several Elvis Presley films, was asked to buy a page ad at $2,500 to appear in the book. He did. Several film moguls paid the requested fee. When it seemed the book was not progressing fast enough for a publication date, several writers approached The Colonel's office or sent letters offering to ghost the book for The Colonel. To their astonishment, and with true Colonel Parkerism, he sent word that any writers who wanted to write a chapter in his book could bid on it. "The one who pays the most money to write it, gets it." The offers cooled. To date, the book is still in he process of collecting more ads. Or is it a way to keep other people from engineering the hope of writing the "Elvis and The Colonel" epic.

It was in 1956, when I was the featured columnist on the *New York Herald Tribune,* during an interview with Hal Wallis, who first signed Elvis for motion pictures, that Mr. Wallis suggested I should interview Elvis Presley. Feeling the *Herald Tribune* had no space for such a highly controversial figure who was being preached against in the pulpits of the nation and who was considered generally to be crude, vulgar, and a bad influence on the young, I declined.

"No one gets to interview Elvis," said Mr. Wallis.

"I'd like one person of the press to get to know him as he is." The challenge of "an exclusive" brought about my first meeting with Elvis, and later with The Colonel. Ever since I have been compiling notes and interviews with Elvis to the present time. Elvis has sat down with me and answered questions, one time a list of a hundred. Even The Colonel gave me one of his extremely rare interviews to set the records straight. At no time, however, could I (or any writer) ask for cooperation or help with a book, nor has such cooperation been given. For the time Elvis and The Colonel have given me, it is only natural that I should write this one— which I am certain they believed would eventually transpire.

CHAPTER THIRTY-SEVEN

The Colonel Turns Down a Million Dollars a Show for Elvis in 1975; "You Haven't Seen Anything Yet"

"THE ONLY TIME I can be me—is when I walk through that door and lock it from the inside," Elvis said. "Everything else is show commitments. And my responsibility to live up to everything everyone else has contracted me for."

It was the last day of an engagement at Lake Tahoe. His voice was tired. He'd had a recurrence of strep throat, and it came through clearly, Elvis was in need of a rest, a long rest. Earlier a cold and hoarseness due to sheer over-work, had forced him to cancel his midnight show in Las Vegas. He gamely kept on going with his dinner show—but he said he wondered, "If I'm going to make it through the night.

"I've never had my voice crack yet. I don't want

281

that to happen. My doctors say I need a rest," he repeated. A slight frown furrowed his brow.

"Why don't you retire? You don't need the money nor the aggravations. Give yourself a good rest. You can always make a great come-back like Frank Sinatra. Take a year off."

"That would put too many people out of work, people who depend on me. If it were just me, I'd walk now. But I can't let the others down."

There was a possibility of a throat node. These happen to all singers who sing too much; who strain their vocal cords. It's a simple operation that Sinatra once had. It requires a six-month's healing process. For the first two months after the operation, the person is not allowed to even talk. Communication is made in writing only. Elvis was hoping to avoid this crisis.

It has been a tough working schedule—shows, concerts and immediate tours these past three years, with no time in between to rest or relax. The pace, which also included two T.V. specials and recordings, had been hazardous.

"A voice is a muscle," Elvis explained. "It can be overworked." Elvis was deep with worry. With the removal of nodes, singers either come through better than ever—after a long rest—or not. It's a gamble. It can be a whole career.

Elvis has been singing for over twenty years. The work load on his vocal cords in the past three years has been heavier and more tightly scheduled than of any other singer in history. Now Elvis was facing it head-on. His mentors continued booking him on immediate tours following all of his engagements. Some said they were afraid to stop, lest the trend of his tremendous success and demand would be lost by a long absence. Others said, with Tom Jones coming high now on the fan polls, Elvis dared not stop.

Elvis mentors pooh-poohed those rumors with the facts: Elvis had yet to invade Tom Jones' territory in England and the European continent, which have made the highest bids to get him there in person!

Elvis has the whole world to explore on an international tour whenever he signs the multi-million dollar contracts offered.

Elvis said, "I would like to take a rest for awhile and go to Europe, travel as a tourist and see the world. I've only seen it in pictures in books.

"I'd like to shed all of the glad rags, the fringe, and jewelry, put on a plain pair of jeans, a jacket, a shirt, and bum around the world on my own."

"If I could walk around and see things without mobs of people, be free, it would be worth a million dollars, if for only a couple of weeks. Just be plain little old me instead of 'the image', would be a big relief after almost twenty-one years of it."

Would Elvis and Priscilla ever go back together again? "She has her life. I have mine."

The next night, Elvis had to bow out of his Lake Tahoe engagement due to his worsening throat condition. He flew straight to Los Angeles and the next morning he flew to Memphis. "It's the only place I can relax."

Linda Thompson, his constant companion, reaffirmed she loved Elvis, and wasn't afraid to say so. "We are constantly together, but we have never discussed marriage. Elvis isn't ready to marry now—and maybe not for a long time."

Perhaps Elvis has been pushed too far; the golden goose might stop laying those golden eggs. Elvis is a human being, not a machine. Friends and fans who taped Elvis' recent shows were more than worried. The tapes revealed his golden voice needed care and rest. Critics, the few who remarked on this, upset Elvis which registered his own vital concern for his future.

It is interesting that no one who knows Elvis Presley ever refers to him as "El." Family and friends and business associates call Elvis by his full name. It is an open secret that those who refer to him as "El" are strangers in Elvisland.

"The Lord sure loves Elvis Presley," wrote one reviewer. After two months' complete rest, Elvis bounded back at the Forum in Inglewood, California, in glorious

283

voice and filled with boundless energetic vitality. He was in great form physically and emotionally. Long live the King!

Elvis was now at the very best he had ever been, not only in voice, but he worked hard and wanted to please his audience. His quips were spontaneous and witty. He received continuous standing ovations. "Fever" brought ecstatic screams and yelling. Every time Elvis moved his legs, women screamed. Elvis laughed, "Anyone can do that, all you do is—adjust your pants belt!"

Elvis talked between songs. "When I was ten years old I grew sideburns. I was the only ten-year-old in the world with sideburns! My mother and father kept me in the house—didn't want nobody to see me. He's weird—watch him!"

The hotel had given Elvis a gold necklace with a ram pendant for his birthday: Capricorn. When the audience remarked on its gold flashing in the lights, Elvis switched to a sing along "this is a ram - a - ram - a lam - a - ding - dong - ding!" He began throwing stuffed hound dogs into the audience as he sang "Hound Dog". Leaning way down with a sexy movement, he quipped, "I did this on the Ed Sullivan Show way back when I was first starting out and it caused Mr. Sullivan to retire early! Ed looked at me and said, 'Sonofabitch!' No, he didn't say that—I'm making it up, he called me something else. I gotta lean over or I'll strip my gears." People laughed and Elvis explained, "No man, really, some people don't know where you sing from. It's gotta come from the bottom up!"

In the next instance Elvis sang "What Now My Love" with such deep dramatic sensitivity that he seemed possessed and singing in a world of his own—one apart from his audience. A hush stilled the entire audience as though this were sacred and they were interlopers to even listen. Such was the charisma of Elvis Presley: the beauty of voice and pure showmanship.

In 1974, Elvis again was voted on the Record Mirror Poll in England: No. 1 international male singer,

"Aloha from Hawaii" was voted No. 1 international album; the top five international singles were all by Elvis Presley: "Burning Love," "Fool," "Steamroller Blues," "Polk Salad Annie," and "Always on my Mind," which again cornered the world market.

Rock concerts sprang up all over the country in the sixties. Promoters made offers "that Elvis and The Colonel can't possibly resist." The Colonel proved he could resist such offers with the greatest of ease. His astonishing reply to Sydney, Australia, which was reported by wire service around the world, was typical. Dated April 4, 1974, it read, "A Sydney newspaper reports Elvis Presley has turned down a one million offer from an Australian promoter to do two shows down-under." The response from Presley's agents was "Thank you, but if ever we need a million bucks that badly, we'll give you a ring!" I personally was present when The Colonel turned down a million-dollar offer made by the emissary of a British promoter for Elvis to do one show in London. I felt at the time, The Colonel had plans for some of the sixty or more arenas in America with respective seating capacities of 20,000 to 80,000. Those are still ahead beckoning to Elvis and The Colonel.

Rock concert promoters at the start, hired farm fields far away from towns and cities, hoping to draw at least five thousand paid admissions. Instead ten and then twenty thousand rock fans showed up. The Red Cross had to be called in, for there were accidents, no toilet facilities, and less food. Highways and roads were jammed, while traffic was backed up for miles. Movies were made of the concerts and a few promoters grew wealthy overnight.

No money could induce Elvis nor The Colonel to sign up. The rock concerts caused pure bedlam. Damage to property along with traffic jams suddenly ended the rock concert craze by 1973. Laws, licenses, and requirements made them prohibitive.

Elvis, being a drawing capacity, sold out two hours after any box office opened for ticket sales and in the biggest auditoriums around the country, including

Madison Square Garden, had promoters figuring how to get such a money-maker! Extended Elvis engagements, two a couple of days at the Garden and in Texas to meet the public demand, only whetted the appetite of rock promoters.

In spite of the gasoline shortage in the spring of 1974, a new rock concert blossomed in Ontario, California. A third of a million people jammed traffic for miles. Police reserves, doctors, nurses and ambulances were sent. Makeshift toilet facilities were put up, and the Red Cross was called, while food and barrels of water had to be imported. Such was and is the rock craze, twenty-one-years after Elvis began it.

There isn't a place in the world big enough to hold "An Elvis Rock Concert," it was decided after 250,000 paid admissions were reported in Ontario. The deserts outside Las Vegas or in Africa or Egypt were considered, for Elvis would easily draw a million people according to statistics.

"Easily a million people would turn out for an Elvis Rocker," stated the news media.

The Colonel just smiled. He had his plans well laid for the future. And all around the world too. "You haven't seen anything yet!"

Elvis Presley celebrated his fortieth birthday on January 8, 1975, with a miserable case of virus which had kept him confined to his suite in Graceland for over two weeks. While millions of fans from all over the world sent birthday cards, wires, and birthday gift packages that jammed the Memphis, Tennessee, post office. Local friends poured offerings and congratulations in big receptacles on Graceland's famous gates. But Elvis remained alone with his cold.

Even so, Grandma Presley, his aunt, his little daughter Lisa Marie (almost seven), and his father Vernon had prepared a family party in a small way. Elvis made a brief appearance.

There were many thoughts that pursued Elvis' nostalgic recall that day of his twenty-one years as the biggest star show business has ever known. He was still on top, unrivaled by anyone in his field. He has fifty-six gold single records and twenty-one gold albums. A gold record represents the sale of one million records. Elvis Presley record sales number fifty-six million singles plus twenty-one million albums. He had made thirty-three motion pictures with his salary never less than half a million dollars plus all music rights and many other special concessions for each one. His rare television appearances and specials have all been in the top ratings. In Las Vegas where he plays to over 111,000 paying customers at the International Hotel, he is the super-star of all time in show business. He would next open the Hilton's 20-million-dollar new tower addition in March, 1975. The world's number-one entertainer has multi-million dollar personal appearance and concert offers waiting on his selection all over the world.

Elvis has always been and is generous in sharing his money and his good fortune with those close to him. Two years in succession, he has given his personal physician a $37,000 Stutz Bearcat. He has distributed Rolls Royces, Cadillacs and other makes of expensive cars annually to co-workers, girl friends, as well as members of his family. When he visits his tailors, he casually orders equally expensive suits and clothes for them also. Expensive gold lockets, bracelets, watches, cuff links and diamond rings are also favorite gifts. Just before his birthday during the Christmas holidays, he casually, as per custom, bought five new Cadillacs and five new Lincoln Continentals, handing the dealers $100,000 completing the purchase in a fast fifteen minutes.

There is nothing in the world Elvis can't have, except his two personal goals for happiness. First there is still the loss of his beloved mother, Gladys, and his dream of a devoted domestic wife and several children. Instead he finds himself alone, divorced, his only child growing up in divided homes, his father legally separated from his wife Dee after fourteen years of marriage. Was it the touring and constant absences away from home that broke up his marriage with Priscilla and his father's with his stepmother, who is enjoying a career under the Presley name charisma of becoming a song writer and celebrant, who loves the spotlight; while Priscilla has become a highly successful couture designer. With all of the millions of women, young and old, who idolize Elvis Presley, there is a great fear in his heart that he will never find one who will love him for himself only, as his mother loved his father.

AFTERWORD

In 1975, Elvis began avoiding his gate fans who stand at all times outside his residence at Graceland, Beverly Hills, and Palm Springs. He no longer stopped to chat, as he had always done for his twenty-one years as a super-star in show business. He could no longer trust them all: which ones were friends, which ones were foes? There had been the pretty girl jumping up and down excitedly, calling, "Please, Elvis, you're the King . . . please I beg you, give me an autograph." Smiling, he had stopped and she handed him a subpoena. "I'm a process server," she jeered, then made suggestive remarks, too suggestive, in their appraisal of Elvis as a sex symbol rather than a person.

The press continued filling their space with hot Elvis rumors, as they'd been doing all of those years. Since Elvis didn't give interviews and news couldn't be checked, the press printed whatever they liked—which sold papers.

Elvis now shocked and surprised everyone on the last night of his Las Vegas engagement—by blowing his top. Fed up, he eyed the house, saw no press but a lot of fans and personal friends.

After the last show, Elvis stepped to the microphone. He said, "I want to share with you—the facts—the truth, at last, about me! All of the stuff you've been reading about me—is junk—pure bunk!"

"The other night I had the flu real bad—the flu that's going around. Someone started the report that I was strung out! If I ever find out who started that, I'll knock their G.D. head off! I've never been strung out in my life—!!"

Elvis' indignation mellowed as suddenly as his forceful vent of words. He gave pause, however, so everyone would know he was dead serious. "For too long, things are made up about me!" He reiterated, "They are all bunk!" Elvis, who has always been so closely guarded that his personal life behind the scenes had remained deep mystery and haunted by reports on pure conjecture, no matter how wild or implausible, suddenly decided to blow the lid!"

"Now," he continued, "I've always been an open and honest man. I will always continue to be. I am not putting down the people who've written so much junk about me, because I realize that they have to fill their columns and pages with something. But right now I'm setting the record straight, as it is!"

Elvis stood there defiant, while closing his again record-smashing appearance at the International Hilton (packing in over 2,700 people, with 900 to 1,000 people turned away at every show). There was no press, no one to record this news-shattering talk straight from the shoulder from Elvis. It just happened he was in the mood. Elvis decided for once and all to have his say—in a way, in confidence, actually, since Elvis obviously felt very close and dear to everyone in the room.

After a few minutes of by-play, he was serious, making every word count. He has never taken drugs nor been strung out in his life! He reminded everyone, "I'm not trying to show off or brag, that I'm now an eighth-degree Black Belt karate holder, and I'm trying for my ninth and tenth!" He is well able to take care of himself and any problem besetting him, he assured. The measure of his words (and the tone) in spite of their portent then became friendly and gentle.

Turning on his special brand of magic warmth and affection, and with a hand extended towards a certain center-down-front booth, Elvis invited, "Priscilla . . . stand up and take a bow!" When they were married this had never happened. Priscilla was always brought into the booth after the house lights were lowered for show time and whisked off before the house lights came on again. Now Elvis' ex-wife, stunningly lovely

290

and chic, rose, smiling and confident. "Isn't my ex-wife a real beauty?" Elvis observed proudly. "And our daughter Lisa," he announced. Priscilla had little Lisa, whose natural beauty is the pride of her father and her mother, arise and take a bow. "I'll say the same for my daughter," he smiled with paternal pride. While everyone was gasping with amazement, for Elvis had always objected to any photographs being made public of Lisa. Certainly he never introduced her from the stage. But he now turned with a smile and said, while pointing to the same booth, "My new girl friend, I want you to meet my new girl friend, Sheila." A young girl with long blonde hair arose.

Elvis said, "Stand there a minute, Sheila, show the ring I gave you." The girl raised her finger. And there on the fourth finger of her right hand was a big diamond flashing in the lights.

It was a fact! Elvis was telling everyone that what had been appearing as "factual" news for the past year —that he was engaged to marry Linda "Miss Tennessee" Thompson, simply was in error.

Linda, his long-time companion since Priscilla, had flown in with Elvis for his opening night. Then she'd gone back to Memphis . . . and there were easily three or four other Elvis girl friends who could show off rings and new cars from Elvis.

Sheila (no one knew nor discovered her last name) was not a new girl friend, but actually one of many and had been for several months. Clearly all of this on Elvis' part and his sudden disclosures was to show that he was not dating any one girl, but several, and the fact that he had no immediate plans to marry, and for years to come most likely he would not remarry.

"Priscilla and I are close friends, and we'll always be together—after all we have a daughter to raise." His tone was gentle and affectionate. Then with typical humor, Elvis laughed, "What do you think? Tonight Priscilla gave me, now get this folks, a $42,000 white Rolls Royce." With an aside wink, he said, "We're friends, it's nice we can do that. Well, I got part of it back, didn't I?" (Referring to the two-million-dollar divorce settlement he'd given Priscilla?)

Indicating close friends, Telly Savalas, Vicki Carr, and so many fans—many who'd flown in from Japan, England, China, Australia, Canada, France—some who'd caught Elvis' show for a whole week of successive nights—he spoke a word of greeting individually. "Hello, Judy! take a bow!" This was Judy Spreckles, the sugar heiress, whom he had first met some twenty years before, when he first came to Hollywood to make films. "Judy in 1956 gave me a black star sapphire ring. That means I wore it a lot of years," he added with affection. (Judy had visited Elvis and his mother at Graceland in 1956 and 1957.) Taking his time, Elvis talked to everyone. It was a time to be remembered, for never before in the history of the entertainment world had a performer bared his heart and his emotions on such a personal level to share them and himself so completely! And every single person well knew it!!

Then Elvis sang his heart out!! For an hour and a half. "I've got no place to go, and I don't think you have at this hour," he said. It was by now 1:30 A.M.

Never in better form physically, he was hard and muscular with good color. Vocally his voice was at its peak of perfection in spite of an occasional slight hoarseness on some numbers due to the recent bout with flu.

Colonel Parker, his mentor, who had been reported so ill in hospitals, also disproved those rumors. The Colonel was in fine form and fettle and not ill at all. Elvis' father, Vernon, took a bow from back stage, his usual handsome smiling self, although he dodged all questions about his legal separation from his wife Dee, having six months previously moved out of their lavish home, back fencing Graceland, to reside once more with Elvis.

Yes, Elvis was putting it all together.

"ALL WE HAVE IS TIME!" Elvis repeated. "So how about me singing you some of my new favorites

292

instead of the old 'Polk Salad Annies?' The audience roared approval.

With a mischievous laugh, Elvis began clowning. "See this ring?" he said, pointing his finger up into the spotlight. "It's the ring I wore on the *Aloha Special.* I'm going to explain it. It's one large diamond stone in the center with a lot of little ones around it. I'm explaining all this because you all helped to pay for it!"

The audience sat electrified. Elvis was telling them straight about everything he could think of that his friends might want to know. "I've signed a contract here to 1977." He was going to Lake Tahoe to make up the four days he was off due to the flu during his last engagement. Elvis' lively, happy mood was contagious. Everyone was caught up in his high, happy spirit, and began to clap time and laugh and beat time and just have one wonderful good time, because Elvis was having the best time of all time!!

"This is my life's blood up here on stage. I love it. I love every minute of it," he said. When he and Priscilla were divorcing, Elvis was so unhappy and beside himself that one night he ran off stage after twenty minutes, too upset to continue. Now the wide contrast with this new open, carefree Elvis—the place was falling apart!!

"All those stories about why Priscilla and I split up," he said, "it was because of my career. I was away so long. But Priscilla and I will always love and care for and about each other with our daughter," he said. Without directly mentioning the mind-boggling settlement of two million dollars he gave Priscilla he added, "I gave her a couple of things too, after the divorce."

There was nothing more anyone could want to know. Elvis said he was going right along in show business, he hopes, forever. "It is my life's blood," he repeated. Then he began singing songs like, "If you love me, let me know; if you don't, then let me go." His dramatic interpretation of "Big Boss Man," and "Let Me Be There" was moving and memorable and even brought tears. "This Time You Gave Me a Mountain" was another. "I appreciate the gesture of people calling me 'the

King.' I've never taken that serious, for there is only one King: Jesus Christ." Elvis loves to talk religion, and is referred to as "the evangelist." "I'd go to church, except when I do the congregation stares at me instead of listening to the minister. I get embarrassed."

Elvis then went to the apron of the stage and shook hands with everyone joyfully, purposefully, and freely. He signaled the security guards away, to be left on his own.

Everyone loved Elvis. While in the hotel lobby everyone stood around and talked about it; talked about his sudden openness, his renewed vitality, the happiness he radiated—and quite remarkably too, his ability and his diplomacy at having a new girl friend, his ex-wife and child all happily sitting together in a booth out front.

"I didn't plan to say anything. But it's been bothering me for a long time—all the bunk stuff written up. I know they have to fill pages with print—but I had to get it together for once and all as it is."

Elvis smiled. "Time will tell," he said, as he went upstairs to his private suite for a little family party to celebrate Lisa coming to Las Vegas to hear her daddy sing.